Touring Texas Wineries

If you drink alcoholic beverages, do so in moderation and when consumption does not put you or others at risk.

TOURING
TEXAS
WINERIES

Scenic Drives Along Texas Wine Trails

THOMAS M. CIESLA ▪ REGINA M. CIESLA

LONE STAR BOOKS
Lanham • New York • Toronto • Plymouth, UK

Satellite image of Texas on title page: *Shaded Relief Map*, courtesy of Ray Sterner, Johns Hopkins University. Reprinted by permission.

LONE STAR BOOKS, 4501 Forbes Avenue, Suite 200, Lanham, Maryland 20706

Distributed by National Book Network
1-800-462-6420

Library of Congress Cataloging-in-Publication Data

Ciesla, Thomas M.
    Touring Texas wineries : scenic drives along Texas wine trails / Thomas M. Ciesla, Regina M. Ciesla.—[2nd ed.].
       p. cm.
    Includes bibliographical references and index.
    ISBN 1-58907-004-6 (alk. paper)
      1. Wineries—Texas—Guidebooks. 2. Wine and winemaking—Texas.
    3. Texas—Guidebooks. I. Ciesla, Regina M. II. Title.

TP557 .C5 2003
641.2'2'025764—dc21   2002042589

♾™ The paper used in this publication meets the minimum requirements of American National Standard for Information Sciences—Permanence of Paper for Printed Library Materials, ANSI/NISO Z39.48—1992.
Manufactured in the United States of America.

The Publisher wishes to thank the individual wineries, bed & breakfast inns, and restaurants for the use of their photographs. In addition, the Publisher appreciates the photo contributions from the Texas Department of Agriculture and Austin Convention and Visitors Bureau.

CONTENTS

Chapter 1
About Texas Wines   1
The Beginnings—17th and 18th Centuries, The Formative Years—
The 19th Century, The Modern Years—The 20th Century and
Beyond, Recognition for Texas Wines, Looking Toward
Tomorrow, Touring Texas Wineries, Tours and Tastings.

Chapter 2
North Central Wineries   13
The Munson Trail, Homestead Winery, Hidden Springs Winery,
Cross Roads Vineyards, Lone Oak Vineyards, Brushy Creek
Vineyards, Cross Timbers Winery, Cap*Rock Winery, La Buena Vida
Winery, Homestead Winery, Delaney Vineyards, La Bodega Winery,
Kiepersol Estate Vineyard, Bed and Breakfasts Along the Munson
Trail, Restaurants Along the Munson Trail.

PREFACE TO THE SECOND EDITION

*T*exas winemakers and wine tourists alike are caught in a liminal moment; each seasoned by past experiences and each looking toward the promise of tomorrow with anticipation and excitement. Texas is poised to take its place alongside the great winemaking regions of the world.

What does this mean to you as a wine tourist and reader of this book? As a wine tourist, the recent growth in the Texas wine industry has provided you with more wineries and wine trails to explore. At the time of this writing there are forty-one wineries distributed along our seven wine trails.

We hope that our readers will enjoy this revised edition, featuring fourteen new wineries, internet website listings, and enhanced maps to help you find the wineries along these trails. To fulfill our goal of providing you, the reader, with fun casual trips, we have increased our wine trails by one—the Balcones Trail—to help balance your touring experience.

Besides great wineries full of friendly and informed people, each Texas wine trail offers the wine tourist a great variety of activities; shopping, multicultural foods and entertainment, great places to stay, great music, and that Texas hospitality that makes everyone feel welcome.

Thanks for your support of Texas wine, it just keeps getting better and better.

Enjoy the adventure.

ACKNOWLEDGMENTS

*N*aturally, when you write a book on wineries in a state the size of Texas, you run into a few folks along the way. The individuals that make up the Texas wine industry are by far some of the nicest people we have ever met, and we wish to thank all of them for directly and indirectly helping us with writing this book. Of course, we have to say the same to those folks we met along the way during our travels across the state. Whether it was a hotel in Dallas, a bed and breakfast in Fredericksburg, or a State Trooper in West Texas, the Lone Star State should be proud of the people who live within its borders—thank you all for making our journey safe and pleasant.

Of all those who helped along the way, a few stand out above the rest. A special thanks to Paul Bonnarigo of Messina Hof Wine Cellars for his encouragement in the early and final phases of this work. His gracious moral support along the way was invaluable. We also thank Russell Smith, Lisa Allen of the Texas Wine and Grape Growers Association, Tim Dodd of the Texas Wine Marketing Research Institute, and Susan Dunn and associates at the Texas Department of Agriculture.

To the vintners and grape growers of Texas, we say "Cheers!" Don't let that Texas pioneer spirit die.

INTRODUCTION

*I*f you enjoy drinking wine, learning about wine, or visiting friendly places where wine is made, you might want to try something new from the Lone Star State—Texas wineries and the unique people and places that form the Texas Wine Trails.® Whether you are looking for a fun trip with family or a romantic weekend in a cozy cottage in the Texas Hill Country, *Touring Texas Wineries* has something for you.

What is a Texas wine tour? While the wine touring concept is an old one, the sheer size of Texas, and until recently, the relatively small number of wineries, made the idea of a wine tour difficult to imagine in this state where everything seems larger than life. The explosive growth of Texas wineries in the late 1980s and early 1990s has allowed us to outline for the very first time seven wine trails. Along the way you will taste the wines, meet the people who create them, and enjoy the attractions of the surrounding communities. As you will see, it is impossible to separate the wine from the history, culture, and romance of the location where it is created.

These trails are a casual, fun way to visit Texas wineries and allow you to plan a day, a weekend, or a holiday trip through picturesque areas of the state. By focusing each tour on a small number of wineries, we hope your trips will be fun-filled and free of frantic schedules. You will have the extra time needed to personally meet the winery owners and winemakers to discuss their techniques and passion for winemaking. Then, after visiting the wineries, you can enjoy the shops and restaurants in the surrounding communities, and perhaps even stay the night to sample some good old Texas hospitality. The best of the Texas wine industry and all of what makes Texas itself so special can be experienced along these wine trails.

Who ventures along these wine trails? Reports from the winery owners tell us that just as many Texans as non-Texans are likely to visit these wineries. You will find singles, couples, families, newlyweds, retirees, wine lovers, and folks new to wine at these wineries. By the way, the smiles you'll see on the faces of these folks aren't from too much wine tasting, but from the kind, friendly treatment of the staff at all the Texas wineries. Texas winemakers are proud of their state and of the wine they create. This pride is probably best summed up in an old Texas saying: "Two kinds of people in this world, son—folks that live in Texas, and those not fortunate enough." A trip down one of the Texas wine trails will definitely help you understand that pride.

"Why take one of these trips? I don't know very much about wine!" One of the best things about a trip along a Texas wine trail is that you don't have to be a wine expert! You don't even have to know anything about wine. No one cares. No one will snicker when you ask a question or wonder what wine to serve with a meal. You no longer have to feel intimidated about tasting wine. If you are new to wine, folks at the wineries will be happy to explain wine and winemaking techniques. If you are an experienced wine drinker, traveling these trails will be a great way to find out more about Texas wines, and learn to appreciate the challenges these vintners face.

Perhaps you want to do more than just sample some great wine. Maybe you need a Saturday out of town, just to get away from it all. Or you may be looking for a romantic weekend with that special someone to enjoy fine wine, good food, and each other's company. Or perhaps, you are a visitor from another state, trying to decide on the best way to see this giant state they call Texas. The Texas Wine Trails® can fulfill any of these needs. One thing is certain, you will come away with memorable wines, great food, and good times with the people you will meet along the way.

Where do we begin? Before we get too excited and start running down one of the wine trails, join us for a brief story of wine production in Texas. Remember that the Texas wine industry is a young, dynamic one. As it evolves, new wineries appear as quickly as others fade away. Though we have made every effort to make this an accurate collection of Texas wineries, it is almost impossible for any book written on the subject to remain current for an extended length of time. Keeping that in mind, we have created an Internet Web site, called oddly enough, the Texas Wine Trails. It will serve our readers to update listings of Texas wineries between revised editions of this book. The Internet address for our Web site is: http://www.texaswinetrails.com

STOPPING AT RESTAURANTS AND BED AND BREAKFASTS ALONG THE WAY

What better way to experience the fun of a Texas wine tour than to stop off for a relaxing meal at one of the restaurants along the way or to spend the night at one of the local bed and breakfasts?

We have included with each of the wine trails a short description of many of the fine bed and breakfasts and restaurants you may encounter. Be sure to check them out, but remember, prices are subject to change, so you may want to call ahead.

RESTAURANTS

The following symbols indicate the cost of a typical meal for one person, exclusive of drinks, tax, and tip.

$	under $7
$$	$8–$17
$$$	$18–$25
$$$$	over $25

BED AND BREAKFASTS

The following symbols indicate the price range for a double room.

$	under $60
$$	$61–$80
$$$	$81–$100
$$$$	over $100

For a more complete listing of bed and breakfasts in Texas, pick up a copy of the *Lone Star Guide: Texas Bed & Breakfasts* by Gail Drago, Marjie Mugno Acheson, and Lyn Dunsavage, ISBN 0-89123-027-0, available from Gulf Publishing Company or your local bookstore.

How to Read a
Wine Label

Brand or
Proprietary
Name

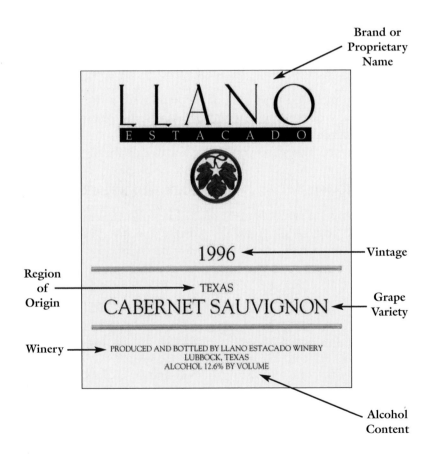

1996 ← Vintage

Region
of
Origin → TEXAS

CABERNET SAUVIGNON ← Grape
Variety

Winery → PRODUCED AND BOTTLED BY LLANO ESTACADO WINERY
LUBBOCK, TEXAS
ALCOHOL 12.6% BY VOLUME

Alcohol
Content

2002 LONE STAR INTERNATIONAL WINE COMPETITION

The Lone Star Wine Competition, renamed the Lone Star International Wine Competition for 2002, was hosted by the Texas Wine and Grape Growers Association at the Hilton DFW Lakes Conference Center. The competition featured forty-five wineries from thirteen states and three countries, entering two hundred and fifty-five wines. The competition judges awarded one hundred and eighty-three medals, including eighteen Gold, fifty-four Silver and one hundred and five Bronze.

Becker Vineyards:	Chardonnay–2001 *BRONZE*
	Chenin Blanc–2001 *BRONZE*
	Viognier–2001 *BRONZE*
	Cabernet Sauvignon–1999 *GOLD*
	Merlot–2000 *GOLD*
	Gewurztraminer–2001 *SILVER*
	Fumè Blanc–2001 *SILVER*
	Claret–2000 *SILVER*
Blue Mountain Wines:	Cabernet Sauvignon–2000 *SILVER*
Buffalo Creek Winery (Missouri):	Red Table Wine–2001 *SILVER*
Casa Madero:	Merlot–2000 BRONZE
	Cabernet Sauvignon–1999 *GOLD*
	STAR OF THE NATION
	GRAND AWARD
Cedar Creek Winery (Wisconsin):	Vidal Blanc–20001 *GOLD*
Chatham Hill, Inc. (North Carolina):	Riesling–2001 *BRONZE*
Chisholm Trail Winery:	Texas White–2001 *BRONZE*

Cross Roads Vineyards:	Chardonnay–2000 *BRONZE*
Cross Timbers:	Merlot–2001 *BRONZE* Blush–NV *BRONZE*
Daniel Vineyards (West Virginia):	Blackberry–NV *BRONZE* Cayuga White–2001 *BRONZE*
Delaney Vineyards:	Texas Rosé–NV *BRONZE* Sparkling Wine–NV *BRONZE*
Dry Comal Creek Vineyards:	Sauvignon Blanc–2001 *BRONZE* Cabernet Sauvignon–2000 *BRONZE* Comal Red III–NV *BRONZE* Rosé–NV *BRONZE* Sauvignon Blanc–2000 *SILVER* Cabernet Sauvignon–2001 *SILVER* Merlot–2001 *SILVER*
Escondido Valley Cordier Estates, Inc:	Pinot Noir–2000 *BRONZE*
Fall Creek Vineyards:	Granite Reserve–2001 *BRONZE* Reserve Merlot–1999 *BRONZE* Chardonnay–1999 *BRONZE* Chenin Blanc–2001 *SILVER*
Fredericksburg Winery:	Chardonnay–2001 *BRONZE* Muscat Canelli–2001 *BRONZE* Ehrenfelser–2001 *BRONZE* Cabernet Sauvignon–2001 *BRONZE* Cabernet Sauvignon–2001 *BRONZE* Cabernet Sauvignon–2001 *BRONZE* Orange Muscat–2000 *GOLD STAR OF TEXAS GRAND AWARD*
Georgia Wines (Georgia):	Muscadine–NV *BRONZE* Blush–NV *GOLD* Concord–NV *SILVER* Southern Blush–NV *SILVER*
Gray Ghost Vineyard (Virginia):	Chardonnay–2001 *SILVER*
Gray Monk Cellars (Canada):	Gewurztraminer–2001 *BRONZE* Pinot Auxerrois–2001 *BRONZE* Pinot Blanc–2000 *BRONZE* Rotberger–2000 *BRONZE* Pinot Gris–2000 *SILVER* Kerner–2000 *SILVER*
Homestead Winery:	Homestead Red–NV *SILVER*
Kiepersol Estate Vineyards:	Merlot–2000 *BRONZE*
La Bodega Winery:	Cabernet Sauvignon–2001 *BRONZE* Merlot–2001 *BRONZE* Chardonnay–2000 *SILVER* Merlot–2000 *SILVER*

La Buena Vida Vineyards:	Chardonnay–1998 *BRONZE* Merlot–1998 *BRONZE*
La Buena Vida Vineyards Walnut Creek Cellars:	Tawny Port–NV *BRONZE* Vintage Port–1998 *BRONZE* Vintage Old–1985 *GOLD*
La Buena Vida Vineyards Springtown:	Cabernet Sauvignon–1998 *BRONZE* Cabernet Sauvignon–1998 *BRONZE* Sweet Ruby Proprietor–NV *BRONZE* Springtown Mist Blush–NV *BRONZE*
Les Bourgeois Winery (Missouri):	Chardonel–2001 *BRONZE*
Llano Estacado Winery:	Chenin Blanc–2001 *BRONZE* Sauvignon Blanc–2001 *BRONZE* Signature White–2001 *BRONZE* Merlot–2000 *BRONZE* (Syrah) Shiraz–2001 *BRONZE* Passionelle–2000 *BRONZE* Chardonnay–2001 *GOLD* Chardonnay–2001 *SILVER* Johannisberg White Riesling–2001 *SILVER* Signature Red–2000 *SILVER* Port–NV*SILVER*
Lone Oak Vineyards:	Merlot–2000 *BRONZE* Merlot–2000 *SILVER*
Lynfred Winery (Illinois):	Pinot Gris–2001 *BRONZE* Zinfandel–2000 *BRONZE* Syrah–2000 *SILVER*
Magnotta Winery (Canada):	Chardonnay–2001 *BRONZE* Merlot–2001 *BRONZE* Icewine–2000 *GOLD* Icewine–2000 *SILVER* Icewine–2000 *SILVER*
Messina Hof Winery:	Chardonnay–2000 *BRONZE* Gewurztraminer–2001 *BRONZE* Muscat Canelli–2001 *BRONZE* Port of Call Ivory–NV *BRONZE* Sauvignon Blanc–2001 *BRONZE* Pinot Grigio–2001 *BRONZE* Merlot–2001 *BRONZE* Pinot Noir–2000 *BRONZE* Gamay Beaujolais–2001 *BRONZE* Port of Call Ebony–NV *BRONZE* Shiraz–1999 *BRONZE* Muscat Canelli–2001 *BRONZE* Johannisberg Riesling–2001 *BRONZE*

Port–1999 *BRONZE*
Johannisberg Riesling–2001 *GOLD*
Proprietary Blend–2000 *GOLD*
Merlot–2001 *GOLD STAR OF
TEXAS GRAND AWARD*
Chenin Blanc–2001 *SILVER*
Cabernet Sauvignon–1999 *SILVER*
White Zinfandel–2001 *SILVER*
Sparkling Wine–NV *SILVER*

Oak Glenn (Missouri):
Vidal Blanc–1999 NV *BRONZE*
Husman's Heritage–NV *BRONZE*
Blush–NV *BRONZE*

Piney Woods Country Wines:
Muscadine–NV *BRONZE*
Muscadine–2001 *BRONZE*
Light Ruby Port–NV *SILVER*

Pleasant Hill Winery:
Fumè Blanc–NV *BRONZE*

Sharpe Hill Vineyard (Connecticut):
Chardonnay–2000 *BRONZE*
Proprietary Blend–NV *BRONZE*

Sistercreek Vineyards:
Chardonnay–2000 *GOLD*
Muscat Canelli–2001 *GOLD STAR
OF THE TEXAS GRAND AWARD*

Spicewood Vineyards:
Chardonnay Dulce–2001 *BRONZE*
Bluebonnet Blush–2001 *BRONZE*
Chardonnay–2000 *SILVER*
Cabernet Sauvignon–2000 *SILVER*
Merlot–2000 *SILVER*

St. James Winery (Missouri):
Chardonel–2001 *BRONZE*
Velvet Red–NV *BRONZE*
Norton–1999 *BRONZE*
School House Red–NV *BRONZE*
Vignoles–2000 *BRONZE*
Seyval–2001 *SILVER*
Vignoles–2001 *SILVER*
School House White–NV *SILVER*
School House Blush–NV *SILVER*

Ste. Genevieve Cordier
Estates, Inc.:
Chardonnay–NV *GOLD*
Cabernet Sauvignon–NV *SILVER*

Stone Bluff Cellars (Oklahoma):
Cheval Blanc–2001 *BRONZE*
Royale–2001 *BRONZE*

Stone Hill Winery (Missouri):
Catawba–NV *BRONZE*
Seyval–2000 *BRONZE*
Chardonel–2001 *BRONZE*
Steinberg–2000 *BRONZE*
Hermannsberger–2001 *BRONZE*
Hermannsberger–NV *BRONZE*

Steinberg Red–2001 *BRONZE*
Blush–NV *BRONZE*
Sparking–1997 *BRONZE*
Brut–1998 *BRONZE*
Sparking Spumante–NV *BRONZE*
Concord–NV *GOLD*
Vignoles–2001 *GOLD STAR OF
    THE NATION GRAND AWARD*
Shery–NV *GOLD STAR OF THE
    NATION GRAND AWARD*
Golden Rhine–NV *SILVER*
Seyval–2001 *SILVER*
Vidal Blanc–2000 *SILVER*
Vidal Blanc–2001 *SILVER*
Steinberg–2001 *SILVER*
Norton–1999 *SILVER*
Norton–2000 *SILVER*
Rosé Montaigne–NV *SILVER*
Vignoles–2001 *SILVER*
Port–1999 *SILVER*
Port–2000 *SILVER*
Vignoles–2000 SILVER

Tabor Family Winery (Iowa): Vidal Blanc–2001 *BRONZE*

Texas Hills Vineyard: Due Bianco–2001 *BRONZE*
Merlot–2000 *BRONZE*
Cabernet Sauvignon–2000 *SILVER*
Moscato–2001 *SILVER*

Travis Peak Select–Flat
Creek Estate: Muscato Blanco Muscat–2000
    BRONZE
Cabernet Sauvignon–2000 *BRONZE*
Cabernet Sauvignon–1999 *SILVER*

Winzer Krems (Austria): Riesling–1999 *BRONZE*

Wollersheim Winery (Wisconsin): White Riesling–2001 *BRONZE*
Prairie Fume–2001 *SILVER*

WINE TASTING

The difference between tasting wine and drinking wine revolves around how much attention you pay to the wine. Here's a few examples to show you the difference.

You're poolside on a hot Texas afternoon with a glass of iced-down Ste. Genevieve White Zinfandel by your side. It's 100° in the sun, you're thirsty, so you reach for the glass and take a big refreshing gulp. That's *drinking* wine!

You're at a party. The host pours you a glass of Pheasant Ridge Pinot Noir that you sip and say, "Mmmm, that's nice." Then for the remainder of the evening, you take a sip now and then while engaged in conversation. That's *drinking* wine!

You're at a tasting room of a Texas winery. A dozen or so people are huddled around the wine bar as the vintner holds two glasses of Chardonnay in the light so everyone can see the subtle differences in color. The vintner explains that one Chardonnay has undergone barrel fermentation and the other has not. Oak aging imparts a slightly darker hue to the wine. He pours a small sample of each for everyone and asks them to taste and comment on the difference between the two. That's *tasting* wine!

The obvious difference between the first two examples and the last one is the wine drinker's focus. When wine is a prop in a larger production (such as the pool or party), it is impossible to concentrate on the smells and tastes within the wine.

There are five basic steps to use when visiting a tasting room that will make it seem as though you've done this a thousand times. These steps that focus on the senses of sight, smell, and taste, include color, swirl, smell, taste, and savor.

Color—It's the first thing we notice about a wine, isn't it? If you are new to wine you may simply be able to tell if it's a white, blush, or red wine when you hold the glass. After some experience the color might tell you if it's a young or an aged wine. White wines gain color as they get older, and red wines lose color. Other wines like Zinfandels (not white Zinfandels) have a deep, almost purple color, and are sometimes called the "inky" Zins.

Swirl—Have you ever wondered why people swirl their wine? Are they just trying to look cool and sophisticated? Well, maybe some of them are, but swirling actually releases compounds from the wine allowing them to react with oxygen that enhances the "nose" of the wine. The "nose" is the combination of the aroma and bouquet each wine carries as a clue to the grapes and the winemaking process that produced the wine.

Swirling is easy to do, but use small motions, taking care not to "swirl" onto your tasting partner. There is of course a danger with swirling that we should mention. As you become adept at the motion you'll find yourself swirling everything! My wife has caught me on many occasions absent-mindedly swirling milk that I've poured into a wine glass.

Smell—Now that you have the swirling part down pat, we examine the reason for the swirl: the "nose." Most of us don't spend enough time at this stage, which is a pity, because as with most foods, wine usually tastes the way it smells. Take your time, we recommend bringing the glass of wine up to your nose at least twice before tasting. Remember the longer the wine is exposed to the air, the more changes occur in the "nose." Compounds in the wine create the wine's "signature," be it woody, fruity, vinegary, or like "burnt matches." As your experience grows, you may eventually be able to use these clues to identify bad wine *before* you taste it. And life is too short to drink bad wine!

Taste—Finally, we get to taste this stuff! Remember though, we're not *drinking* the wine, we're tasting. Take a small sip and hold it in your mouth for a moment. Different parts of the tongue are sensitive to different tastes. For example, the tip of the tongue contains the cells that recognize sweet tastes. For red wines or oak-aged white wines, you'll want the wine to swish around to the sides and center of the tongue to judge the amount of acidity or tannin flavors. Remember too, that wine is a complex substance and often contains more than one of these flavors in one sip. About 20 seconds after you've tasted the wine, a distinct aftertaste may linger, quite different from your initial taste. Really good wines will have a pleasing aftertaste.

Savor—You've looked, swirled, smelled, and finally tasted the wine. Now what? It may have seemed like a lot of work but in reality all four steps probably took only 30 to 40 seconds total. Now you have to ask yourself if you liked the wine. Is it a wine you would buy for yourself? What was it about the wine that you liked or didn't like? Was it too acidic? ("It tastes like a battery.") Was it too sweet? ("It tastes like a spoonful of sugar.") This reflection on what you just tasted will help you in future tastings and wine purchases. Finally, is the wine worth the price?

A NOTE ABOUT THE LOVE-HATE RELATIONSHIP BETWEEN OXYGEN AND WINE

During the winemaking process, oxygen is the devil for a vintner. Too large of a surface area exposed to oxygen inside of a barrel will ruin the wine. That is why vintners are constantly "topping off" barrels during the fermentation process to keep the amount of wine exposed to oxygen as small as possible.

For the consumer however, oxygen is the wines' friend—at least temporarily. Swirling a glass of wine to allow oxygen to mix with it is similar to removing the cork from a bottle in advance of pouring—allowing the wine to "breathe." You can try this at home. Open a bottle of wine and immediately taste a small amount. Taste another sample after the bottle has remained open for 10–15 minutes. You'll be amazed at the difference.

But there is still a dark side to oxygen. The benefits gained from that initial contact with the air when you open a wine bottle will be overshadowed by the forces set in motion to spoil the wine. If you have wine remaining in a bottle and want to save it, refrigerate it as soon as possible to slow the spoiling process. You can expect wine to stay drinkable for up to a week when refrigerated. Left on a countertop, you won't like the flavor within just a few days.

Buying Texas Wines

Ten Do's and Don'ts for the Informed Wine Traveler

Chances are that as you travel these wine trails you will find yourself carrying home a few bottles of Texas wine—we always do even though we've traveled these trails many times. Here are a few tricks we've learned over the years.

DO purchase one of the cardboard wine carriers if available at the winery. They are a convenient way to carry and pack bottles of wine and reduce the chance of breakage.

DO leave sufficient room in the trunk for extra wine bottles, especially if you plan on buying a case or more.

DO ask the winery staff about distribution of their wines. Many of the smaller wineries only sell from the tasting room or in the local town. If you taste a wine from a small winery that you enjoy, buy it. Chances are it will not be available in your hometown.

DO plan for the future. As you sample these wines think about the next six months. Will you be giving a dinner or a barbecue for friends? Is there a special occasion coming up such as a birthday or anniversary? A Texas wine would go nicely with any of these.

DO ship home the larger wine accessories you purchase in the tasting rooms. Some wineries offer a broad selection of wine accessories such as handmade wine racks, which can be quite large. Ship the accessories home to save trunk space for the wine.

DON'T take the smallest vehicle you own or rent a compact car. In addition to the items available in the wineries, each trail offers many shopping opportunities. For example, during one innocent trip along the Enchanted Trail, we came home with a butcher block table for the kitchen that we bought in Fredericksburg!

DON'T forget the strength of the Texas sun. Summertime temperatures in automobiles can ruin a wine in a matter of hours.

DON'T buy wine before you shop. If you are visiting wineries located in historic downtown districts such as Grapevine or Fredericksburg, it's likely that you will want to walk around to visit local shops and restaurants. Purchase your wine at the end of the day or have the winery hold your purchase until you return. One or two bottles of wine will feel ten times heavier after being carried around town for hours.

DON'T travel with open bottles in your automobile. If you've enjoyed a Texas wine while staying in your Bed and Breakfast or hotel room and would like to take the rest home, cork the bottle firmly and place it in your trunk. Do not carry an opened bottle of any alcoholic beverage with you in the passenger compartment.

DON'T be afraid to ask about personalized wine labels. Most Texas wineries now offer their customers the ability to purchase select wines with labels personalized for special occasions.

Chapter 1

ABOUT TEXAS WINES

*M*any of us today are startled when we hear that Texas has a wine industry. When most Americans think of Texas, they think of horses, cowboys, cattle, or oil, not wine and vineyards. The phenomenal growth of the Texas wine industry during the last few decades was preceded by a winemaking history dating back to the mid-1600s.

THE BEGINNINGS—17TH AND 18TH CENTURIES

By 1650 Spanish Franciscan monks had established a viticulture hold in the area around Paso Del Norte, which is now El Paso, by planting the Spanish black grape. This grape was hardy enough to grow in the Texas environment and produced a palatable wine. The monks did not think that wines made from native wild grapes were suitable for consumption. However, a readily available water supply and the development of irrigation systems made it possible for them to maintain extensive vineyards of the Spanish black grape.

In 1680 the Pueblo Revolt in the territory of New Mexico forced the Spaniards to flee for their lives and settle into the area now known as El Paso. The countryside, rich with flood plain

◄ THE CLEAR SIMPLE BEAUTY OF A GLASS OF TEXAS WINE.
(COURTESY OF THE TEXAS DEPARTMENT OF AGRICULTURE)

1

soil and adequate water, was turned into a garden paradise of fruit trees and vineyards that supplied the local missions with sacramental wines. These vineyards flourished throughout the eighteenth century and produced wines and brandy. In the early nineteenth century, however, objections were beginning to be raised concerning the quality of the wines from the El Paso area. As American wine consumers became increasingly familiar with the taste of vinifera-based wines, the flavor of wines based on native grapes became less desirable. At the same time, many growers were beginning to discover that few of the European vinifera grape varieties were capable of surviving the harsh environment of far West Texas.

THE FORMATIVE YEARS—THE 19TH CENTURY

Around the same time that West Texas was seeing a decrease in vineyard acreage, a second wave of European immigrants began to populate the Hill Country and northeast areas of Texas. German immigrants settled into the central Texas Hill Country and quickly established vineyards and wineries. The Steinberger Winery operated in this area of Texas from 1880 until Prohibition.

As German immigrants were settling the Hill Country, Italian immigrants were settling into the eastern half of Texas. They too brought a heritage of winemaking with them by importing grapes from California to produce homemade wine. Northern Italians began to settle in the areas northwest of Dallas and established vineyards and orchards. The Carminati Winery operated from 1887 to 1919 and the Fenoglio Winery existed from 1900 until Prohibition in 1919. The Fenoglios were influenced by T. V. Munson whose work with viticulture eventually saved the French wine industry. Using standard Concord grapes and Munson-developed hybrids, the Fenoglios produced first-class wines from an increasingly prolific grape producing area.

The Prohibition Act in the United States broke the back of the wine industry in Texas, closing all but one winery—Val Verde Win-

TYPICAL TRELLIS WORK USED IN TEXAS VINEYARDS.
(COURTESY OF THE TEXAS DEPARTMENT OF AGRICULTURE)

ery in Del Rio, Texas. Val Verde was established by the Qualia family in 1883. Unlike other wineries around the state, the Qualias continued to maintain their vineyard, using their grapes for jellies, jams, sacramental wines, and table grapes. Their grapes were hardy enough to withstand rail shipment to major centers such as Galveston and Houston. Although Prohibition brought a close to an era for commercial winemaking in Texas, the time between the Civil War and Prohibition served as a foundation for the winemakers that were to follow.

Three generations of the Qualia family and the work they performed with a variety of grapes after Prohibition provided a critical link between past winemaking efforts and today's commercial wine industry in Texas.

Two experts in the field of raising grapes and making wines lived in Texas during this formative era. A. J. Winkler, born in Waco, went on to head the Department of Viticulture and Enology for thirty years at the University of California at Davis. The other internationally known authority was T. V. Munson. After a decade of researching, categorizing, and experimenting, Mr. Munson established a vineyard near Denison, where he classified over 300 varieties of grapes. His goal was to determine the best native grape rootstock onto which he could graft the European vinifera.

In the late 1800s, France's vineyards were devastated by the plant louse, *phylloxera,* which was introduced into France accidentally by Americans in the 1860s. Hearing of Munson's work, the French sent representatives to consult with the Texas expert. The French representative returned to France with disease-resistant Texas rootstock on which the French grafted their vines. French wines, which are so popular today, owe a large debt to native Texas rootstock.

Today you can visit the T. V. Munson Memorial Vineyard at Grayson County College in Denison, Texas. This vineyard was established in 1979 as a memorial and as a viticulture center. Grayson County College serves the Texas wine industry as a viticulture and enology center of education. Call for class information or visit them on their Web site: www.grayson.edu.

THE MODERN YEARS— THE 20TH CENTURY AND BEYOND

By the early twentieth century, the vast vineyards of the El Paso area had disappeared. Nature and economics played a role in the demise of these vineyards. Floods devastated the crops, and raising vegetables to feed an increasing population became more profitable. El Paso's last winery, Isleta Winery, closed its doors in 1919, after more than eighty years of operation.

Research efforts around the state continued between the 1940s and the early 1960s and produced a renewed promise and interest in Texas grape production. California entered the wine industry in the 1960s and America discovered wine in the 1970s. So where was Texas? Texas winemakers were cautiously learning about growing grapes in Texas. It is true that Texas rootstock is resistant to *phylloxera*, but it has other enemies such as cottonroot rot and Pierce's disease that can destroy a vineyard in short order. Combine these diseases with the excitable weather in Texas and, if you are not cautious, you have a recipe for easy disaster.

However, Texans have always been famous for their pioneer spirit. That same tough determination they used to make oil flow from the Texas plains came into play again when they made wine flow from the Texas vineyards at the end of the twentieth century. In the 1970s, a handful of individuals tempered that famous Texas pioneer spirit with a little patience and common sense. While the rest of America ran headlong into vineyard expansion, these Texans took a deliberate, methodical approach to planting small test vineyards across the state. These pioneers began laying the groundwork, both in the vineyards and the halls of legislation, for a resurgence of commercial wine production in Texas.

Dr. Bobby Smith, owner of La Buena Vida Winery, is an advocate for Texas wine legislation. In 1977 he was instrumental in the passage of the Farm Winery Act that permitted winemakers to produce and bottle wine in dry counties (counties in which the sale of alcoholic beverages is prohibited) as long as distribution occurred outside of the dry county. This was a giant step for the wineries and growing regions of North Texas.

Ed Auler is another pioneer of Texas wine legislation. He and his wife Susan have played an important part in the marketing of Texas wines. From lobbying for legislation to establishing wine and food festivals, the Auler's continue to play a large part in the growth of the Texas wine industry.

The 1980s saw a dramatic expansion in vineyard acreage and the number of bonded wineries. Texas has forty wineries at this writing, and more plan to open within the next few years. Ironically, there were as many wineries in Texas in the late 1980s as there were in 1900. It is somewhat poetic that as we enter the new millennium, we are finally expanding beyond the number of wineries Texas had at the turn of the last century.

RECOGNITION FOR TEXAS WINES

Another major advance for the Texas wine industry in the 1980s was the recognition of viticulture areas in Texas. In November 1986, the U.S. government announced the establishment of the Bell Mountain Viticulture Area. This honor recognized the Bell Mountain area of the Texas Hill Country for its ideal soil and climate conditions. It was the first Texas wine-growing appellation and a great addition to Bell Mountain's wine labels. Today there are seven viticultural appellation areas—Texas High Plains, Mesilla Valley, Escondido Valley, Texas Hill Country, Bell Mountain, Fredericksburg in the Hill Country, and Texas Davis Mountains.

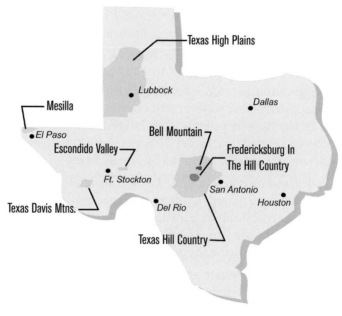

TEXAS VITICULTURE AREAS

LOOKING TOWARD TOMORROW

As wine seems to play a more important role in many of our lives, results of numerous studies indicate that moderate wine consumption is beneficial when included in a healthy lifestyle. The increase in wine-related activities in Texas, such as wine festivals, wine seminars, wine society chapters, and vintner dinners, bears witness to the state's desire to become connected to a myriad of elements of Western civilization that for over 8,000 years have maintained wine as a key cultural thread.

In the 1990s, Texas rallied to become the fifth largest wine-producing state in the nation, just behind California, New York, Washington, and Oregon. Texas' 1999 production was 1,200,000 gallons from 3,200 acres of wine grapes. Vineyard managers are learning how to apply and adapt the techniques used in the Old World and in California to the unique Texas environment. Where the experts once thought that only hybrid grapes would survive, vinifera varietals are flourishing across the state to produce wines that regularly capture awards in international competitions.

Texas vintners produce a wide array of classic and specialized wines. For red wine lovers there is a very good selection of robust Cabernet Sauvignons with blackberry, vanilla, and toasty flavors; Merlots with a more silky flavor to the palate; Zinfandels with rich, thick, woody, nutmeg flavors; and Pinot Noirs that offer the wine lover a lighter, yet full-bodied wine. White wine drinkers will appreciate the diverse selection of Chardonnays that range from light and fruity to full, oaken creations that fill the mouth with a buttery explosion. Vintners across the state also offer Sauvignon Blanc, Chenin Blanc, and Muscat Canelli. The German heritage we spoke of earlier is wonderfully showcased in the fine selection of Reisling and Gewurztraminer, especially from the Hill Country wineries.

For those of you who enjoy something out of the ordinary, that famous pioneer spirit has given Texas vintners the courage to experiment with both technique and grape selection. Texas vintners now offer peach wines, a robust selection of Meads,

**THE FERMENTING OF WHOLE-BERRY CLUSTERS IS BECOMING
INCREASINGLY POPULAR WITH TEXAS WINEMAKERS.**
(COURTESY OF THE TEXAS DEPARTMENT OF AGRICULTURE)

Blush Merlots, and late-harvest, sweet wines. We can expect
to see this trend continue in the future as new wineries and
winemakers join the Texas bunch to make their mark on the
industry.

TOURING TEXAS WINERIES

Texas is almost a country of its own. In fact, it was an independent republic for almost a decade in the mid-1800s (1836–1845), and it was during that time that Texas acquired the moniker of "The Lone Star State," because of the single star in the republic's flag.

Second only to Alaska in size, Texas offers a landscape that is hard to match. In East Texas you will find over 23 million acres of forest, while in West Texas the rugged Davis Mountains stand with more than 90 peaks over a mile high. South Texas is a water recreation dream with over 600 miles of coastline along the mild Gulf of Mexico. In the vast expanses of the High Plains region of the Panhandle area, it's rumored that on a clear day, you can see all the way up into Canada.

This diverse geography is divided into five wine-grape-growing regions by the Texas Agricultural Department: High Plains, North Central, Trans Pecos, Hill Country, and South Eastern. Each region has a unique climatic, geographic, and cultural character that defines the wines produced within. When it comes to touring Texas wineries, however, the state's infamous size and diversity have proved to be a hindrance in the past. For wine tourists, finding a winery in a state measuring 900 miles from east to west is like trying to find a needle in a haystack.

We have created seven wine trails that we believe will give you the tools you need to find not only the haystack, but the needles within. These trails are the Munson Trail in North Central Texas; the Enchanted Trail, the Highland Trail, and the Balcones Trail in the Hill Country; the Brazos Trail in South Eastern Texas; and the Palo Duro Trail and the Pecos Trail in West Texas. Each wine trail is your map to wine tasting and fun in the towns along the trails. The scale of the vineyards and the capacities of the wineries increase as you travel from East to West Texas.

The Munson Trail takes you through the agricultural area of North Central Texas and includes eleven wineries. The Hill Country, which is assuredly the most romantic area in Texas, is divided

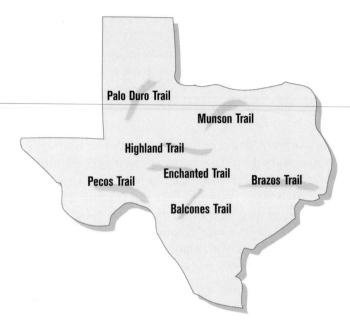

TEXAS WINE TRAILS

into three trails: the Enchanted Trail that tours nine wineries, the Highland Trail that includes stops at six wineries, and the Balcones Trail that visits three wineries south of Austin. This area has something for everyone: lakes, rivers, sleepy enclaves, beautiful vistas, and cozy Bed and Breakfast accommodations. The Hill Country is host to roughly fifty percent of the wineries in the state.

In southeast Texas is the Brazos Trail that includes seven wineries. Further west are wineries whose scale and grandeur befit the vastness of West Texas. Along the Palo Duro Trail, which includes three wineries, you will encounter the architectural grandeur of Cap*Rock Winery near Lubbock, and along the Pecos Trail, which includes three wineries, is the sprawling 1,000+ acre vineyard of Ste. Genevieve Wines in Fort Stockton.

TOURS AND TASTINGS

The details of winery tours and tastings vary greatly across the state. Many of the wineries established in the late 1970s and early 1980s were built in dry counties. These wineries, especially in the Dallas area, were forced to move their tasting rooms to another county, sometimes many miles from the wine-producing facilities. Because of this, the wineries can offer the public a taste of their wines, but winery tours are either not available, or only available by special arrangements. The majority of the wineries however have tasting rooms located within the wineries themselves and offer tours of their facilities, often with a stop in the vineyard.

We begin our tour in the lush agricultural area north of the Dallas/Ft. Worth area, as we travel along the Munson Trail.

Chapter 2

NORTH CENTRAL WINERIES

THE MUNSON TRAIL

*T*he ghosts of great winemakers and viticulturists past haunt this region. Many of the early grape pioneers have long been forgotten, but one stands out in these parts: T. V. Munson. This trail—the Munson Trail—has many unique characteristics, beginning with its name. It is the only trail that is not named after a geographical or geological feature in Texas. It is named instead to honor the groundbreaking work done by Munson and the legacy he left for Texas.

In more modern times, this passion for the grape is found in the likes of Dr. Bobby Smith of La Buena Vida Vineyards and Gabe Parker of Homestead Winery. These men, with wineries in dry counties, were pioneers in the resurgence of the Texas wine industry. Both have been active over the decades in working with the Texas legislature to enact laws to keep Texas competitive with other state wine industries. But, more about them later!

We will visit eleven wineries along this north central trail: Homestead Winery, Hidden Springs Winery, Cross Roads Vineyards, Lone Oak Vineyards, Brushy Creek Vineyards,

◄ **THE WINE INSIDE THESE BARRELS SLOWLY ABSORBS THE CHARACTER OF THE WOOD.** (COURTESY OF THE TEXAS DEPARTMENT OF AGRICULTURE)

THE MUNSON TRAIL

- Homestead Winery
- Hidden Springs Winery
- Cross Roads Vineyards
- Lone Oak Vineyards
- Brushy Creek Vineyards
- Cross Timbers Winery

- Cap*Rock Winery—
  Grapevine Tasting Room
- La Buena Vida Winery
- Delaney Vineyards
- La Bodega Winery
- Kiepersol Estates Vineyard

Cross Timbers Winery, Cap*Rock Winery, La Buena Vida Vineyards, Delaney Vineyards, La Bodega Winery, and Kiepersol Estate Vineyards. This trail is a unique mix of wineries: off-site tasting room, a one-of-kind airport winery, and an architectural jewel—a diversity befitting the Dallas/Ft. Worth area. The Munson Trail is also the only one where you visit one winery twice; Homestead Winery has tasting rooms in Denison and Grapevine.

The Munson Trail, with its roots in the forest and farmland near Denison, delights the wine tourist by offering quiet, bucolic pastures and loads of history in the many small towns, as well as the beauty and excess of the Dallas/Ft. Worth area. The trail will take you over approximately one-hundred-seventy miles of scenic landscapes, and stops at towns such as Denison, Denton, Grapevine, and Dallas. You will also pass through smaller towns such as Whitesboro, Collinsville, Tioga, and Pilot Point.

Using Dallas as our base camp, our first stop is the Homestead Winery tasting room in the town of Denison, seventy-five miles north of Dallas on US 75. Our next stop is Hidden Springs Winery in the town of Pilot Point. Approximately sixty miles north of Dallas, this winery is located on SH 377, in the middle of town. "Just past the Texaco station," as one of the staff told us on the phone—and she was right. It serves as a good landmark. Winemaker Lela Banks, educated at Grayson County College, produces wine that reflects the warmth of her personality. From Hidden Springs we head

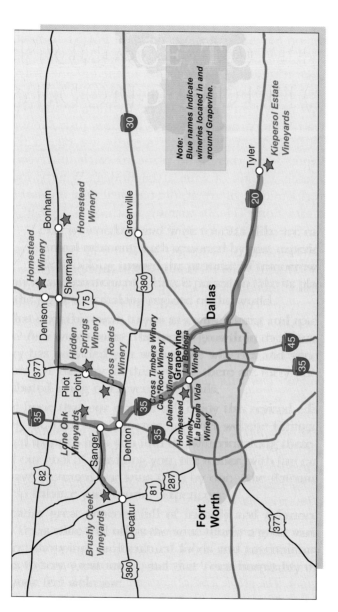

Note:
Blue names indicate wineries located in and around Grapevine.

Kiepersol Estate
Vineyards

Tyler

20

30

Greenville

380

Dallas

Bonham

Homestead
Winery

Homestead
Winery

Sherman

Denison

75

Hidden
Springs
Winery

Cross Roads
Winery

377

Pilot
Point

35

Cross Timbers Winery

Cao*Rock Winery

Grapevine
La Bodega
Winery

Delaney Vineyards

Homestead
Winery

La Buena Vida
Winery

Lone Oak
Vineyards

35

Sanger

Denton

35

35

45

82

81

287

Decatur

Brushy Creek
Vineyards

380

Fort
Worth

377

THE MUNSON TRAIL WINERIES

south on SH 377 a few miles to visit Cross Roads Vineyards. Then we head west on SH 380 and north on IH 35 to visit Lone Oak Vineyards. After tasting some fine Merlot there, we head west on SH 455, turning south on FM 51 to north on SH 81 for a few miles to visit Brushy Creek Vineyards on FM 2798. Then it's back towards Dallas to the historic district of Grapevine, where we will stop at the tasting rooms of Cross Timbers Winery, Cap*Rock Winery, La Buena Vida Winery, Homestead Winery, and Delaney Vineyards just a few miles down SH 121. From Delaney Vineyards, we take a trip to DFW Airport. No, there's no plane to catch, but you may want to catch a *flight* of wine at La Bodega Winery, located smack in the middle of an airport terminal. For our last stop, we head east along IH 20, turning south on SH 69 in Tyler to visit Kiepersol Estate Vineyards.

After enjoying these wineries, we will end our journey in Dallas/Ft. Worth. This metropolis will entice you with culinary delights, incredible shopping excursions, stockyards, fine arts, theater, museums, and subtle (and not-so-subtle) entertainment spots. Local restaurants are also big supporters of Texas wines. Be sure to ask for them.

We begin our tour with Homestead Winery in one of two ways. If you're a Type-A personality who "just likes to get there already," then heading north on US-75 is the way to go. If one the other hand, you would like to take a backroad to Denison, even though it will take slightly longer, try SH 289, which parallels IH 75, about eleven miles to the west. SH 289 delights the traveler with sights and sounds of small towns like Frisco, Prosper, and Gunter.

Once in downtown Denison, you can find Homestead Wineries' tasting room on Main Street. A little warning for you, plan on spending more time than you may have thought in Denison. The people and atmosphere will make you want to linger to take in all the historic sites and sample some of the food and shopping available.

❧Homestead Winery

www.homesteadwineries.com
P.O. Box 35,
Ivanhoe, Texas 75447

Phone: (903) 583-4281,
Fax: (903) 583-2024

Denison Tasting Room
220 West Main St.,
Denison, Texas 75020

Phone: (903) 464-0030

OPEN: WEDNESDAY–SATURDAY
11:00 A.M.–5:30 P.M.

TOURS AND TASTING
BY APPOINTMENT

Homestead Winery is a small boutique-style family operation located on the grounds of the Parker Homestead, which gives the winery its name. Because the winery facility is off the beaten path, the owners decided to take their wine to where the people are by opening three tasting rooms. You can sample their wine in Denison and Grapevine.

Gabe and Barbara Parker came to winemaking from a heritage that includes more than 100 years of farming in North Texas.

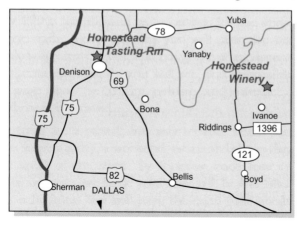

HOMESTEAD VINEYARDS AND WINERY

This gives the family a level of expertise unmatched by other grape growers in the area. Gabe is a rancher, businessman, and farmer. After spending years in the corporate world, he decided to go back to his roots and started his vineyard in 1983. The winery was bonded in 1989 and with the help of wine consultant Roy Mitchell has grown consistently, and in 1996 produced 3,000 cases of wine. Gabe's heritage in farming quickly helped him establish a robust vineyard and made the Homestead name a label of quality and distinctive wines.

The winery has intentionally been kept small over the years, which allows greater control of the winemaking process. Gabe's philosophy is simple: The quality of the wine starts with the quality of the vineyard. Gabe feels that the awards his wines continue to win are the results of the skill of his winemaker and the quality of his grapes.

Gabe's efforts in defining and enhancing the Texas wine industry have led him, like Bobby Smith of La Buena Vida Winery, to be a catalyst for new legislation to help the wine industry flourish in the state. He also assists with a variety of festivals to promote the industry in this and other areas of the state.

The Denison Tasting Room is located in a renovated 1890s structure and houses both a tasting room, and a production facility. When we spoke with winery owner Gabe Parker, he told us that the business has outgrown the production capacity of the winery, and it made sense to move some of the production out to where visitors were the tasting room. Most of Homestead Winery's red wines are now being made in the Denison tasting room, which within three years is projected to have a 20,000-gallon capacity. "Eventually," Gabe told us, "all oak fermentation will be done in the Denison facility."

THE WINES

Roy Mitchell is Homestead's winemaker and is well-known in the Texas wine industry. A pioneer of the early 1970s research in grape production, Dr. Mitchell helped to establish the first new commercial winery in Texas—Llano Estacado. He has been a consultant to numerous wineries in the state and has assisted growers with grape production problems. Roy knows how to grow grapes in Texas, perhaps better than anyone. He brings a classic sense of winemaking to Homestead Winery, and working with Gabe, produces blended wines with grapes picked from the Homestead Vineyard and vineyards around the state. Some of Homestead's most popular wines include Muscat Canelli, Roses of Ivanhoe, Cabernet Sauvignon, and Chardonnay, all of which enjoy distribution across a large area of Texas. Gabe is especially proud of the success of his Muscat Canelli. It was one of the first wines ever produced in this area of Texas. Homestead has added some exciting wines since the opening of their Denison tasting room—a Fume Blanc and a White Rosé in 1999, and Desert Rosé and Bodega de Mitchell in 2000. The Bodega de Mitchell, Cream Del Sol Texas Cream Sherry is a mederized white wine aged and blended to a constant taste in Homestead Winery's solera. A solera is a barrel system set up for the specific purpose of creating this wine. The Desert Rosé is one of the few dry Muscat Cannelli wines produced in Texas.

DIRECTIONS: AFTER TOURING HOMESTEAD WINERY, WE HEAD WESTWARD ON SH 82 FOR 48 MILES. TURNING SOUTH ON SH 377 IT IS A SHORT TRIP OF 18 MILES TO THE TOWN OF PILOT POINT AND HIDDEN SPRINGS WINERY.

❧Hidden Springs Winery

www.hiddenspringswinery.com

256 North Highway 377
Pilot Point, Texas 76258

Phone: (940) 686-2782
Fax: (940) 686-4206

OPEN: 12:00 P.M.–5:00 P.M.
TUESDAY–SATURDAY

2:00 P.M.–5:00 P.M. SUNDAY
TASTINGS, RETAIL SALES, AND GIFTS
TOURS BY APPOINTMENT ONLY

Turning onto SH 380, you will probably breathe a sigh of contentment as you travel through this north Texas agricultural area. The roadsides are awash in green, be it from untouched trees or the meticulously planted fields of the local

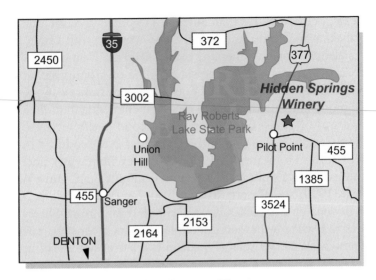

HIDDEN SPRINGS WINERY

farmers' vegetables. The fast pace of big-city life is far behind you and the tranquil agricultural area will have a calming effect, putting you in just the right mood for Hidden Springs Winery.

This unassuming facility, which looks like a remodeled office building from the road, is full of Victorian charm and elegance. You know in the back of your mind that you just turned off a busy highway, and you are also vaguely aware that in the backrooms of this winery, people are feverishly working on setting up a private party or bottling this year's new crush, but it doesn't seem to matter. Jim and Lela Banks, along with the wonderful staff working with them, have cleverly created a remarkably calm and friendly environment in which to sample their wines.

Lela Banks, winemaker and co-owner, had been an amateur winemaker for years prior to her formal education at Grayson County College in the early 1990s. She was awarded a scholarship at Clos du Vougeot in France to complete her studies for an Associate of Applied Science in Viticulture and Enology. The vineyard in Whitesboro had been in existence long before the opening of Hidden Springs Winery. In fact, the winery owes its name to the springs located on the property. As Lela tells it, when she and her husband purchased the property, they were told that it had a number of natural springs. During excursions on the property their first year, they managed to find three springs, but were told by neighbors that there was a fourth.

After moving in, Lela and Jim noticed that a car would often drive slowly by their home, but never stop. Finally, when Lela was in the front yard one day, the driver, an elderly woman, stopped to talk. As the conversation went on, Lela learned that this woman was part of the original family that started the farm, and she knew exactly where that last "hidden" spring was located. After finding what turned out to be the prettiest of the springs, according to Lela, they decided that Hidden Springs would be the name of their yet-to-be-formed winery.

The winery is located in a building that has gone through many reincarnations: an office, a restaurant, and even a honky-tonk saloon. After extensive remodeling, the Bankses have created a comfortable atmosphere filled with antiques from Europe. The tasting room features a massive turn-of-the-century bar from a Texas saloon, backed by a marble credenza surrounded by oversized walnut-framed mirrors. The magnificent chandelier is festooned with over 300 lead-crystal drops.

After sampling their wines, you may embark on a tour of the winery facilities by passing through a gothic-styled solid-oak

THE UNMISTAKABLE SIGN FOR HIDDEN SPRINGS WINERY.

door brought here from an Austrian wine cellar. The tour culminates with a pass through the function room and the gift shop, both well appointed in the Victorian theme. The function room is available for wedding receptions, teas, luncheons, corporate functions, and other special events. The gift shop is a comfortable unpretentious display of food items intermixed with arts and crafts of some fine Texas artists.

Hidden Springs Winery celebrates their anniversary on the Fourth of July. Keep that date in mind when you're planing a trip around that holiday, because their multi-day celebration features food, music, and of course, wine. As a testament to the quality of their wines, they have expanded their production capacity to seven thousand gallons to keep up with demand, and plan to go to ten thousand shortly.

THE WINES

Hidden Springs is a young winery, though you couldn't tell that by tasting the wines. Opened in 1996 on the Fourth of July, it offers a good range of red and white wines. Though somewhat guarded about her winemaking techniques, Lela admits that she prefers making "lighter" wines. She uses stainless-steel fermentation for her whites, even the Chardonnay that she only "ran the roots of the oak tree through." The Chardonnay is a light, fruity creation, quite different from the oakey, buttery wines that are created by barrel fermentation. Lela also prefers just a little oak fermentation for her reds to avoid a heavy tannin flavor. When she does use oak, Lela uses both French and American oak at Hidden Springs, but prefers the flavor of the French.

With only eighteen acres of their own grapes, the Bankses must rely on vineyards from other areas of the state to supplement a growing demand for their wine. This has forced Lela to be a more creative winemaker, in that she does a large amount of blending for her wines. Her Ruby Glow, a particular favorite of ours during our visit, is a blend of 80 percent Ruby Cabernet, 10 percent Cabernet Franc, 5 percent Cabernet Sauvignon, and 5 percent Merlot. This blend produces a nice smooth taste, with just a hint of a tannin aftertaste to fill out the mouth. A similar blending experiment—the Crystal Red—is a mixture of 50 percent Cabernet

Sauvignon, 20 percent Mixed Red (it's a secret!), 15 percent Cabernet Franc, 12 percent Ruby Cabernet, and 3 percent Merlot. New for 2000 is a Vintner's Red, Vintner's White, and a 1997 Cabernet Sauvignon.

As Lela promised two years ago, she did indeed produce a Merlot to meet her customer's demands. This one hundred percent Merlot is made from grapes grown in nearby Lone Oak Vineyards. The high quality of these grapes allows Lela to create a smooth wine with intriguing texture and wonderful fruit flavors. A good-natured individual with a quick smile, Lela brings a strong sense of professionalism to her craft and isn't afraid to admit when she is wrong about something. Traditionally, Lela used Merlot as a blending wine, feeling that it lacked enough of a presence to stand on its own. The results of her 1997 Merlot, however, changed her mind. As always, the wines are always made to her tough standards. In her words, "Nothing will go behind our label that is not quality and consistent."

THE QUALITY WINES OF HIDDEN SPRINGS WINERY.

In 2000, Hidden Springs Winery released a new label for their wines featuring bold colors and a sleek design. Look for them to incorporate glass etching on their bottles, a process that carves a design into the glass. They also offer private labeling of their wines, a service seeing a sharp rise in popularity. If you are a member of their Patrons Privilege Club, membership includes twelve free custom labels per year. Benefits of the Club also include discounts on wine and non-wine purchases

When you buy their wines, the staff will ask if you would like the optional gift-wrap service they offer. We suggest you have at least one bottle wrapped this way. They do a wonderful job. The wrapping was so attractive, in fact, that two of the three bottles we had wrapped, never made it out of Dallas. Friends we visited saw the bottles and just had to have them. While we hated to part with Lela's wine, we were happy to introduce our friends to delicious Texas wine.

DIRECTIONS: FROM HIDDEN SPRINGS WINERY, WE SLIDE SOUTHWARD ALONG SH 377 FOR JUST A FEW MILES TO VISIT CROSS ROADS VINEYARDS.

☙Cross Roads Vineyards

www.crossroadsvineyards.com

8400 Fishtrap Road
Aubrey, Texas 76227

Phone: (940) 440-9522

> OPEN: THURSDAY–SUNDAY
> 1:00 P.M.–SUNSET
> TASTINGS, RETAIL SALES, AND GIFTS

Charmed by the bucolic scenery of this agricultural paradise in North Texas, Fernando and Laura Sanchez purchased some acreage along SH 377 to enjoy the area all year long. After visiting Hidden Springs Winery, which is just up the road from them, Lela Banks told Fernando about the winemaking courses available at nearby Grayson Community

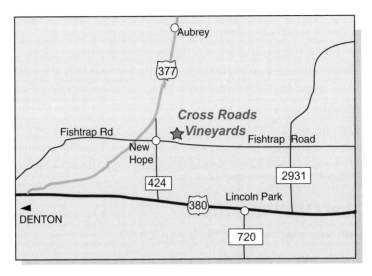

CROSS ROADS VINEYARDS

College. Excited by the possibility, Fernando threw himself into the curriculum, anxious to learn all he could and launch his own vineyard and winery.

Fernando and Laura first planted an experimental plot of 75 vines that are now in third leaf. Based on the success of this small vineyard, the couple followed with an additional 1,600 vines in the Spring of 2001. The two-acre vineyard now includes Zinfandel, Merlot, Chenin Blanc, Sangiovese, Chardonnay, and Shiraz. The Sanchez's are patient folks, planting small amounts of each grape to see how well the grapes grow in the soil conditions of their vineyard.

THE WINES

Cross Roads Vineyards offers a Sweet Muscat, Sweet Red Table wine, Chardonnay, Merlot, Cabernet Sauvignon, a Blush, and a Dry Red Table wine from their tasting room and gift shop. The 2000 Chardonnay took a bronze medal in the 2002 Lone Star Wine Competition. To help visitors enjoy these wines, an outside Gazebo tasting bar allows folks—weather permitting—to sip wine and enjoy the beautiful surroundings of the winery.

Initial production will be about 400 to 500 cases a year. As with all small lot releases, if you taste something you like, you'd better buy it before you leave. Chances are, the wine will be sold out the next time you visit. Cross Roads Vineyards is the perfect place to leave big city stress behind you, buy a bottle of wine, and sit by the winery's two-acre pond and enjoy life a little.

Directions: We head west on IH 30, turning north on IH 35. Once past the town of Sanger we will exit on Lone Oak Rd., heading east to Lone Oak Vineyards—entering the second "Flying W" ranch gate on your left.

❧Lone Oak Vineyards

www.texaswinetrails.com/lone.htm

4781 E. Lone Oak Road
Valley View, Texas 76272

Phone: (940)-637-2612

Open:
Thursday–Saturday
2:00 p.m.–7:00 p.m.
Other times by
appointment
Tastings, retail sales,
and gifts

The day we visited Lone Oak Vineyards, a warm breeze from the south slid up the hillside making the landscape come alive, turning the vineyard into a green undulating mass. As we talked with Jamie and Robert Wolfe, owners of Lone Oak Vineyards, we admired the panoramic view of the countryside. To the west, fisherman carefully guided their boats amongst the ghost-white trunks of dead trees that now provide some of the best fishing spots on Rayburn Lake.

To the north and east we are surrounded by a vast complex of stair-step hills awash in a palette of green hues from recent spring rains. Jamie remarks that the land and the vineyard have provided a sort of spiritual cleansing and rejuvenation, teaching her not to sweat the small stuff in life. Dressed in jeans and a denim shirt, her long hair pulled back, Jamie exudes a wholesome beauty that seems to be nurtured by the countryside. Her dark eyes flash with excitement as she talks about the vineyards that have become a labor of love over the years.

THE VINEYARD

Robert Wolfe, who bears a striking resemblance to Kevin Costner, surveys the vineyard with pride as we inspect the appearance of new grape clusters on a healthy Merlot grapevine. Texas wine notables, such as Roy Mitchell and Roy Renfro have helped the Wolfes accomplish what many said couldn't be done in this area in terms of vineyard design. Utilizing five-foot spacing between rows and a unique diagonal trellis design, the vineyard contains 3,000 vines over three acres. At this spacing, the use of commercial-sized equipment is impossible. As a consequence, the Wolfes have developed an intimate relationship with their vineyard, having to do much of the work by hand. Orientated to take advantage of the steady southern breeze, this vineyard has consistently produced record-breaking crops. Though

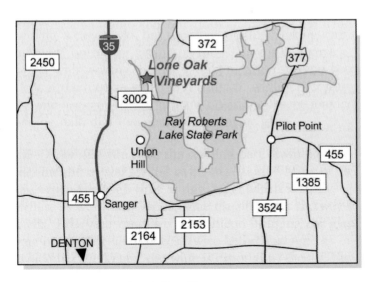

LONE OAK VINEYARDS

dominated by Merlot grapes, the vineyard also includes Cabernet Sauvignon, Cabernet Franc, and small amounts of Malbec and Petit Verdot.

Opposed to unnecessary chemistry, Robert minimizes herbicide usage but maintains a religious schedule of fungicide spraying. He also is against allowing vegetation to grow between the rows, preferring to allow all the soils nutrients to concentrate in the vines. It must pay off, the seven-year-old vineyard has never had a problem with the diseases typical in this part of Texas. Through the Wolfes' constant attention their vineyard not only provides tremendous fruit, it is a true pleasure to the eye with thick green foliage and magnificent clusters.

THE WINES

Robert's motto for the winery is, "to do one thing very well." For Lone Oak Vineyards, that one thing in producing only red Bordeaux-style wines. With the help of winemaker Jim Evans, Lone Oak Vineyards offers hand-crafted red wines that include Merlot, Cabernet Sauvignon, and, at the time of our visit, a still unnamed blend.

Jim Evans, one of the early pioneers of the Texas wine industry, nurtures the fermentation and blending of these premium reds in a long row of French oak barrels. The barrel room is located in a former horse barn that has been magically transformed into a state-of-the-art wine production facility. The wines are, so far, unfiltered, which is a style preferred by both winemaker and owner. However, Robert later told us that a decision was made by Jim to lightly filter the wine.

A visit to this winery is a real pleasure, both in the wines and in the environment the Wolfe's have created. As Robert explained, he wants people to stop by and "know the wines, know the history of the wine, and enjoy tasting the wine." Indeed! He's definitely off to a good start; his 2000 Merlot took two bronze medals in the 2002 Lone Star Wine Competition. Based on our barrel tasting of future releases, we can expect to enjoy a long line of marvelous red wines from Lone Oak Vineyards.

In the future, Robert plans his vineyard by planting in what is now hayfields along the curving drive up to his house. "The new vineyard," Robert says, "will be planted to allow commercial-sized equipment between the rows. I've got all the hand labor grapevines I need."

To help folks acquire a better appreciation of Texas wine, Lone Oak Vineyards now offers eight wines from four other Texas wineries. Stop by and enjoy their hospitality and great selection of wines.

DIRECTIONS: FROM LONE OAK VINEYARDS, WE BACKTRACK TO SANGER AND HEAD WEST ON FM 455 TO FM 51 AND HEAD SOUTH TO THE TOWN OF DECATUR. IN DECATUR WE HEAD NORTH ALONG SH 81, PAST THE TOWN OF ALVORD, UNTIL WE REACH COUNTY ROAD 2798, TURNING RIGHT TO VISIT BRUSHY CREEK VINEYARDS.

♣Brushy Creek Vineyards

www.brushycreekvineyards.com/
572 County Road 2798
Alvord Texas 76225-3026
Phone: (940) 427-4747

OPEN: SEVEN DAYS A WEEK 10:00 A.M.–6.00 P.M.

TASTINGS, RETAIL SALES, AND GIFTS

Brushy Creek Vineyards

Black Venus

Les Constable, Winemaker

Grapes from Oak Creek Vineyards, Red River Valley

Surrounding Brushy Creek Vineyards is the inspiring beauty of the 20,250-acre Lyndon B. Johnson National Grasslands. Containing over 400 lakes and ponds, this grassland area is a refuge for a variety of wildlife. As Les Constable, owner and winemaker for Brushy Creek Vineyards explained, "Being surrounded by the Grass-lands, we have a lot of wildlife on our property, as well as some excellent bird-watching conditions." According to Les, it is not unusual to spot birds such as the Mississippi Kite, the Painted Bunting, and numerous Hawks on the winery grounds.

As a retired nuclear engineer, once responsible for nuclear re-actor operations aboard U.S. submarines, Les is detailed orient-ed and big on research. Not surprisingly, he looks at his vineyard as one big research project. His career in winemaking began as a child helping his botanist father make homemade wines. Later, Les went on to become an amateur winemaker, experimenting with many varietals while earning numerous awards at amateur winemaking contests.

In anticipation of opening his own winery, Les and his wife Ann began planting their vineyard in 1996. Today, they have five acres planted with thirty-six varieties of grapes. Why so many different grapes? That is where the research part comes into play. The win-ery's vineyard contains a sandy loam soil known as Crosstimbers soil, perfect for growing grapes. Taking advantage of this soil, Les sees his vineyard as a grape growing experiment; he wants Brushy Creek Vineyards to be, "a small neighborhood winery that spe-cializes in research for growing grapes in this part of Texas."

WINDMILL.

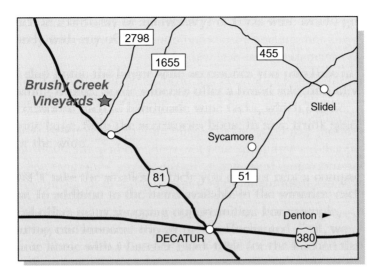

BUSHY CREEK VINEYARDS

THE VINEYARD

Les is focusing on hot climate grapes such as the Spanish Tempranillo and Carnelian varietals. He has also introduced a new grape to the area, the Rkatsiteli, which is a Ukrainian grape from the Black Sea area. The grape develops a beautiful floral nose and seems to have the perfect chemistry for the Texas climate. If you want to hear a good story, ask Les to tell you about the Ukrainian monk who is helping him grow this grape.

THE WINES

As a winemaker, Les is passionate about developing a unique winemaking style for Texas. He feels that, "If we follow what others [Europe and California] have done we will never make anything out of our wine industry." He believes that rather than copying a certain winemaking style "we should adapt the best of European and California winemaking techniques that best fit our soil and climate conditions." When asked if he thought Italian grapes would do well in Texas, his response was, "No, I think Spanish grapes will eventually prove themselves superior." Les draws attention to the fact that Italy's narrow land width surrounded on each side by water is vastly different from conditions in Texas. Spain's larger landmass and similar climatic conditions are a better match to what Texas winemakers must deal with.

Brushy Creek Vineyards will produce small amounts of Sherry, Port, "Big Reds," and a variety of white wines in the 2,000-gallon capacity winery. Using both stainless-steel and oak for fermentation, Les hopes to gradually raise the capacity to around 8,000 gallons within the next few years. To help the public learn about and enjoy Texas wines, Brushy Creek Vineyards will also carry wines from many other Texas wineries in its tasting room.

DIRECTIONS: WE HEAD BACK TO DECATUR AND TURN EAST ONTO SH 380 TO IH 35E, THEN HEAD SOUTH TO THE TOWN OF GRAPEVINE. TURN LEFT ON N. MAIN SREET TO VISIT THE FIRST GRAPEVINE AREA WINERY— CROSS TIMBERS WINERY.

&Cross Timbers Winery

www.crosstimberswinery.com

**805 N. Main Street
Grapevine, Texas 76051**

Phone: (817) 488-6789

HOURS: SUNDAY–FRIDAY
12:00 P.M.–5:00 P.M.

SATURDAY
11:00 A.M.–5:00 P.M.

TASTINGS, RETAIL SALES,
AND GIFTS

CROSS TIMBERS
W I N E R Y

Blush

Table Wine
TEXAS
2000

Cross Timbers Winery, 805 North Main Street, Grapevine, TX 76051
Phone: 817-488-6789 • E-mail: Crosstimberswinery@Directlink.net

750 ml   Alc. 11.5% by Vol.

The pace of life changes as you drive north of the Northwest Highway in the Grapevine area. Though only spittin' distance from Opry Land, Grapevine Mills and the bustling Historic District of Grapevine, you enter into a quiet country settlement. That is exactly the atmosphere Don Bigby was looking for when scouting a winery site. The Cross Timbers Winery tasting room opened in the summer of 2001, offering wines from all Texas wineries. It is the first step in

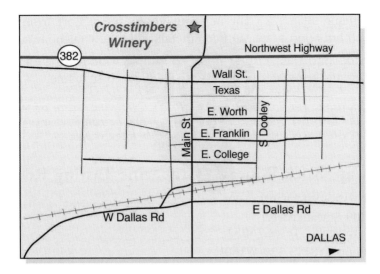

CROSS TIMBERS WINERY

Don's ambitious plan to intermingle wine and unique events with the ambiance of the Grapevine area.

When we spoke with Don, he was out in the acreage behind the tasting room working on a 4,000-square-foot wine production facility. Designed after an original pole barn on the land, this building system will allow Cross Timbers Winery to easily expand as additional production space is needed. In addition to the tasting room and production facility, Don's master plan includes the construction of gazebos, cabins, and even a chapel.

THE WINES

Don is the first to admit that he is not a farmer, though he admires the tenacity and dedication of Texas grape growers who risk heartache and finances to bring grapes to Texas winemakers. Grapes gathered from the his small vineyard in Grapevine and from numerous growers in the state are handed over to Les Constable, wine consultant for Cross Timbers Winery. Together with Don, Les is developing a vision of wines to be produced by this winery. Cross Timbers Winery plans to initially offer a Blush, a Chenin Blanc, a Cabernet Sauvignon, and a Port from the Chambourchin grape. Other varietals will follow in the future.

Stop into their tasting room to sample wine from all across Texas and see what special events are on their schedule.

DIRECTIONS: FROM CROSS TIMBERS WINERY, WE HEAD SOUTH ON MAIN STREET INTO THE HISTORIC DISTRICT OF GRAPEVINE FOR OUR NEXT STOP: THE GRAPEVINE TASTING ROOM OF CAP*ROCK WINERY.

❧Cap*Rock Winery—Grapevine Tasting Room

www.caprockwinery.com

**409 S Main Street
Grapevine, Texas 76051**

**Phone: (817) 329-WINE
Fax: (817) 410-2014**

OPEN: TUESDAY–SATURDAY
11:00 A.M.–4:30 P.M.
SUNDAY
12:00 P.M.–5:00 P.M.

Those of you familiar with the Lubbock area probably recognize the name of Cap*Rock Winery. Don't worry, they haven't decided to abandon their gorgeous Lubbock facility to move to Grapevine; the winery decided to open a second tasting room. Sales and Marketing director John Bratcher explained that the winery owners wanted to develop a higher profile in the Dallas/Ft. Worth area and Grapevine seemed like the ideal place.

Located on Main Street directly across from the Opry House, Cap*Rock's tasting room opened in September of 1999. The manager told us that the response has been tremendous, "During festivals, it's shoulder-to-shoulder in here, within minutes of opening the doors."—a fitting testament to the quality of Cap*Rock's wines and their decision to open the Grapevine tasting room.

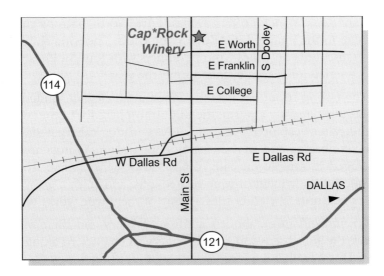

CAP*ROCK WINERY

**WINEMAKER KIM MCPHEARSON
BARREL SAMPLES A MATURING RED WINE.**

Cap*Rock Winery offers Dallas/Fort Worth patrons membership in the unique Cap*Rock Wine Club. The wine club features discounts on wines, vintner dinners with Kim McPhearson, and a variety of special events during the year.

The tasting room has been designed in an elegant, understated fashion, creating a warm, friendly atmosphere for tasting wine. Handcrafted cabinetry and a custom-made, cabernet-stained concrete bartop add to the cutting edge design. Visitors are encouraged to sample the line of Cap*Rock wines, select from a wonderful assortment of wine-related gifts, and enjoy a great display of custom labeled bottles—many of them true works of art.

To find out more about Cap*Rock Winery and their wines, check the full discussion of this winery in chapter 5, along the Palo Duro Trail.

DIRECTIONS: FROM CAP*ROCK WE CONTINUE ALONG MAIN STREET, TURNING LEFT ONTO COLLEGE STREET TO VISIT THE TASTING ROOM OF LA BUENA VIDA WINERY.

❧La Buena Vida Winery

www.labuenavida.com

**416 College Street
Grapevine, Texas 76051**

**Phone: (817) 481-9463
Fax: (817) 421-3635**

OPEN: MONDAY–SATURDAY 10:00 A.M.–5:00 P.M.
SUNDAY 12:00 P.M.–5:00 P.M.
TOURS, TASTINGS, AND GIFTS $5 FOR TASTING

Welcome to La Buena Vida Winery in Grapevine, Texas. In the Texas wine industry, historic Grapevine is akin to sacred ground. Town fathers requested, and re-

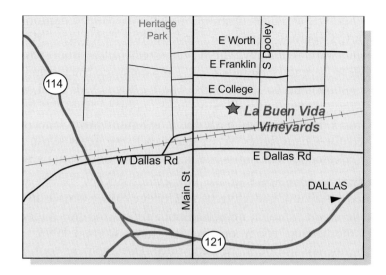

LA BUENA VIDA WINERY

ceived, special legislation that allows wineries to sell wine by the glass for consumption on the premises in counties designated as wet counties.

It is fitting then, that Dr. Bobby Smith, owner of La Buena Vida, decided to move his tasting room to Grapevine since he was a key promoter of the Farm Winery Act of 1977. This bill permits winemakers to produce wine in a dry county, as long as it is sold in a wet county. A secondary, but no less important benefit of this legislation, was that it opened the doors for the creation of small wineries across the state of Texas.

This small family-owned winery, the first to establish a tasting room in Grapevine, has been making wine since the early 1970s. It is the third-oldest winery in Texas and the first in the northeastern section of the state. It is also the last of three wineries originally established in Parker County.

Bobby and his son Steve, the winemaker for La Buena Vida Winery, produce wines under five separate labels: Springtown, Walnut Creek Cellars, Grapevine, La Buena Vida, and Smith Estates. Each label focuses on a certain segment of the wine market.

The Springtown label includes Springtown Mist, Chardonnay, Merlot, Cabernet Sauvignon, Red, Merlot l'Elegance, Muscat Canelli, and Sweet Ruby. The Walnut Creek Cellars label includes a reserve Port and a vintage Port. The Grapevine label includes a Mist (Blush) and La Dulce Vida. The La Buena Vida label, used for wines made from bulk wine juice imported from Chile, includes a Chardonnay and a Merlot. The Smith Estates label is reserved for Champagnes. A separate label, the Texas Blush is a wine released for Christmas and is always a favorite with patrons.

Eager to participate in the Grapevine concept, Bobby purchased an abandoned church on College Street, smack in the middle of a residential neighborhood. After extensive remodeling, the tasting room opened its doors in mid-1995, and Grapevine has not been the same since. Development continues to this day as Bobby enhances the grounds around the building with greenery, shady arbors, fountains, herb gardens, and a beautiful adjoining patio area for special functions.

We met Bobby on a recent visit to the tasting room. At an age when most men would prefer a leisurely round of golf or a cigar with the guys, Bobby was out back driving posts, stringing trellis wire, and planting vines in 90° plus heat. He is developing an experimental vineyard on the property to produce Grapevine select wines.

Bobby told us that it has been somewhat of an uphill battle to bring the wine industry back to this part of Texas, but he has had plenty of help over the years convincing legislatures. Humbly, he is quick to point out that it took the efforts of much more than one man to bring about the needed changes, and he is happy to participate in the Grapevine concept.

Camille McBee has been with the winery from its early days and is responsible for public relations, arranging special events and corporate functions and deftly organizing the winery's participation in various festivals and competitions.

Her effervescence and enthusiasm is infectious as she describes the winery and its participation in the city of Grapevine. Camille sees La Buena Vida as unique in that it fills a niche market in the

LA BUENA VIDA WINERY TASTING ROOM.

industry. The winery is one of the true experimental wineries in the state, offering an esoteric mixture of table wines, traditional varieties, and dessert and specialized wines.

THE WINES

To satisfy the increasing demand for their wines, La Buena Vida Winery uses grapes from their own Springtown vineyard and other vineyards in Texas to produce their quality wines. The Springtown vineyard is planted with a variety of grapes: Chambourcin, Chenin Blanc, Riesling, Pinot Noir, and Pinot Blanc. Long range plans call for expanding the vineyards by five acres each year. Now this may not sound impressive, but considering the effort required for the trellis work, the irrigation, and the vines themselves, it is quite ambitious.

After twenty years as a Texas winemaker, Bobby Smith is still pushing the envelope of exactly what is a Texas wine, constantly refining and occasionally redefining his wines. They continue to produce their popular Springtown label wines (such as Springtown Mist, Springtown Rain and Springtown Red), which are all light, fruity, highly drinkable wines with wonderful aromatics.

The Merlot l'Elegance, a newcomer to the Springtown label, is one of the few blush Merlots available from a Texas winery. You'll find it especially enjoyable during the hot Texas months when it is served over ice. Camille explains that this wine has been one of their most popular since its first appearance.

Exciting new wines are available under two new labels: Grapevine and La Buena Vida. The La Dulce Vida, bottled under the Grapevine label is a blend of Cabernet Sauvignon, Ruby Cabernet, and Merlot. With a residual sugar level of 5.3, this is a sweet wine similar to the Springtown Sweet Ruby.

The La Buena Vida label was created just for wines produced by La Buena Vida Winery, using bulk grape juice brought in from Chile. With the ongoing shortage of grapes in the United States, Bobby plans to continue importing juice from Chile to help maintain his production levels. Bobby is also experimenting with grape varietals from Portugal in his experimental vineyard behind the tasting room. These grapes will be used to produce a Port made from only the grapes grown in the Grapevine vineyard.

The Walnut Creek Cellars label is used for the winery's Ports, which have been their most decorated wines over the years. The Smith Estates label offers two champagnes, the Blanc De Blanc Brut and the Blanc de Blanc Ultra Brut. Bobby was one of the first winemakers to offer a champagne made in Texas.

This versatile array of varietals, dessert wines, table wines and specialty wines like the Texas Blush and Scarbourough Mead, is indicative of the adventurous spirit at La Buena Vida Winery. Expect much more of the same in the future.

DIRECTIONS: FROM LA BUENA VIDA WINERY, WE TURN RIGHT FROM THEIR PARKING LOT, TAKING A LEFT ONTO SMITH STREET AND ANOTHER LEFT ONTO EAST WORTH STREET TO VISIT THE SECOND TASTING ROOM OF HOMESTEAD WINERY.

☙Homestead Winery—Grapevine Tasting Room

www.texaswinetrails.com/home.htm

211 East Worth
Grapevine, Texas 76051
Phone: (817) 251-9463

OPEN: WEDNESDAY–SATURDAY
11:30 A.M.–5:30 P.M.
SUNDAY
1:00 P.M.–5:30 P.M.

We have the opportunity to sample Homestead Winery's wines for a second time along the Munson Trail, this time in a magnificently restored house in the historic district of Grapevine.

The Grapevine tasting room at 211 East Worth is located in an 1890s Texas Victorian folk-style home. As you step onto the front porch, a generous treatment of architectural gingerbread prepares you to step back in time and enjoy the country charm and

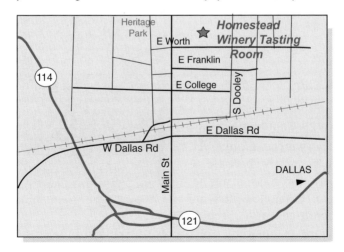

HOMESTEAD WINERY—GRAPEVINE TASTING ROOM

atmosphere of long ago. Inside, you can sample Homestead's most popular wines, browse their selection of wine-related gifts, and even check out their extra room that is available for special events.

Tasting room representative John Hatcher will captivate you with his quick smile, charisma, and impressive knowledge of Homestead's wines. Ask him about tips on pairing these wines with different foods and special events, he is always ready to help you plan a great presentation.

DIRECTIONS: FROM HOMESTEAD WINERY WE TAKE A LEFT ONTO MAIN STREET AND TRAVEL A FEW SHORT BLOCKS TO SH 114, HEADING WEST TO SH 121, THEN SOUTH TO GLADE ROAD, TO VISIT THE ARCHITECTURAL DELIGHT THAT IS DELANEY VINEYARDS.

❧Delaney Vineyards

www.delaneyvineyards.com

**2000 Champagne Boulevard
Grapevine, Texas 76051**

**Phone: (817) 481-5668
Fax: (817) 251-8119**

OPEN: MONDAY–FRIDAY 9:00 A.M.–5:00 P.M.
SATURDAY 10:00 A.M.–5:00 P.M.
TOURS 12:00 P.M.–5:00 P.M.
TASTING, RETAIL SALES, AND GIFTS
$7 FOR A TASTING

Since opening in 1995, the Delaney winery along SH 121 has already become a landmark for folks living in the area. Fashioned after an eighteenth-century French winery, the magnificent structure is surrounded by a century-old stand of oak trees and a lush, ten-acre vineyard. Passersby could easily mistake this site for a European winery on a picture postcard.

THE EUROPEAN AMBIANCE OF DELANEY VINEYARDS.

Passing through the massive doors of the winery, you are swept back in time to the Renaissance period by the hand-painted frescos that adorn the vaulted ceiling of the entry. The masterful paintings incorporate images of cherubs, who supposedly guard the winery from evil at night. Once inside the winery, the eighteen-inch thick walls block out all outside sounds, as a winery greeter points you toward the well-appointed gift shop where you are encouraged to browse through their wines and gifts while you wait for the next tour to begin.

A tour through the facility gives you a better appreciation of the meticulous planning that went into the design and construction of this facility. Owner Jerry Delaney, toured wineries across France for a number

DELANEY VINEYARD'S ATTENTION TO DETAIL IS EVEN EVIDENT IN THE WINERY'S WOODWORK.

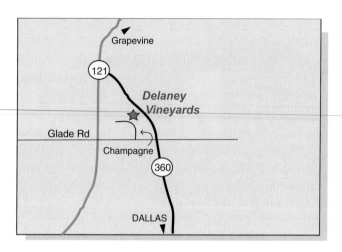

DELANEY VINEYARDS

of years to help him incorporate the essential elements of a grand French winery. A bell tower chime, set at a volume that will not disturb the neighbors, is their attempt to capture the atmosphere of a winery in a small village of France.

The tour finishes in the Barrel Room, which contains a generous 5,000 square feet and seems even larger as you look upward at the soaring vaulted ceiling. The massive stacks of American and French oak fermenting barrels are themselves dwarfed by the shear size of this room. At the far end is the tasting bar that is attended by the well-educated staff who will assist you with a wine tasting.

THE WINES

Delaney uses grapes from the ten-acre vineyard that surrounds the winery as well as grapes from their seventy-eight-acre vine-yard near Lamesa, Texas, which was established in 1987. Wine is produced at both the Lamesa and Grapevine wineries using a combination of stainless-steel tanks and oak barrels to achieve the proper fermentation qualities, depending on the variety.

The 1994 Cabernet Sauvignon, a blend of Cabernet Sauvignon, Merlot, and Cabernet Franc, was produced following the traditional Bordeaux methods, using egg whites for finning, or clarifying, the wine prior to bottling. After more than fifteen months of oak aging, the wine has a delicate bouquet with cherry undertones. Jerry Delaney expect this wine to continue to age in the bottle over the next ten years. The 1995 Cabernet Sauvignon bears the distinction of having been completely produced in French oak.

Between these bursts of wine activity, the Barrel Room plays host to a number of catered events and private parties and has had the honor of hosting numerous weddings. Jerry continuously expands the events calendar in this facility. In 1997, the room served as a backdrop for filming a series of perfume commercials. Look for more creative happenings over the next few years.

The 1996 barrel-fermented Chardonnay, made with Chardonnay grapes from the Delaney's High Plains vineyards was fermented to dryness in French oak and matured "surlies," sediment at the bottom of the fermentation vessel. It possesses a soft creamy taste with a buttery bouquet, which would go well with seafood and cheeses.

Delaney Vineyards also produce a Texas Rose Blush wine that is a combination of Chardonnay and Cabernet Franc. Promoted as a good summer red wine, it is sweet enough to almost be a

THE WINES OF DELANEY VINEYARDS AGING IN FRENCH OAK.

dessert wine and goes well with barbecue. Their Texas White table wine, on the other hand—a combination of Chardonnay and Sauvignon Blanc—has a spicy, nutmeg flavor, and is good for picnic meals. Under the watchful hand of French winemaster Jacques Recht, Delaney Vineyards also offer a Merlot, a Riesling, a Pinot Noir, and a Zinfandel.

DIRECTIONS: OUR TRAIL WILL CONCLUDE WITH A VISIT TO THE ONLY WINERY IN AN AIRPORT—LA BODEGA WINERY IN DFW. WE WILL TRAVEL ON SH 121 TO SH 114 AND HEAD EAST TOWARD THE AIRPORT. THE WINERY IS LOCATED IN TERMINAL 2-E, GATE 6.

La Bodega Winery

www.texaswinetrails.com/bodega.htm

Terminal A, P.O. Box 613136
Dallas/Fort Worth Airport, Texas 75231

Phone: (972) 574-1440
Fax: (972) 574-3635

OPEN: MONDAY–SATURDAY
7:30 A.M.–10:00 P.M.

SUNDAY
11:00 A.M.–10:00 P.M.

TASTINGS, RETAIL SALES, GIFTS

$4 FOR 3 TASTES
(WINE BY THE GLASS: $4.95–$7.95)

A winery in an airport? Yes, welcome to the world's first and only (as far as we know) bonded winery to be located in an airport. Located within the city limits of Grapevine, the DFW Airport is included in the legislation that makes Grapevine attractive to wineries.

A visit to La Bodega is just plain fun. The hustle and bustle of the airport terminal, with people off to strange (or not-so-strange) lands, serves as an exciting backdrop for this small niche of space carved into Terminal A. While it is a real bonded winery, La Bode-

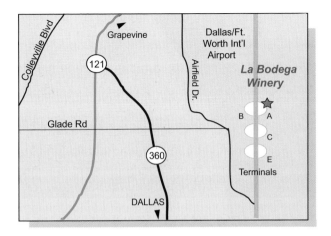

LA BODEGA WINERY

ga is at present a small tasting room that features La Bodega's wines and more than thirty Texas wines from across the state.

Gina Puente-Brancato, owner of La Bodega explains that initially she produced her wines by using the facilities of a nearby Texas winery, while she developed a small facility of her own within the airport tasting room.

Despite the lack of a vineyard and traditional stainless-steel vats and oak barrels one expects to see at a winery, Gina and her staff have created a warm, inviting area to sit and sample Texas wines. Just a step away from the river of humans and transport carts that whiz by, we found ourselves lingering by the tasting bar longer than we had anticipated. There is something infectious about the place—something about relaxing and sipping a glass of wine as the world seems to rush by.

THE WINES

La Bodega Winery offers a limited number of wines under their label: Cabernet Sauvignon, Chardonnay, Merlot, and a Blush. When we spoke with Gina, she was enthusiastic about the future of the winery and of the airport over the next few years. DFW is undergoing a transformation into a larger, state-of-the-art airport, and Gina plans for the winery to follow in those footsteps.

**LA BODEGA WINERY OFFERS YOU A CALM PLACE IN THE HECTIC
AIRPORT TERMINAL.**

Along with her husband John Brancato, who is responsible for blending their wines, La Bodega maintains an active calendar of featured winemakers for bottle signings and tastings. The Texas wine industry is happy to support La Bodega Winery's efforts and is excited about this cutting-edge approach of placing a winery in an airport.

DIRECTIONS: FROM LA BODEGA WINERY, WE HEAD NORTH ON SH 121 FOR A FEW MILES TO LOOP 635 EAST, WHICH TAKES US AROUND TO IH 20 EAST AS WE SET OUR SIGHTS ON THE CITY OF TYLER AND THE KIEPERSOL ESTATES VINEYARD.

❧Kiepersol Estates Vineyard

www.kiepersol.com

**21081 CR 113
Tyler, Texas 75703**

Phone: (903) 530-0321

MONDAY–SATURDAY
BY APPOINTMENT ONLY
TASTINGS, GIFTS, TOURS

"Wine begins in the vineyard," a phrase we have often heard in conversations with winemakers around the state. This statement was never truer than with the de Wet family, owners of Kiepersol Estates. After immigrating to the United States from South America where the family was in the agricultural business, the de Wet's established vineyards in California and Washington State before establishing the Texas homestead.

Kiepersol Estates is a storybook collection of a Bed and Breakfast, a five-star restaurant, a vineyard, a secluded chapel, and, now, a winery. Completed in 2000, the winery is simply the icing on the cake for visitors who stay at Kiepersol Estates. Complete with carriages to provide guests with tours of the estate, vineyards, chapel, and winery, a stay at Kiepersol Estates is a memorable experience.

As Pierre, patriarch of the family, was quick to point out, this operation is truly a family affair since both of his daughters are intimately involved with running the estate. Daughter Marnelle is responsible for the winery and serves as resident winemaker, while daughter Velmay runs the Bed and Breakfast and restaurant.

Marnelle served her apprenticeship with a number of Napa valley wineries before returning to Texas to take the helm of Kiepersol Estates Vineyard. The family is also trying a unique approach to wine consulting during the first few years by bringing in notable winemakers from around the world each year to assist Marnelle in creating handcrafted signature wines.

Kiepersol Estates Vineyard plans to place their wines in various retail outlets in the Dallas Metroplex and Tyler areas. The family plans to keep the winery small, producing about 4,000 cases annually, from premium estate-grown grapes. The twenty-two acre vineyard contains a selection of thick-skinned varietals to survive in the highly humid conditions such as Syrah, Sangiovese, and Barbera, along with Cabernet Sauvignon and a smaller planting of other grapes for blending.

THE WINES

Kiepersol Estates Vineyard plans to focus on Italian/Bordeaux style wines that are a little earthy, yet mild enough to drink for

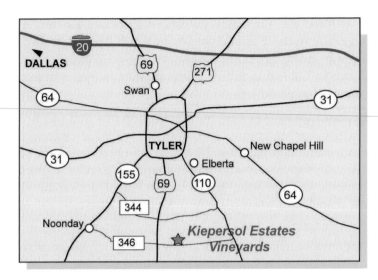

KIEPERSOL ESTATES VINEYARD

fun or to compliment Texas cuisine. Expect to see a Syrah, a Cabernet Sauvignon, a Sangiovese, and a blended red from their 2000 harvest.

ALONG THE TRAIL

The Munson Trail winds through a rich patchwork of forests and grassland that offers farming, ranching, winegrowing, as well as the charisma of small towns and the excitement of a major metropolis in America. Quite a mixture, wouldn't you say?

What exactly does this mean to you? For starters it means that by traveling along the Munson Trail you will experience some of the best scenery and will meet some of the friendliest people in Texas. Take Denison, Texas, for example. Just spitting distance from the Red River, Denison is a place where folks know each other by name on the streets and are likely to say hello to you even though you're a stranger. Folks here are cordial, so please, say hello in return! And here's a tip for you city folks—

when an approaching driver waves to you, wave back—it's only neighborly.

Further south, the land is filled with the trademarks of Texas: horses and cattle. Horse ranches dominate your trip back toward Dallas, and Fort Worth is proud of its stockyard heritage. But Fort Worth is much more than stockyards these days: museums, water gardens, restaurants—the city is more than capable of surviving in the shadow of Dallas. Then there's Dallas! Immortalized by oil, the Dallas Cowboys, and J. R. Ewing, like many other major American cities, you either love it or hate it. Yes, Dallas is a modern behemoth of glistening skyscrapers, but it also has a softer side. Dallas is also about Victorian homes, tree-lined streets, wonderful restaurants, nightclubs, and fashion. Dallas has—dare we say—areas that will simply charm you! Stay at the Stoneleigh Hotel for a weekend and explore the area—you'll see what we mean.

Finally, nestled between Dallas and Fort Worth, in the shadow of DFW airport, is the historic town of Grapevine. From our perspective, the outstanding efforts that the city fathers have made to bring the wine industry to the forefront of tourism in the area has given Grapevine a new focus. It seems that every season, Grapevine has a wine-related event, whether it's the Texas New Vintage Wine and Food Festival in April, Main Street Days in May, Grapefest in September, or the Christmas Parade of Lights in December.

Grapevine also has plenty to offer in terms of history, food, and shopping. Numerous historic buildings, restaurants, and shops will capture your imagination; the Grand Old Opry will make you dance; and Grapevine Mills will offer you an incredible shopping experience found in only a handful of locations around America. For amusement park fans, Opry Land is currently under construction just down the road from Grapevine Mills. For you train buffs, the historic, steam-driven Tarantula Train will take you from the restored train station in Grapevine to downtown Fort Worth. With all this trail has to offer, you might want to give yourself a few extra days to enjoy the wineries, and sights and sounds along the way.

BED AND BREAKFASTS ALONG
THE MUNSON TRAIL

Denison

IVY BLUE

Hosts: Lane and Tammy Segerstrom, 1100 W. Sears, Denison 75020, (888) IVY-BLUE, (903) 463-2479, fax (903) 465-6773. 4 guest rooms, 4 baths, Carriage House (2 suites), Garden House (1 suite), gourmet breakfast, $$, children only in Carriage House, no pets, smoking in designated areas outside, MC, V, AE, D.

THE MOLLY CHERRY

Hosts: Regina and Jim Widener, 200 Molly Cherry Lane, Denison 75020, (903) 465-0575. 1 suite, 2 guest rooms, 2 baths, 4 suites in 2 hideaway cottages, full breakfast, $$–$$$$, no pets, designated smoking areas, all credit cards.

Denton

GODFREY'S PLACE INN

Hosts: Marjorie and Dick Waters, 1513 N. Locust, Denton 76201, (940) 381-1118, fax (940) 566-0856, or contact Bed & Breakfast Texas Style (972) 298-8586. 4 guest rooms, 4 baths, heart-healthy gourmet breakfast, $$–$$$, no children, no pets, no smoking, MC, V.

Dallas

AMERICAN DREAM B&B

Hosts: Pat and Andre, P.O. Box 670275, Dallas 75367, (800) 373-2690 or (214) 356-6536, fax (214) 357-9034. 2 suites, gourmet breakfast, $$, children by special arrangement, no pets, smoking only on patio, MC, V.

COURTYARD ON THE TRAIL

Host: Alan Kagan, (972) 553-9700, or contact Bed & Breakfast Texas Style, (972) 298-8586. 2 guest rooms, 2 baths, full breakfast, $$$, no children, no pets, no smoking, MC, V.

THE CLOISTERS

Contact Bed & Breakfast Texas Style, (972) 298-8586. 2 guest rooms, 2 baths, full breakfast, $$, no children, no pets, smoking outdoors only, MC, V.

Fort Worth

AZALEA PLANTATION

Innkeepers: Martha and Richard Linnartz, 1400 Robinwood Drive, Fort Worth 76111, (800) 68-RELAX, (817) 838-5882. 2 guest rooms, 2 baths, 1 cottage with 2 suites, buffet style full breakfast (weekends), continental plus breakfast (weekdays), $$–$$$, no pets, outside smoking only, MC, V, AE, D.

ETTA'S PLACE

Hosts: Bonnie and Vaughn Franks, 200 W. Third Street, Fort Worth 76102, (817) 654-0267, fax (817) 878-2560. 4 suites, 6 rooms, choice of continental or full breakfast, $$$–$$$$, children and pets welcome, smoking on balconies, all credit cards.

MISS MOLLY'S HOTEL

Host: Mark Hancock, 109½ West Exchange Avenue, Fort Worth 76106, (800) 996-6559, (817) 626-1522, fax (817) 625-2723. 8 rooms, 4 baths, continental plus breakfast, $–$$$, no pets, no smoking, MC, V.

THE TEXAS WHITE HOUSE

Hosts: Grover and Jamie McMains, 1417 Eighth Avenue, Fort Worth 76104, (800) 279-6491, (817) 923-3597, fax (817) 923-0410. 3 guest rooms, 3 baths, gourmet breakfast, $$–$$$, no children, no pets, smoking on front porch, MC, V, AE, D.

Grapevine

THE 1934 BED AND BREAKFAST

322 E. College Street, Grapevine 76051, (817) 251-1934. 3 guest rooms, Motor Car Room for meetings and receptions, five-course gourmet breakfast. $$$–$$$$.

RESTAURANTS ALONG THE MUNSON TRAIL

Denison

THE POINT RESTAURANT AND CLUB

On Lake Texoma (take US 75 north to FM 84, then west about 10 miles and follow signs), Denison, (903) 475-6376. Steak and seafood, breakfast on Saturday and Sunday, Bar. $$.

Denton

LOCUST ST. GRILL

104 N. Locust, (940) 566-3614. Denton. Burgers, Steaks, Seafood, Pasta, Bar. Open daily. $$.

RICK'S AMERICAN CYBER GRILL

501 W. University Dr. at Carroll, Denton, (940) 382-8260, http://www.cybergrill.com. Burgers and steaks, Bar. Open daily. $$.

TWO BROTHERS ITALIAN RESTAURANT

1125 E. University, Denton. (940) 591-9215. Italian. Bar, Texas wines. Open Monday–Saturday. $$.

Dallas

ADELMO'S RISTORANTE

4537 Cole Avenue at Knox, Dallas. (214) 559-0325. Italian bistro. Bar, Texas wines, Lunch and dinner Monday–Friday, dinner only on Saturday. $$.

ALESSIO'S

4117 Lomo Alto, Dallas, (214) 521-3585. Italian. Semi-formal dress requested. Bar, Texas wines, Lunch Monday–Friday, dinner daily. $$–$$$.

ANTARES

300 Reunion Blvd. in Reunion Tower, Dallas, (214) 712-7145. American. Bar, Texas wines, Lunch Monday–Saturday, Sunday brunch, dinner daily. $$.

CHEZ GERARD

4444 McKinney at Armstrong, Dallas, (214) 522-6865. French bistro. Bar, Texas wines, Lunch Monday–Friday, dinner Monday–Saturday. $$–$$$.

DEL FRISCO'S DOUBLE EAGLE STEAKHOUSE

5251 Spring Valley Road, Dallas, (972) 490-9000. Steak, Bar, Texas wines, dinner Monday–Saturday. $$–$$$.

THE FRENCH ROOM

1321 Commerce Street at Akard in The Adolphus Hotel, Dallas, (214) 742-8200. Bar, Texas wines, dinner Monday–Saturday, closed Sunday, reservations required. $$$.

PAN-SEARED BEEF TENDERLOIN SERVED WITH A SHALLOT TART IN BASIL CABERNET SAUCE IS JUST ONE MENU CHOICE THAT MAKES THE FRENCH ROOM AT THE ADOLPHUS HOTEL A AAA FIVE-DIAMOND RESTAURANT.

LA TRATTORIA LOMBARDI

2916 North Hall Street near McKinney Avenue, Dallas, (214) 954-0803. Italian. Bar, Texas wines, Lunch Monday–Friday, dinner seven days. $$–$$$.

LOCATED INSIDE A SMALL, LUXURY HOTEL, THE MANSION ON TURTLE CREEK IS THE ONLY RESTAURANT IN TEXAS TO CONSISTENTLY EARN A FIVE-STAR RATING FROM MOBIL AND A FIVE-DIAMOND RATING FROM AAA.

THE MANSION ON TURTLE CREEK

2821 Turtle Creek Blvd., inside The Mansion on Turtle Creek Hotel, (214) 559-2100 or (800) 527-5432. Continental. Bar, Texas wines, lunch and dinner seven days, reservations required. $$$.

STAR CANYON RESTAURANT

3102 Oak Lawn, in The Centrum at Cedar Springs, Dallas, (214) 520-STAR (520-7827). Texas cuisine. Bar, Texas wines, lunch Monday–Friday, dinner seven days, reservations required. $$$.

STAR CANYON'S BONE-IN COWBOY RIBEYE WITH RED CHILE ONION RINGS IS A STAR EXAMPLE OF CHEF STEPHAN PYLES NEW TEXAS CUISINE.

Fort Worth

THE BALCONY OF RIDGLEA

6100 Bowie Blvd., at Winthrop, Fort Worth, (817) 731-3719. Continental. Bar, Texas wines, lunch Monday–Friday, dinner Monday–Saturday, closed Sunday. $$.

CAFÉ ASPEN RESTAURANT AND BAR

6103 Camp Bowie Blvd., Fort Worth, (817) 738-0838. American. Bar, Texas wines, lunch and dinner Monday–Saturday. $$.

CATTLEMEN'S STEAKHOUSE

2458 North Main, in the Stockyards, Fort Worth, (817) 624-3945. Steaks and seafood. Bar, Texas wines, lunch and dinner seven days. $–$$.

CELEBRATION

4600 Dexter Avenue, at Camp Bowie and Hulen, Fort Worth, (817) 731-6272. American. Bar, Texas wines, lunch and dinner seven days. $–$$.

JOE T. GARCIA'S MEXICAN DISHES

2201 North Commerce, near the Stockyards, Fort Worth, (817) 626-4356. Mexican. Bar, Texas wines, lunch and dinner seven days. $–$$.

REFLECTIONS

200 Main Street, in The Worthington Hotel, Fort Worth, (817) 882-1765. American and French. Bar, Texas wines, dinner Monday–Saturday. $$$.

REATA

500 Throckmorton Street, Bank One Tower Building, Fort Worth, (817) 336-1009. Steak, seafood, Tex-Mex. Bar, Texas wines, lunch and dinner Monday–Saturday. $–$$.

Chapter 3

HILL COUNTRY WINERIES

*I*magine a two-lane road twisting and turning through a valley of shrub-covered limestone hills. Now visualize sparkling lakes nestled in these valleys, slow-moving rivers, fields of wildflowers, and communities rich in German heritage. Welcome to the Texas Hill Country. Welcome to Texas' largest concentration of wineries and holiday destinations. A rich mixture of people, culture, and landscape, this picturesque area serves as the backdrop for the most exciting and romantic wine trails the state has to offer. Once a land of cultural and geological clashes, the Hill Country today is a vibrant viticultural area where past diversities contribute to the character of the region's wine.

THE TRAILS

The Hill Country wineries are found along three wine trails: the Enchanted Trail, the Highland Trail, and the Balcones Trail. We use the city of Austin, Texas' state capital, as our starting point for each trail. The Enchanted Trail offers wine tourists an exciting tour of nine wineries, plus an overnight stay in the town of Fredericksburg—always a welcome treat. The Highland Trail, with six wineries, offers magnificent views of the Highland Lakes as you cruise the twisting, turning roads that connect these wineries. The Balcones Trail stops at three wineries and offers an

◀ HARVEST TIME IN A TEXAS VINEYARD IS STILL A LABOR OF LOVE. (COURTESY OF GRAPE CREEK VINEYARDS)

THE ENCHANTED TRAIL	THE HIGHLAND TRAIL
♠ Texas Hills Vineyard	♠ Flat Creek Vineyards
♠ Woodrose Winery and Retreat	♠ Fall Creek Estate
♠ Becker Vineyards	♠ Alamosa Wine Cellars
♠ Grape Creek Vineyards	♠ Pillar Bluff Vineyards
♠ Bell Mountain Vineyards	♠ Spicewood Vineyards
♠ Fredericksburg Winery	♠ McReynolds Winery
♠ Chisholm Trail Winery	
♠ Comfort Cellars Winery	THE BALCONES TRAIL
♠ Sister Creek Vineyards	♠ Cana Cellars Winery
	♠ Dry Comal Creek Vineyards
	♠ Poteet Country Winery

exciting opportunity to stop in San Antonio, where music, culture, and food come together beautifully.

THE ENCHANTED TRAIL

Tall cedars, stubby pines, peach orchards, and Old-World style towns dominate our weekend trip along the Enchanted Trail. This ambitious trail is named after Enchanted Rock State Park, located just north of Fredericksburg, and will take us to nine wineries: Texas Hills Vineyard, Woodrose Winery and Retreat, Becker Vineyards, Grape Creek Vineyards, Bell Mountain Vineyards, Fredericksburg Winery, Chisholm Trail Winery, Comfort Cellars Winery, and Sister Creek Vineyards.

Our first stop after leaving Austin is the town of Johnson City, home to Texas Hills Vineyard. Then we head out to Stonewall, located just east of Fredericksburg on SH 290 and home to the newly formed Woodrose Winery and Retreat and two established wineries, Becker Vineyards and Grape Creek Vineyards. From there, we drive directly to Fredericksburg to visit Bell Mountain Vineyards, located on the slopes of Bell Mountain, fourteen miles north of Fredericksburg, and only open on Saturdays, so plan accordingly.

You may want to stay overnight in Fredericksburg, and stroll among the antique and specialty shops and restaurants that line Main Street. With a strong German heritage, this town offers a

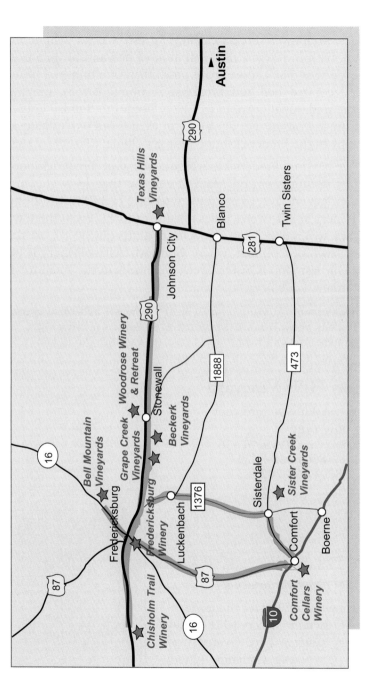

THE ENCHANTED TRAIL WINERIES

Austin

Texas Hills Vineyards

290

Blanco

Twin Sisters

281

290

Johnson City

Woodrose Winery & Retreat

Stonewall

1888

Beckerk Vineyards

473

16

Bell Mountain Vineyards

Grape Creek Vineyards

Fredericksburg

Fredericksburg Winery

Luckenbach

1376

Sisterdale

Sister Creek Vineyards

Comfort

Boerne

87

87

Chisholm Trail Winery

16

10

Comfort Cellars Winery

variety of German restaurants and bakeries to tempt even the strongest willpower. Fredericksburg is also a pure delight for lodging, with the largest concentration of bed and breakfasts in Texas. Visitors may choose from more than one hundred beautifully decorated bed and breakfast accommodations, ranging from the traditional (a room in a large home) to Sunday houses and rustic log cabins. For a preview of what is offered, call ahead for a copy of the Fredericksburg Visitor's Guide: 830-997-2155.

Before leaving Fredericksburg, we will visit Fredericksburg Winery's tasting room on Main Street. We then leave this historic German enclave, to continue west on SH 290 to Chisholm Trail Winery about twelve miles outside of town. From there we backtrack to Fredericksburg and head south on SH 87, to the historic town of Comfort, where Comfort Cellars Winery is located. Our last stop is Sister Creek Vineyards in the small town of Sisterdale. Let's begin the tour!

DIRECTIONS: FROM AUSTIN WE HEAD WEST ALONG SH 290 TO JOHNSON CITY. ONCE IN TOWN, TURN EAST ON RR 2766, WHICH IS THE SAME ROAD TO PEDERNALES STATE PARK. TEXAS HILLS VINEYARD IS ABOUT ONE MILE DOWN THE ROAD ON YOUR RIGHT.

❧Texas Hills Vineyard

www.texashillsvineyard.com
P.O. Box 1480
Johnson City, Texas 77636
Phone: (830) 868-2321
Fax: (830) 868-7027

> OPEN: MONDAY–SATURDAY
> 10:00 A.M.–5:00 P.M.
>
> SUNDAY
> 12:00 P.M.–5:00 P.M.
>
> TASTINGS, RETAIL SALES, AND GIFTS

A cave above the ground!

A fitting description for this environmentally friendly winery that Kathy and Gary Gilstrap have created near Johnson City, using a building system known as "rammed earth." A combination of earth, cement, and moisture

TEXAS HILL COUNTRY
PINOT GRIGIO

TEXAS ☆ HILLS
Vineyard

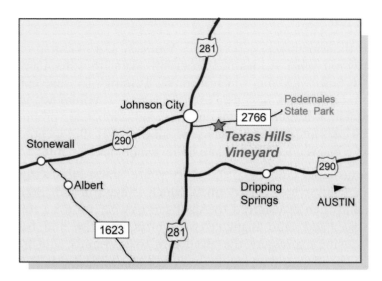

TEXAS HILLS VINEYARD

are placed into forms and compacted under hydraulic rams to form twenty-four inch thick walls. The resulting walls have a remarkable ability to resist thermal transfer of heat or cold, creating a stable interior environment, much like that in an underground cave.

The Gilstraps became interested in wine while traveling through the wine regions of Europe, particularly the Tuscany area of Italy. When they found the rolling hills outside of Johnson City, the area reminded them of the Tuscany countryside. At that point they decided to purchase the land and create a winery with a decidedly Italian influence. Their son, Dale Rasset, then joined them as vineyard manager.

The seventeen-acre vineyard is planted with Pinot Grigio, Sangiovese, Moscato, Cabernet Sauvignon, Chardonnay, Merlot, and Chenin Blanc—all of which allow wines to be produced with an Italian influence. Nine acres are currently in pre-production and ultimately the vineyard will grow to thirty-five acres. In the winery and in the vineyard, the Gilstraps advocate the environmentally correct way and grow their vineyard in a "sustainable organic fashion." They use natural fertilizers and remove weeds with a mechanical device called a Clemens.

THE WINES

As the winemaker at Texas Hills Vineyard, Gary Gilstrap relies heavily on what he learned from his many trips to Italy to spend time with the winemakers of Tuscany. To supplement this knowledge, he also uses Enrique Ferro—a well-known wine consultant—as his consultant on wine production. Gary produced 6,500 cases in 2000 and close to the same in 2001. Production for 2003 remains uncertain because of low grape yields in 2002.

Texas Hills Vineyard offers three white wines: Pinot Grigio, a dry fruity wine; Chardonnay, which is aged first in French oak and then transferred to American oak barrels for a touch of spice; and Duo Bianco "two whites," a crisp and fruity white wine expressing the essence of toast, vanilla, and fresh pear. Their sweet white wines include Texas Hills Blush, White Zinfandel, and Moscato. The Blush is a semisweet wine made from a blend of two white wines and a touch of Merlot. The White Zinfandel is a unique blend of California wine with estate made Chenin Blanc and Pinot Grigio. Their Moscato has proved to be one of the most popular and award-winning wines, garnering a silver medal in a New York City competition and a gold medal at the Spring Texas Wine and Art Festival.

Texas Hills Vineyards red wines include Cabernet Sauvignon, Merlot, and Sangiovese and three new wines: Tre Paesano, Novello Rosso 2000, and a Cabernet Franc. The majority of their red wines are produced using the old European technique called "d'eletage," a time-consuming process that removes the seeds from the wine in the early fermentation stages. Once a "cap" forms and floats to the top of the fermentation tank, Gary opens the drain at the bottom of the tank and captures the first fifty-five or so gallons into a barrel, which removes the seeds from the fermentation tank. Then the entire contents of the fifteen-hundred-gallon tank are pumped over to an empty tank to allow the "cap" to sink to the bottom. Then the wine is pumped back into the original tank, and the cap slowly floats to the top, helping remove more seeds from the wine. This process is done daily until the majority of the seeds have been removed. Gary feels that by using this process, he can better control the amount of tannins in the wines, ultimately producing a fruitier, tastier wine.

The Sangiovese is a mild wine, perfect for those who are trying to like red wines but don't like the heaviness of Merlot or Cabernet Sauvignon. The Cabernet Sauvignon is a rich full-bodied estate cabernet. Let the black cherry and blackberry tease your taste buds as this Cabernet shows its Texas Hill Country heritage. It has been aged in new American Oak for twelve months, then bottle aged for another twelve months. Of the newer wines, the Tre Paesano is a particular favorite with visitors. Tre Paesano is Italian for "three fellow countrymen." This wine is a pleasant blend of three estate wines: Cabernet Sauvignon, Merlot, and Syrah. Each component provides a distinct flavor to the blend; you will recognize blackberry, mulberry, plum, and white pepper in the flavors.

Novello Rosso—Italian for "new, tender red"—is a Pinot Noir with complexity that did not dictate the long barrel aging, but the flavor of this wine in its young state provides a superior product. You will pick up cherry and cinnamon with a fruity finish. Finally, the Cabernet Franc was aged for fourteen months in American Oak, then bottle aged for another fourteen months. With a production of only ninety cases, this wine is sure to sell out quickly.

In addition to producing award-winning wines, Gary told us that Texas Hills Vineyard, "has become sort of a focal point for local area growers." Seminars on grape growing and disease research are offered, and Kathy Gilstrap chaired a group to create the sixteen-member Hill Country Wineries Association to help promote Texas wine. As production increases and time goes on, you can expect to see a number of great wines nurtured by Gary's hands in the winery and Dale's hands in the vineyard.

DIRECTIONS: FROM TEXAS HILLS VINEYARDS, WE CONTINUE WEST ALONG SH 290 TO THE TOWN OF STONEWALL. ON THE WESTERN EDGE OF TOWN, WATCH FOR A SIGN POINTING TO WOODROSE WINERY AND RETREAT AND TURN LEFT ONTO WOODROSE LANE.

❧Woodrose Winery and Retreat

www.woodrosewinery.com

**Woodrose Lane
Stonewall, Texas 78671
Phone: (830) 644-2111**

OPEN: LATE SPRING 2003

TASTINGS AND RETAIL SALES

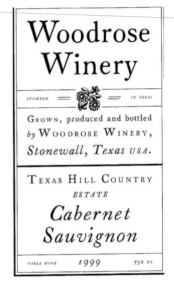

Woodrose Winery

STOMPED === 🌹 === *IN TEXAS*

GROWN, produced and bottled
by WOODROSE WINERY,
Stonewall, Texas USA.

TEXAS HILL COUNTRY
ESTATE
*Cabernet
Sauvignon*

TABLE WINE   *1999*   750 ML

Susan Benz and Brian Wilgus, proprietors of Woodrose Winery and Retreat, seem to have a knack for making history. You may remember them from the first edition of this book, as owner of the first winery established within Austin's city limits: Oak Hill Cellars. At that time, they told us they were looking for good vineyard land to build a winery facility. After looking around the country, their search led them back to Texas and to Stonewall. Oak Hill Cellars was closed in 1999, and Woodrose Winery and Retreat was born.

The metal roof of the winery shimmered in the midday sun, partially obscured by a thick stand of post oaks, as we wound down the road to the building site. At the time of our visit, Woodrose Winery and Retreat was a work in-progress. Brian Wilgus, co-owner and winemaker, balanced precariously twenty feet in the air as he and a helper worked on rough framing the exterior walls of what would be their lodge. Shouting a greeting, he indicated where Susan Benz, winery co-owner, could be found.

As we walked toward the winery itself, Brian and Susan gave us a tour of the vineyard that will be 100 percent dedicated to Cabernet Sauvignon. The first 1,000 vines were planted in March 2000, in what will eventually be a seven-acre vineyard. Recalling the initial planting, Susan flashed a warm smile as she

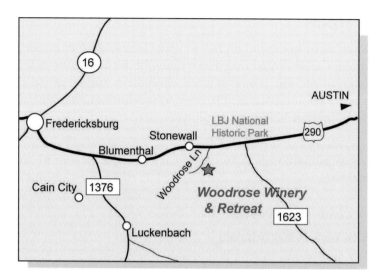

WOODROSE WINERY AND RETREAT

described how hard-working friends helped plant those vines in about four hours. Many now feel a special connection to the vineyard; "our friends call all the time to ask how vine seven in row thirteen is doing. They think it's their baby."

Long-range plans for the winery include a three-building production and tasting room facility, the lodge to serve as an activity center, and six cabins available to guests by advance reservations. Susan and Brian, who are both architects in San Antonio, have designed all of the buildings on the site. Their common architectural background is their inspirational source for the winery's name: the classic "wooden-rose" in architectural design over the centuries was used by Brian to create a plaster relief that serves as the winery's icon. Wooden-rose became Woodrose for the winery's name. The limestone winery is done in the German style that predominates the Stonewall-Fredericksburg area. Their passion for architectural detail is evident throughout this building, the first of three identical structures. Initially this building will serve all production and retail functions until the other structures can be built.

THE WINES

Brian plans to expand on the winemaking techniques he used at Oak Hill Cellars, enhancing and refining his techniques to take advantage of the more sophisticated equipment and larger storage and production capacities. Plans are to produce a Cabernet Sauvignon, Cabernet Rosè, and a still to be determined white wine.

DIRECTIONS: FROM WOODROSE WINERY, WE CONTINUE WEST FOR A FEW MILES ON SH 290, THEN TURN LEFT ON JENSKE LANE TO VISIT BECKER VINEYARDS.

🍇Becker Vineyards

www.beckervineyards.com

P.O. Box 393
Stonewall, Texas 78671

Phone (830) 644-2681
Fax: (830) 644-8689

OPEN: MONDAY–THURSDAY
10:00 A.M.–5:00 P.M.
FRIDAY–SATURDAY
10:00 A.M.–6:00 P.M.
SUNDAY
12:00 P.M.–6:00 P.M.

TASTINGS, TOURS, RETAIL, SALES, GIFTS, AND BED AND BREAKFAST

BECKER VINEYARDS

TEXAS
1996

FUME BLANC

CELLARED AND BOTTLED BY BECKER VINEYARDS,
FREDERICKSBURG, TX BW-TX-91 ALCOHOL 12.5% BY VOLUME CONTAINS SULFITES

Richard and Bunny Becker planted their experimental thirteen-acre vineyard in the overgrown remnants of a peanut farm surrounded by an ancient stand of mustang grapes. As the Beckers' excitement grew, they quickly expanded the young vineyard to thirty-six acres of French vinifera grapes in 1993 and began restoration work on the original German farmhouse. The Beckers developed their site to resemble an early nineteenth-century country farm, complete with windmill, log cabin and barn. The cabin has been remodeled to serve as a bed and breakfast at the winery.

Visitors approach the winery (which was built to resemble a Hill Country German stone barn) through fields of grapevines

**GERMAN INFLUENCE IS EVIDENT IN THE DESIGN OF BECKER
VINEYARDS WINERY.**

with yellow rose bushes planted at the end of each row. The winery has a large covered porch with views of the log cabin Bed and Breakfast and a three-acre field of lavender that extends to the twenty-five-acre vineyard. The Beckers have expanded the original thirteen-acre test vineyard to a thirty-six-acre production vineyard. Richard Becker has planted classic French grapes: Chardonnay, Cabernet Sauvignon, Cabernet Franc, Malbec, Petit Verdot, and Merlot, along with an unusual group of Rhone varietals: Viognier, Syrah, Mourvedre, Grenache, Roussanne, and Marsanne. The Viognier vineyard is the first significant effort of its kind in Texas.

The Beckers have dedicated acreage not planted with vineyards to raising Texas wildflowers for seed harvesting. As a result, each spring their winery has the distinction of being surrounded by vast expanses of some of the most beautiful Texas wildflowers including bluebonnets, cosmos, and Indian paintbrush.

THE WINES

This is truly a winery with a wonderful future. The Beckers opened the doors of their tasting room in June 1996, offering only a limited selection of white wines, a Muscat Canelli and a Sauvignon Blanc, while a full compliment of red wines aged in French oak barrels in the wine cellar.

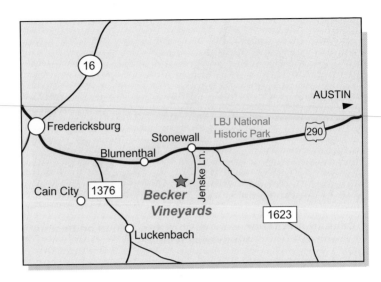

BECKER VINEYARDS

Since 1996, Becker Vineyards has continuously expanded its selection of wines while garnering award after award. In 1999 alone, they captured over sixteen gold, silver, and bronze medals from competitions across the United States. Among those awards were the 1999 Gold, Best of Class, and Grand Star awards for their Muscat Canelli at the Lone Star Wine Competition in Grapevine, Texas.

The selection of red wines includes Merlot, Cabernet Sauvignon Reserve, Cabernet Sauvignon Estate Bottled, a blend of Cabernet and Syrah, and a Claret. All of their red wines are blended in the French tradition and barrel aged. The Merlot was barrel aged in American oak for fifteen months and is a blend of Merlot, Cabernet Sauvignon, and Ruby Cabernet. Both of the Cabernet Sauvignon vintages offered have been barrel aged for twenty months and are a blend of Cabernet Sauvignon, Cabernet Franc, and Ruby Cabernet. Be sure to sample the Becker Vineyards Vintage Port wine when you visit the tasting room—it is fantastic.

Becker Vineyards now offers the wine tourist a selection of signature white wines that include Fumè Blanc, Chardonnay, Chenin Blanc, and a Viognier. The Viognier—the first produced in Texas—is a wine originally made in France during the days of the Roman Empire.

The sweet white wines include a Riesling and a Muscat Canelli. Rounding out this list is a new estate-bottled Rosè called Provence. This dry Rosè is a blend of Mourvedre, Syrah, and Grenache, replicating the Tavel, France, style of dry Rosès.

Every Fourth of July, Becker Vineyards cele-

A MAGNIFICENT TASTING ROOM AWAITS VISITORS.

brates their anniversary with a grand party. Other events include Grape Stomps, Labor Day Weekend, Boxing Day Celebration, Merlot and Chocolate (around Valentines Day), and a summer lavender festival. Consult the website for details.

ROWS OF GLYCOL-JACKETED STAINLESS STEEL FERMENTATION TANKS.

WINE BARRELS ARE OFTEN STACKED TO INCREASE A BARREL ROOM'S STORAGE CAPACITY.

For the wine tourist looking for a cozy Bed and Breakfast at a winery, ask about their Homestead Bed and Breakfast, located beside the winery. The circa-1890 cabin was built by the Heinrich Peese family, who were the original homesteaders of the property. A stay at this snug little cabin includes a continental breakfast and a complimentary bottle of wine.

DIRECTIONS: FROM BECKER VINEYARDS, IT IS A SHORT TRIP WEST ON SH 290 UNTIL YOU SEE THE SIGN FOR GRAPE CREEK VINEYARDS ON YOUR LEFT.

♣Grape Creek Vineyards

www.grapecreek.com

P.O. Box 102
Stonewall, Texas 78671

Phone: (830) 644-2710
Fax: (830) 644-2746

> OPEN: MONDAY–SATURDAY
> 10:00 A.M.–5:00 P.M.
> SUNDAY
> 12:00 P.M.–5:00 P.M.
> TOURS, TASTINGS, RETAIL
> SALES, GIFTS, AND BED AND
> BREAKFAST

Anyone who has driven on SH 290 from Houston to Fredericksburg will no doubt recognize the name Grape Creek Vineyards. This vineyard, planted by owner Ned Simes in 1985, is perhaps one of the most visible and accessible wineries in the Hill Country. The winery's popularity was underscored for us during a visit on a Fourth of July weekend when the holiday rush of visitors was taken in stride by the owners and staff. The gracious hospitality extended in the tasting room and the well-versed tour guide makes a visit to Grape Creek enjoyable any time of the year.

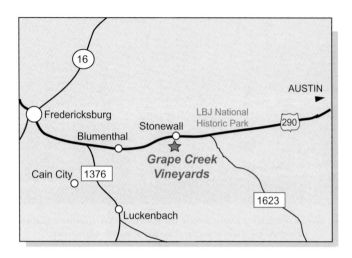

GRAPE CREEK VINEYARDS

Grape Creek is a self-described "boutique winery," a term that may confuse many consumers who associate the word boutique with specialty retail stores. In the context of this industry, a boutique winery is one that specializes in a small number of high-quality wines offered in limited bottling. The efforts of the Simes family fit this definition quite well.

In addition to the fine selection of wines, the Simeses offer possibly the most impressive selections of trinkets available in all the Hill Country wineries. In their tasting room, a visitor may

THE ENTRY TO GRAPE CREEK VINEYARDS ON SH 290.

THE MAGNIFICENT STONEWORK OF EARLY GERMAN SETTLERS IS ECHOED IN THE GRAPE CREEK'S MAIN BUILDING.

choose from an assortment of wine accessories, toys made from corks, flavored vinegars, and even wine-scented soap.

As part of the tour, visitors are led down to the wine cellar to view future wines as they age in oak barrels. Grape Creek has one of the few active, fully functional wine cellars in Texas. It is a particular favorite with visitors because it has an atmosphere most people associate with a winery. Wineries and wine cellars go hand-in-hand in the minds of many, and Grape Creek is uniquely able to provide that imagery.

Ned Simes purchased the property, nestled alongside Grape Creek in Stonewall, following a long search across the United States. After submitting soil samples to A&M University for testing to verify his selection, Ned knew that the climate and soil conditions in this area of the Hill Country were perfect for producing quality grapes. He submitted additional soil samples in 1994 and projected plans to expand the vineyard in ten-acre plots for the next three to four years.

As is the case with many other smaller wineries in Texas, the owner is also the winemaker, vine pruner, harvester, bottler, and sales representative. On any given weekend, you will find Ned and his family in the tasting room giving tours and explaining the different wines being tasted. On any given weekday, you will find Ned and his son Lee in the vineyard tending to the fruit, or in the winery, nurturing the next vintage.

The Simeses deeply believe in the value of family heritage and what it means to producing wines. Ned's son Lee, who shares the responsibility of the vineyard and the winery with his father, was quick to explain the family's commitment to producing fine quality wines. Lee's wife, described by many as having one of the best "noses" in the business, is a major influence in the blending of the wines here.

THE WINES

Grape Creek Vineyards produces fifteen wines made in the French style of winemaking. Their dry white wines include Sauvignon Blanc, Fumè Blanc, Cuvee Blanc (a blend of Sauvignon Blanc and Chardonnay), and a Chardonnay. The Sauvignon Blanc was fermented in stainless steel to enhance the citrus flavors in the wine. Two vintages of the Fumè Blanc were made from 100 percent Sauvignon Blanc and underwent thirty days of fermentation in French oak to soften the citrus flavors and impart a smoky flavor.

Grape Creek Vineyards offers a range of red wines that includes Pinot Noir, Cabernet Trois, Merlot, Cabernet Sauvignon, and Cabernet Sauvignon Barrel Reserve. The Cabernet Trois is the result of a 1993 experiment that turned out to be a huge success. A blend of Cabernet Sauvignon, Cabernet Franc, and Ruby Cabernet, this wine is ideal for the consumer who enjoys a red wine but does not like the heavier taste of a Merlot or Cabernet Sauvignon.

For those consumers who enjoy sweet wines, Grape Creek Vineyards offers White Zinfandel, Riesling Cabernet Blanc, Cabernet Rouge, and a Muscat Canelli. The Cabernet Blanc is "a white wine made from a red grape." Red wine receives its color from contact between the grape juice and the grape skins during fermentation. The longer the contact, the deeper the red colors. To create the Cabernet Blanc, which is made from 100 percent Cabernet Sauvignon, the grapes are crushed and the juice removed immediately to prevent color absorption. The Cabernet Rouge, on the other hand, is a dark garnet red color, semi-sweet wine.

Grape Creek Vineyards also offers Bed and Breakfast accommodations at the winery, above the tasting room. Two rooms are available, each with a kitchen and private bath. Continental breakfast and a complimentary bottle of wine are included. Groups of six can be accommodated by renting both rooms, which includes three complimentary bottles of wine.

DIRECTIONS: FROM GRAPE CREEK VINEYARDS WE TRAVEL WEST ON SH 290 FOR APPROXIMATELY NINETEEN MILES TO THE TOWN OF FREDERICKSBURG. TURNING NORTH ON SH 16, BELL MOUNTAIN VINEYARDS IS ABOUT FOURTEEN MILES NORTH OF TOWN.

♙Bell Mountain Vineyards

www.bellmountainwine.com

HC 61, Box 22
Fredericksburg, Texas 78624

Phone: (830) 685-3297
Fax: (930) 685-3657

> **OPEN: SATURDAYS**
> **10:00 A.M.–5:00 P.M.**
> **(FROM FIRST SATURDAY OF**
> **FEBRUARY UNTIL SATURDAY**
> **BEFORE CHRISTMAS)**

Located north of Fredericksburg on the slopes of Bell Mountain is Bell Mountain/ Oberhellman Vineyards. Originally known as Oberhellman Vineyards, owner/winemaker Robert (Bob) Oberhellman changed the winery's name to honor the areas designation in 1986 as Texas' first appellation area. This identifies the area as possessing unique soil and climatic characteristics for producing quality grapes for winemaking.

Spreading across the rolling foothills of Bell Mountain, the winery's vineyards have slowly grown from thirty acres in

THE WINERY'S ARCHITECTURE MIMICS BUILDINGS FOUND IN GERMANY'S COUNTRYSIDE.

1986 to fifty-five acres in 1993. According to his wife Evelyn, this methodical expansion of the vineyard is indicative of Bob's approach to every aspect of the winery. "The facilities have grown in a similar fashion," Evelyn tells us, "following Bob's master plan." Using a phased approach to expand the facility, the Oberhellmans have incorporated a spacious brick patio to separate the original lab/office building from the

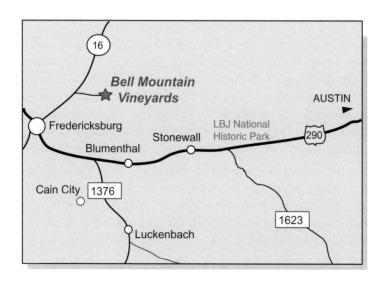

BELL MOUNTAIN VINEYARDS

winery itself and have purchased state-of-the-art winemaking equipment. The patio, equipped with a large masonry barbecue and wine-barrel tables, is enjoyed by visitors to the winery and local organizations who hold charitable functions in this beautiful setting.

Bob Oberhellman's approach to wine has been influenced by the winemaking education he received in both France and California, as well as his work experience in the food industry. It is not surprising that Bob views wine as a food product and considers his estate-bottled wines as fine dinner wines. His food-industry experience provides Bell Mountain Vineyards with another critical business element for a growing winery: marketing expertise. Bell Mountain wines enjoy wide distribution throughout Texas and are easily obtained at major liquor stores.

THE WINES

The careful balancing of European and Californian techniques has been a pivotal factor in the production of Bell Mountain premium wines. Along with the traditional techniques of the European masters that emphasize the "art" of winemaking, Bob uses the latest research and technology from California that have revolutionized modern winemaking.

Planted primarily with Old-World grapes, Bob's vineyard grows Chardonnay, Johannisberg Riesling, Gewurztraminer, Sauvignon Blanc, Semillion, Cabernet Sauvignon, Merlot, and Pinot Noir. Located at an elevation of 2,000 feet, the vineyards are planted at 725 plants per acre and use a six-foot-high trellis for maximum foliage development. These techniques allow Bell Mountain to produce approximately 3,200 cases each year.

The white wines include Chardonnay, Dry Riesling, and a Late Harvest Riesling. The Chardonnay is first cold-fermented in stainless steel to preserve the delicate fruit flavors of the grape. Then it is moved to French oak for eight months to add complexity to the nose and finish.

Bell Mountain Vineyards Rieslings have all of the classic characteristics you would expect from a German wine—blossomy, rich pear and apricot flavors finished with subtle acidity. The Dry Riesling is made in the style and technique of the Rhine Valley, offering delicate fruit flavors with very low sugar levels. In stark contrast, the Late Harvest Riesling is a sweet wine offering exceptionally rich fruit flavors.

Bell Mountain Vineyards red wines include Cabernet Sauvignon, Merlot, and Pinot Noir. These wines are all aged in oak and then bottle-aged for one year prior to release. The 1998 Cabernet Sauvignon was aged in oak for fourteen months to achieve a full fruit character with good balance and pronounced herbaceousness. The Merlot exhibits a bold liqueur flavor after twelve months in French oak. Due to limited production, it is only available at the winery. The Pinot Noir offers a remarkable deep burgundy, brick-red color with floral and raspberry aromas.

The Oberhellmans offer a variety of specialty wines under a second label, Oberhellman Vineyards. These wines tend to be fruitier and sweeter, bearing whimsical names such as KrisKindl and Wildflower Mead.

For Bob and Evelyn, the winery's location has had some surprising benefits. It is not an exaggeration to say that the winery is off the beaten path compared to other wineries in the area; you have to intentionally be going to this winery. Visitors are typically wine lovers who have heard about these wines from friends or from conversations with folks in Fredericksburg. The residents of the town are proud of the local wineries and are generous with directions.

DIRECTIONS: WE STOP OUR TOUR HERE FOR TODAY TO ENJOY THE DOWNTOWN AREA OF FREDERICKSBURG. TOMORROW, AFTER ENJOYING AN OLD-FASHIONED BREAKFAST AT A BED AND BREAKFAST OR AT ONE OF THE LOCAL RESTAURANTS AND BAKERIES, WE WILL VISIT THE FREDERICKSBURG WINERY BEFORE LEAVING FOR THE TOWN OF SISTERDALE.

♣Fredericksburg Winery

www.fbgwinery.com

247 West Main
Fredericksburg, Texas 78624
Phone: (830) 990-8747
Fax: (830) 990-8566

> OPEN: MONDAY–THURSDAY
> 10:00 A.M.–6:00 P.M.
>
> FRIDAY AND SATURDAY
> 10:00 A.M.–8:00 P.M.
>
> SUNDAY
> 12:00 P.M.–6:00 P.M.
>
> TASTINGS, RETAIL SALES,
> AND GIFTS

Fredericksburg, Texas
Baron's Back Burgundy
Texas Cabernet Sauvignon
1993

The road to the Fredericksburg Winery has been a long one for the Switzer family. Along the way there have been long hours, dedication, setbacks, and success. But it has mostly been a story of what a family can do when they believe in each other. Opening in 1995 on Main Street in downtown Fredericksburg, this winery is a showplace for all Texas wines, Texas food products, and a large selection of wine accessories.

The family has put their heart and soul into producing a marvelous selection of wines. Stop by the winery on any weekend and three generations will be behind the counter. On our last visit, the Switzer brothers, their seventy-seven-year-old mother, both their wives, and Jene's five-year-old daughter, Chardonnay, were all helping.

Jene Switzer, winemaker extraordinaire, may possibly be the hardest working winemaker in the Texas wine industry. Prior to opening the family winery, Jene served five wineries in Texas in positions ranging from vineyard manager to winemaker. Over the past twenty years, he has consistently produced some of the best wines in Texas.

We first met Jene in the summer of 1993 at the Hill Country Cellars in Cedar Park, Texas. There he was assisting Russell Smith (winemaker at that time) with a recent harvest. At that time, Jene

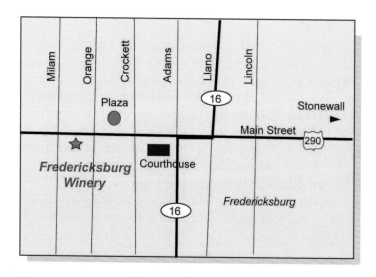

FREDERICKSBURG WINERY

was also working with the Wimberley Valley Winery, producing a small bottling of his own under the name of Falcon Hills Cellars.

The Switzer family was attracted to the exciting atmosphere being created by wineries in the town of Fredericksburg and opened their winery and tasting room on Main Street in a small retail mall. Fredericksburg Winery is a culmination of years of patience and hard work, which has resulted in unimaginable success for the family. After producing 4,400 cases of wine in 1999, production surpassed over 7,000 cases in 2000. Growth has been so fast, in fact, that they took over the entire floor space of the retail mall and were in the process of making room for additional stainless steel fermentation tanks during our last visit.

Phase II of their expansion includes the construction of a 30,000-square foot winery on the family's Falcon Hills Ranch, located just west of Fredericksburg. The preliminary plans on display in their tasting room show a beautiful 10,000-case facility, which will include a tasting room and deli, a banquet area, and pavilions for picnics.

THE WINES

To keep up with production demands (the winery makes forty wines, twenty-one of which are currently available for tasting), the Switzers have had to become creative in their search for grapes. They plan to expand their seventeen-acre vineyard at the ranch to seventy-six acres by the time the new winery opens. In addition to buying grapes from local grape growers, the Switzers acquired the old University of Texas Bakersfield Experimental Vineyard, or the Old Spanish Trail Vineyards as it is referred to now. Under their watchful care, the vineyard is now producing more fruit than at any time in its history, offering over 141 different varietals, rootstocks, and clones to use in creating new,

A WINE'S CHARACTER IS A COMBINATION OF THE GRAPE, THE VINEYARD, AND THE WINERMAKER'S SKILL.
(COURTESY OF THE TEXAS DEPARTMENT OF AGRICULTURE)

unique wines. Several wines offered at Fredericksburg Winery are made from grapes never before released as varietals in Texas: a Sherry from the Palomino grape, Muscat Hamburg, Scheurebe, and Pervella to name a few. How the Switzer's manage to produce such a large selection of wines from such a compact facility is a mystery. They only admit that work often goes on into the night after the winery closes its doors.

Interestingly enough, Jene tells us that acquiring the new vineyard with its expanded variety of grapes to work with has convinced him that the winemaking techniques he has evolved are exactly the right techniques required. He prefers cold soaking and cold fermentation in stainless steel tanks—no barrels are used for the wines. He is also passionate about not using acids or malolactic fermentation—unless the malolactic fermenting occurs naturally.

As the number of awards received increases along with the number of wines being produced, Fredericksburg Winery's zest for experimentation continues unabated. The tradition of using German names for their wines continues, along with the story, or Texas tradition, of the name printed on the label. On January 1, 2000, at the first second after midnight, the winery began bottling a wine called "First Second"—the first wine bottled in the world in the New Millennium. This meritage of Ruby Cabernet, Cabernet Franc, and Cabernet Sauvignon is a very limited release that was hand bottled, hand corked and labeled, and individually numbered.

The family's love for wine shows in all aspects of their work: in the wine itself, in the participation of the whole family in the business, and in the congenial reception each visitor receives on entering the tasting room. Look for many changes to come in the near future for this winery. When the new winery is opened, the current tasting room on Main Street will become a champagne making facility. Fredericksburg Winery is currently making champagne using the true *methode champenoise* system in which riddling and disgorging are done by hand using Old-World methods.

DIRECTIONS: FROM FREDERICKSBURG WINERY, WE AGAIN HEAD WEST ALONG SH 290 FOR ABOUT TWELVE MILES TO VISIT THE INVITING COUNTRY ESTATE OF CHISHOLM TRAIL WINERY.

ꙮChisholm Trail Winery

www.chisholmtrailwinery.com

2367 Usener Road
Fredericksburg, Texas 78624

Phone: (877) 990-2675
Fax: (830) 990-9965

> **OPEN: FRIDAY AND SATURDAY**
> **11:00 A.M.–6:00 P.M.**
> **SUNDAY**
> **12:00 P.M.–6:00 P.M.**

The legend of Vernon Gold lives within the walls of the Chisholm Trail Winery and in the hearts of its owners Paula Williamson and Harry Skeems.

Who was Vernon Gold?

Vernon was one of the early pioneers of the Texas wine industry, though many may not be familiar with his name. He was the winemaker at the old Perdernales Vineyards winery near Fredericksburg, though he usually referred to himself as simply a farmer. He was a man who loved the land, a man with the patience and determination required to nurture a vineyard. He also taught Paula everything he knew about winemaking during the final years of his life.

Today, Paula and Harry use Bob Pepi from Napa Valley as their wine consultant. Bob helped design the winery and an innovative cooling jacket for the stainless steel fermenting tanks to combat the high heat conditions.

On our arrival, we were greeted by a half dozen llamas—yes, we said llamas—as well as a pig, quarter horses, about a hundred cats that call the property home, and the winery's mascot, a longhorn steer. The estate was a busy place, Paula and Harry were awaiting arrival of the remainder of the fermenting tanks, and construction seemed to be everywhere we looked. Harry was in the vineyard while we talked with Paula in the winery. She

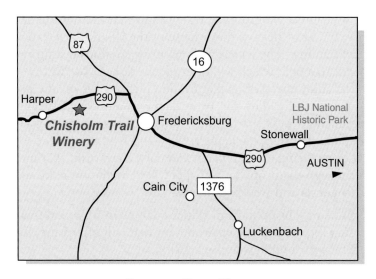

CHISHOLM TRAIL WINERY

explained that the winery grew from a love of wine and their experiences in the European wine regions. After learning all she could from Vernon, Paula attended classes at the University of California, Davis before breaking ground for the winery.

The five-year-old vineyard occupies twenty-five of the estate's eighty acres and is planted with Cabernet Sauvignon, Cabernet Franc, Merlot, and Chenin Blanc. Until recently, the grapes have been sold to local wineries as plans for the winery formalized. Now the grapes will be used to produce Chisholm Trail Winery estate bottled wines.

THE WINES

Eventually the winery will have a production capacity of 18,000 gallons, as well as a barrel cellar for aging. Paula currently offers a Cabernet Sauvignon and a Chenin Blanc, with possible future plans for a Merlot and a still to be named blend of red wines. Her winemaking style will utilize slow, cold fermentation in stainless steel at higher acid levels, then aging in French and American oak. Having had the great opportunity to taste the six-month-old barrel samples, we were sure of some great reds from this winery.

As we toured the grounds, Harry explained their vision of the future, trying to help us make sense of the labyrinth of structural steel framing. The winery will feature a spacious tasting room adjacent to a deli, which will offer picnic baskets for visitors who want to enjoy the various picturesque picnic areas on the property. A series of cabins will be available as a bed and breakfast, complimented by a spa-like activity center that features a pool, sauna, massage stations, game rooms, and a home theater. On a knoll overlooking a magnificent view of a the stream that meanders through the property, a chapel will be built and made available to guests and wedding parties.

Visitors to Chisholm Trail Winery will be in for a real treat as they step into a fairy tale environment that will offer wine, food, beautiful surroundings, and relaxation.

Directions: From Chisholm Trail Winery, we head back on SH 290 into Fredericksburg, then turn right onto SH 87 for a visit to Comfort Cellars Winery in the historic town of Comfort.

❧Comfort Cellars Winery

www.comfortcellars.com

723 Front Street
Comfort, Texas 78013

Phone: (830) 995-3274

> **Open: Daily**
> **12:00 p.m.–6:00 p.m.**
>
> Tastings, retail sales,
> and gifts

We parked at the backside of Comfort Cellars Winery to have the opportunity to stroll through rows of old barn doors and country antiques on one particularly beautiful sunny afternoon in May. We were greeted at the tasting room entrance by Raisin, VP of Public Relations. After sniffing our feet and receiving a generous scratching behind his ears, he permitted us to enter.

Cathie Winmill, owner of Comfort Cellars Winery, said she found Raisin in the local animal shelter when seeking a dog to keep her company while tending to the vineyard. She describes Raisin, now the winery's mascot, as, "a hundred percent mutt, but very lovable." To Cathie's surprise Raisin also has an affinity for wine. The only time he gets upset is when his personalized tasting bowl is empty. Cathie is not sure what his favorite wine is, but she knows he tends to prefer reds.

The atmosphere in the tasting room compliments the town quite well; it is *comfort*able! Set in a renovated 1904 house, the generous woodwork, hardwood floors, soaring beadboard ceilings, and wine rack covered walls invite you to come in and "set-a-spell." Cathie must have had this in mind when she placed an overstuffed couch in one corner of the tasting room. After being handed a tasting of Comfort Cellars Pinot Noir, we drifted over to the couch, which was, of course, quite comfortable.

Winemaking has been in the Winmill family for generations. Growing up in Illinois, Cathie has fond memories of her father making wine, an activity enjoyed by the entire family. After leaving home, the winemaking bug caught her again while attending the University of Arizona. "They were growing grapes in the desert and that fascinated me," she recalled.

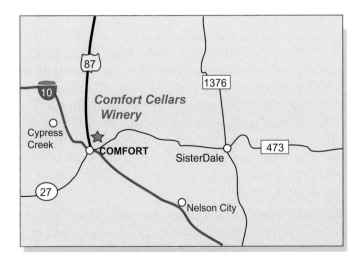

COMFORT CELLARS WINERY

After retiring from the Army Medical Specialist Corps, Cathie purchased land just east of Comfort, near the town of Sisterdale. The two-acre vineyard, which sits at an elevation of 1,500 feet above sea level, has been planted using a terraced design. Cathie told us that, "It's more labor intensive to use the terrace design, but combined with our elevation, it should create a perfect growing environment for our grapes." She also admits that she just enjoys looking at the picturesque pattern that reminds her of the vineyards in Tuscany.

Cathie's brother, Bob Winmill, serves as the winemaker for Comfort Cellars Winery. In addition to winemaking, he has been deeply involved with completing the construction of the new winery facility, located just behind the tasting room. Using a German-heritage design theme, the stone building exudes a casual charm that reflects its owner's personality. Inside, the stainless steel fermenting tanks are dwarfed by the winery's volume, with a ceiling suspended two stories above the production floor. A loft that will be used for special events connects to a second story deck, accessed though French doors.

THE WINES

Bob Winmill's winemaking style leans toward drier wines; he is even planning on releasing a dry Blush. Comfort Cellars Winery's list of red wines includes Pinot Noir, Merlot, and Road Runner Red. The Road Runner Red is a blend of Merlot and Pinot Noir, created to utilize the Pinot Noir, which, Bob felt, was not up to his standards to release as a stand-alone vintage. Their white wines include Chenin Blanc, Orange Chardonnay, White Zinfandel, and Comfort Blush. The Orange Chardonnay is made in sweet style, incorporating orange juice, fresh oranges, and orange peels during the fermentation process. The Comfort Blush, which Cathie calls her "Sunset Sipping Wine," is made in an off-dry style, just perfect for sipping on a hot Texas day.

Comfort Cellars also offers a few specialty wines: two versions of Muscat Canelli, Fredericksburg Peach wine, and a Raisin Wine. The Muscat Canelli is made in both a sweet version and a dry version that pairs well with spicy foods. The Fredericksburg

Peach wine is made from, well, Fredericksburg peaches and has been well received by visitors. The Raisin Wine has become a signature wine of sorts for Comfort Cellars and always sells out shortly after being released.

We should also expect some exciting experimentation with wines in the near future. In the past, Bob has released a raisin wine, and their Orange Chardonnay quickly sold out within days of its release. Cathie is trying to convince Bob to create a Mango-Kiwi wine using Chardonnay as the base. But the experimentation doesn't stop there; with a devilish grin she told us, "There is a Potato wine in our future!" It was hard to tell if she was just kidding us or not!

Comfort Cellars Winery wines are only available for sale at the tasting room, which also offers various wine-related and non-wine-related gift items.

DIRECTIONS: AFTER YOUR VISIT TO COMFORT CELLARS WINERY, YOU MAY WANT TO WALK AROUND THE TOWN'S HISTORIC DISTRICT OFFERING A WIDE SELECTION OF ANTIQUES. THEN, WE HEAD NORTH ON **SH 87**, TURNING RIGHT ON **FM 473** TO SISTERDALE, HOME OF SISTER CREEK VINEYARDS.

&Sister Creek Vineyards

www.sistercreekvineyards.com

1142 Sisterdale
Sisterdale, Texas 78006-7113

Phone: (830) 324-6704
Fax: (830) 324-6704

OPEN: SUNDAY–THURSDAY
12:00 P.M.–5:00 P.M.
FRIDAY AND SATURDAY
11:00 A.M.–5:00 P.M.
TOURS, TASTINGS,
AND RETAIL SALES

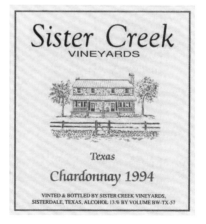

Heading south on Route 1376, we begin the eighteen-mile drive through the Great Divide—the High Hills that separate the Pedernales River watershed from the Guadalupe River watershed. This sparsely populated area offers breathtaking scenery on our drive to the town of Sisterdale. If you own a convertible, this is the perfect road to drive.

Sister Creek Vineyards is hard to miss in this town of twenty-five people. The winery is housed in a renovated one-hundred-year-old cotton gin, the largest structure in Sisterdale. The vineyard, consisting of three acres of lush vines planted along the town's Main Street, dominates the landscape.

Owner Verson Friesenhahn and winemaker Danny Hernandez started the vineyard in the 1986–1987 season, in a valley of rich alluvial soil between west and east Sister Creeks. They originally planted the vineyard at an 8 × 12 density (eight feet between vines and twelve feet between rows); the next year they planted in between the existing vines to double the density. At this double density, Verson and Danny began using an open canopy type of wiring trellis throughout the vineyard. "The open canopy requires more labor," says Danny, "but it opens the vines to more sunlight."

THE WINES

The three-acre vineyard, nestled between the cypress-lined East and West Sister Creeks, is planted with Chardonnay, Pinot

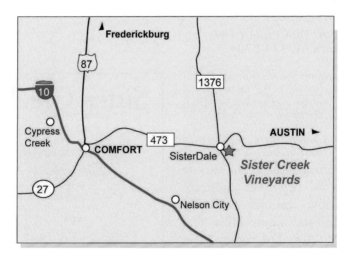

SISTER CREEK VINEYARDS

Noir, Cabernet Sauvignon, Cabernet Franc, and Merlot. The fruit harvested from this vineyard, however, is no longer able to fulfill the winery's production, so grapes are brought in from the Lubbock area. As the popularity, demand, and distribution has grown for Sister Creek's wines, the production capacity has increased to 6,000 gallons, with additional stainless steel fermentation tanks and an expanded barrel room.

Employing French (Bordeaux and Burgundy) winemaking techniques, Sister Creek Vineyards offers a line of subtle, elegant wines that includes two Chardonnays, Cabernet Sauvignon, Pinot Noir, and a Muscat Canelli. The small size of the winery allows Danny to carefully control the winemaking process and test various experimental winemaking techniques. He prefers not to filter his wines when possible to preserve as much flavor and character of the grape as possible.

Sister Creek's Chardonnay remains a consistently remarkable wine from this tiny hamlet winery in the Hill Country. Two Chardonnays are now offered; the traditional barrel aged style with a "buttery" flavor and a crispier more citric style that is fermented in stainless steel.

The Cabernet Sauvignon is a classic production, fruity and clean with a crisp structure and deep ruby color. "The best reception for these Cabs" explains Danny, "has been when they are blended with thirty percent Cabernet Franc." Sister Creek Cabernet Sauvignon is aged for two years in French oak with no filtering. We think the Pinot Noir is one of the best kept secrets about this winery; be sure to try it at their tasting room, even if you are not a lover of red wine—it might just change your mind. The Muscat Canelli is a semisweet wine balanced with intense peach, apricot, and floral aromas. True to Danny's zest for experimentation, a little carbonation has been added to this wine, providing it with a zesty spritz.

Sister Creek Vineyards is our last winery along the Enchanted Trail. For those who enjoy antique shopping or just want to stop for lunch before heading home, travel south on 1376 to the town of Boerne. Another old German town, Boerne is reminiscent of Fredericksburg with its selection of shops, restaurants, and historic downtown district.

Along The Trail

The Enchanted Trail best captures the flavor of the Hill Country's German heritage. Remnants of that past are preserved in towns such as Boerne, Comfort, and best of all, along our wine trail in towns like Fredericksburg and Sisterdale. The Enchanted Trail is a superb combination of the natural beauty that typifies the Hill Country and the excitement of towns rich in the culture, food, art, and the heritage of the Old World. Towns like Fredericksburg fill visitors with a peacefulness born partly of the slower lifestyle there, and partly with their romantic, settled qualities.

Fredericksburg is an enigma, representing different things to different people. For some, it is a wondrous collection of antique shops, for others a charismatic German town, and for yet others, a romantic getaway. In reality, it is all of these and more. The town fathers painstakingly preserved the original architecture of the German immigrants, who were masters in carpentry and masonry. Renovations to storefronts along Main Street preserve original designs; Sunday Homes and log cabins have been converted to bed and breakfasts, and the original extra-wide streets (for turning teams of horses) remain.

The rich assortment of bed and breakfasts and the people they attract help to explain another facet of the atmosphere that fills the town—romance. You can spot it everywhere, couples walking hand-in-hand along Main Street, kissing at intersections, and snuggling close in the beer gardens of German restaurants.

Enchanted Rock State Park lies just to the north of Fredericksburg. Visitors have two routes to reach Enchanted Rock from Fredericksburg: by turning north off Main Street and proceeding eighteen miles on Milam Street, which becomes FM 965. The second route is to drive north on SH 16 for twenty-one miles, then turn west onto FM 965 for another eight miles to the park. Enchanted Rock is the second largest outcropping of pink granite in the United States after Georgia's Stone Mountain. Entrance to the park costs $5, and you can expect crowds during the summer months.

In the springtime, wine tourists are treated to splendid displays of the Texas bluebonnets and Indian paintbrush flowers that carpet the medians and sides of SH 290 between Austin and Fredericksburg. In June, the treat is peaches. The peach harvest is dominant this time of year, with peach stands lining the roads near the Stonewall and Fredericksburg areas.

The harshness and drama of pioneer life in the Hill Country becomes obvious if you tour the city cemetery in Fredericksburg. The German settlers brought their beliefs and traditions with them, as evidenced in the ornate ironworks that box in burial sites. Indications of the devastating epidemics that ravaged pioneer life can be seen in the number of tiny graves of pioneer children who fell victim to these diseases.

THE HIGHLAND TRAIL

The winding roads of the Highland Trail offer you dramatic views of the seven Highland Lakes. These azure blue lakes come into view momentarily, briefly disappear, and then burst into view along the next turn. This trail is a pleasant daylong ride through the hills and valleys that are home to these seven manmade lakes. There are six wineries in the northern section of the Hill Country: Flat Creek Estate, Fall Creek Vineyards, Pillar Bluff Vineyards, Alamosa Wine Cellars, Spicewood Vineyards, and McReynolds Winery. Looking at a map, this may seem like a quick trip to many of you not familiar with the area. Take heed, however; the trail's length can be deceiving. As an example, a direct drive from Austin to Fall Creek Vineyards on the far end of the trail is around two hours. Leave Austin in the morning and take a leisurely drive to enjoy the scenery and still make it to our last winery—McReynolds Winery—before closing time.

Our first stop is the one of the newest wineries, Flat Creek Estate between Lago Vista and Marble Falls. From there, we continue west on RR 1431 to one of the oldest wineries, Fall Creek Vineyards, located on the northern tip of Lake Buchanan, where Ed Auler has been making outstanding wine for two decades. Next, we

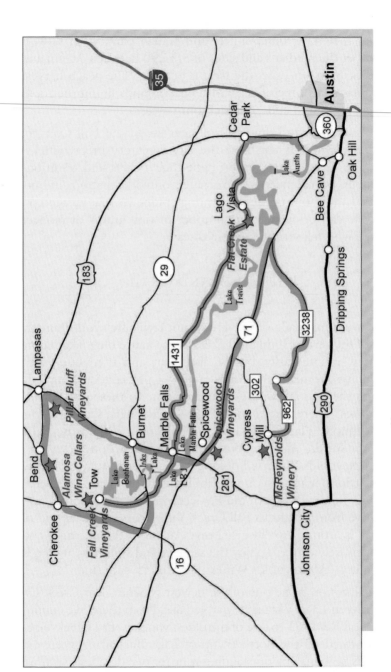

HIGHLAND TRAIL WINERIES

head north on SH 16 to visit Alamosa Wine Cellars near the town of Bend. Then we head east on SH 580 to Lampasas and turn south on 1478 to visit Pillar Bluff Vineyards at the intersection of SH 1478 and CR 111. From there, we head south on SH 281, turning east on SH 71 to visit Spicewood Vineyards in the town of Spicewood. For our last stop, we head south on SH 71 to FM 962 and turn west toward the town of Cypress Mill to visit McReynolds Winery. Let's begin our tour by heading north on SH 183 to the town of Cedar Park, where we will turn west onto RR 1431 to visit Flat Creek Estates, located between Logo Vista and Marble Falls.

❧Flat Creek Estate

www.flatcreekestate.com
24912 Singleton Bend East, Unit #1
Marble Falls, Texas 78654
Phone: (512) 267-6310

> OPEN: TUESDAY–FRIDAY
> 12:00 P.M.–5:00 P.M.
> SATURDAY–SUNDAY
> 10:00 A.M.–4:00 P.M.
> TASTINGS AND RETAIL SALES

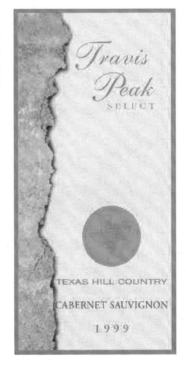

With the town of Cedar Park in our rearview mirror, we head west on RR 1431, a road that epitomizes the term *fun driving*. As we pass the town of Lago Vista, beautiful lake views, challenging turns, and roller coaster hills are sure to bring a smile to even the most jaded of drivers. This undulating landscape perched at the edge of Lake Travis is home to Flat Creek Estate, one of the newest Texas wineries.

Winery owners, Rick and Madelyn Naber fell in love with the

wines and atmosphere of Tuscany during their trips to Europe. Slowly, this turned into passion for wine, prompting the couple to plant a vineyard on their property near Marble Falls. With twelve acres of Italian varietals—Sangiovese, Primitivo, and Pinot Grigio—planted, the Nabers began a search for a winemaker. Ironically, they found an Australian winemaker right in the heart of Texas.

Chris Parker, a trained oenologist with over fifteen years of experience in Australia and Europe, agreed to come on board as winemaker, taking on the additional task of helping with the design of the winery facility. When we spoke with him in the summer of 2001, everyone at Flat Creek Estate was excited about the beginning of construction. The winery will include a conference area, a large spacious tasting room, a restaurant, and a terrazzo patio located under huge oak trees. The Nabers want Flat Creek Estate to be a place where folks want to visit, relax, and stay for awhile. It sounds like this bucolic setting near Lake Travis has just the right elements for just that.

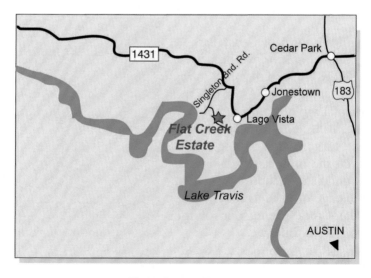

FLAT CREEK ESTATE

THE WINES

Chris told us that the winery will focus on developing small production, high quality, Italian-style wines and an estate Port. Wines available in 2002 included Cabernet Sauvignon and Muscat Blanco. In 2003, the list of wines will expand to include Shiraz, Sangiovese, and Primitivo.

DIRECTIONS: NEXT WE HEAD WEST ON RR 1431 FOR A PICTURESQUE DRIVE TO ONE OF THE OLDEST WINERIES IN TEXAS, FALL CREEK VINEYARDS, AT THE NORTHERN EDGE OF LAKE BUCHANAN.

❧Fall Creek Vineyards

www.fcv.com
Located 2.2 miles north of the Post Office in Tow, Texas
Mailing Address: 1111 Guadalupe Street
Austin, Texas 78701
Phone: (512) 476-4477 or (915) 379-5361

OPEN: MONDAY–FRIDAY
11:00 A.M.–4:00 P.M.
SATURDAY
12:00 P.M.–5:00 P.M.
SUNDAYS
12:00 P.M.–4:00 P.M.
(MARCH–NOVEMBER)

TOURS, TASTINGS, RETAIL SALES, AND GIFT SHOP

If you have never visited the Lake Buchanan area, you will find that this part of the Hill Country boasts some of the most beautiful landscape in Texas. Traveling these winding roads, you will be hard-pressed to run out of unique and beautiful locations to experience. It is in this dramatic setting that we find ourselves, on our way to Fall Creek Vineyards.

Fall Creek Vineyards produces quality wines on sixty-five acres along the sandy loam shore of Lake Buchanan. This entire area rests on a large plateau that provides a special climate for growing

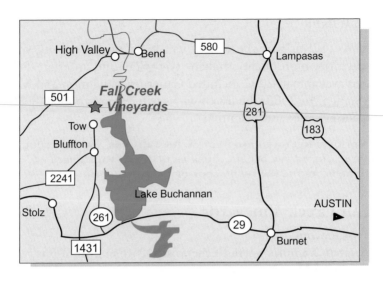

FALL CREEK VINEYARDS

grapes in Texas. The breeze coming from the lake creates an evening cooling effect perfect for vineyard conditions.

Ed and Susan Auler, the owners of Fall Creek Vineyards, have contributed much time and energy to their own endeavor as well as the Texas wine industry. Ed uses his legal background to help develop legislation for the Texas wine industry, while Susan uses her excellent organizational skills to help produce wine events around the state. One event held in early April, The Texas Hill Country Wine and Food Festival, brings together seminars, wine tasting, and an all-day festival of Texas wine and food producers. This event is an enjoyable blending of Texas wines, foods, and music. A weekend of sampling the wines and foods of Texas offers information and culinary treats found only in the Austin area.

Ed Auler's original experimentation with grafting in 1980 proved to be rewarding. By grafting onto champanel rootstock, he brought together the quality of his performing vinifera with the disease resistance of the rootstock to produce a superb grape capable of withstanding attack from diseases such as phylloxera and nematodes. This proved to Ed that vineyards in Texas could grow the best known selections of wine-producing grapes. In 1990, preferable rootstocks were introduced to Fall Creek, and since then the entire vineyard has been regrafted to improve the quality and production.

Along with the vintners of northeast Texas, the Aulers work to enact favorable wine legislation and have made a great contribution to the wine industry in Texas. It became evident to these visionaries that the best wine area of Texas just happened to be located in dry counties and legislation would be needed to change the law in these areas for growth and development of the industry. The production and sale of wine is against the law in these areas. Some dry counties have adopted their laws to allow the growing of grapes, but not the consumption of the alcohol product. These same visionaries are still active today in the legislative process to help make the changes needed to produce and market their wine products in these select areas of Texas.

THE WINES

The Fall Creek Vineyards site on the Colorado River has a history as old as Texas. The Indians that lived on this land left behind a variety of artifacts along their burial mounds and in the Fall Creek Vineyard fields. The burial mounds have been left undisturbed, but arrowheads are often found after heavy rains and are on display in the Fall Creek tasting room. This land was understandably in demand even back then. The property contains innumerable microclimates and rich soils, perfect for grape maturation. After the Aulers spent more than a decade of growing premium grapes at Fall Creek Vineyards, however, a severe frost in 1991 destroyed most of their premier vines. Inspired by the adversity, the Aulers shifted focus, found other sources in Texas for grapes, and continued to produce premium wines while they replanted their vineyard in stages.

Today Fall Creek Vineyards award-winning wines are in such great demand that its sells all it produces. Their Chardonnay enhances the grape's character through cold fermentation and about 30 percent oak aging for four months. A great Chardonnay substitute is their Vintner's Cuvee, which is a blend of Chardonnay and Chenin Blanc, fermented in oak and having undergone partial malolactic fermentation. Just prior to bottling, a small amount of Muscat Canelli is added, giving the wine a slightly fruitier taste.

The Fall Creek Vineyards red wines undergo oak aging in a combination of American and French oak. The Merlot is a blend of Merlot, Malbec, and Cabernet Franc, resulting in a fruity, medium-bodied wine. The Cabernet Sauvignon—which has a habit of selling out very quickly—is a wine with soft tannins that allow for immediate consumption, but it is also able to age for years to come.

Additional wine favorites include Cascade, White Zinfandel, and the "Granite" wines: Granite Reserve and Granite Blush. The Granite wine series has been particularly popular with consumers and usually quickly disappear. The Granite Reserve is a blend of Cabernet Sauvignon, Merlot, and Malbec, which produces a soft wine that is ready to be consumed with less bottle aging. The Granite Blush is a blend of Johannisberg Riesling, Chenin Blanc, and Cabernet Sauvignon and is slightly drier than most blush wines.

Since its inception, Fall Creek has made a commitment to quality wines by harmonizing the best European winemaking techniques with the best modern technological innovations. Its success is underscored by the demand for its wines, which greatly exceeds the supply.

Fall Creek also maintains an active schedule of events during the year. The most popular by far is the Grape Stomp Celebration held every August on the last two Saturdays prior to Labor Day weekend. The event features food, music, lake cruises, and fun activities for the kids.

ACTIVITIES IN THE AREA

If you enjoy outdoor activities, you may want to linger in this area after your visit to Fall Creek Vineyards. There are a variety of state parks and recreational areas around Lake Buchanan and Inks Lake offering camping and water sports. The Inks Lake State Park is a beautiful area that draws many artists to reflect and paint. Golf, swimming, boating, and fishing provide entertainment to please the whole family. A small admission fee is charged for the state park. One of the highlighted attractions in this area is the Vanishing Texas River Cruise. Tours along the banks of Lake Buchanan offer some of the best picturesque scenery in the Hill Country. Tours are two and a half or four hours long. Special cruises running from November through February feature a close look at the American bald eagle that migrates to this area.

DIRECTIONS: FROM FALL CREEK VINEYARDS, WE HEAD NORTH ON SH 16 TO THE TOWN OF CHEROKEE, TURNING RIGHT ONTO CR 501 TOWARD THE SMALL TOWN OF BEND. THEN TURN LEFT ONTO CR 508 AND RIGHT ONTO CR 430. ALAMOSA WINE CELLARS IS ABOUT ONE AND A HALF MILES DOWN THE ROAD.

❧Alamosa Wine Cellars

www.alamosawinecellars.com

P.O. Box 212
Bend, Texas 76824

Phone: (915) 628-3313

OPEN BY APPOINTMENT ONLY
TOURS AND TASTINGS

The word *alamosa* is Spanish for "cottonwood," a tree that grows vigorously along most creeks in the southwestern part of the state. When proprietor and winemaker, Jim Johnson, saw the Cottonwood trees growing along Cottonwood Creek, which borders his vineyard, Tio Pancho Ranch Vineyards, he knew what the winery should be called. Besides, if it was good enough for the legendary Alamo in San Antonio, it must be good enough for his winery.

Jim is no stranger to winemaking or to the Texas wine industry. After interning at several well-known California wineries, Jim graduated from University of California, Davis in 1991 and headed back to Texas to join his fellow pioneers in the wine industry. Some of you may recognize his name from the work he did as winemaker to Slaughter-Leftwich and Becker Vineyards. When he reflects on his experiences, Jim feels that he is somewhat unique in the business, "I came to winery ownership through winemaking, not winemaking through winery ownership."

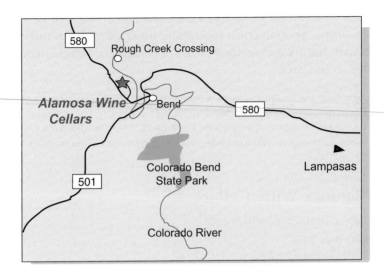

ALAMOSA WINE CELLARS

After establishing Tio Pancho Ranch Vineyards in 1996, Jim was soon ready to realize his goal of owning his own winery. The ten-acre vineyard contains nine varietals: Viognier, Sangiovese, Cabernet Sauvignon, Ruby Cabernet, Tempranillo, Granache, Syrah, Mourverde, and Lavasia Blanca. Future plans call for more Rhone white, Orange Muscat, and Grignolino.

THE WINES

Under Jim's guidance, Alamosa Wine Cellars focuses on using warm climate grapes, which he feels are perfect for south Texas. After looking around the world, he was impressed by the wonderful wines of Spain, Italy, and Northern Rhone and decided to concentrate on those varietals in his vineyard. His winemaking style? "Not apparent," Jim explains, "I prefer to allow the vineyard voices to be expressed in my wines." That philosophy bears fruition as you taste the wines. For the 2001 Viognier, Jim used a new style, aging 25 percent of the wine in French oak and the rest in stainless steel. The result is a crisp, aromatic wine full of apricot, pear, and lemon. As Jim likes to say, "a wine made mostly in the vineyard."

For the reds, blending is a big part of Jim's winemaking approach; he believes that blending creates a more complex wine, worthy of bottle aging. The Palette 2000 Rhone Blend is a combination of Mourvedre, Syrah, Grenache, and Viognier, creating berry aromas with a rustic "gigondas" style. The 2000 El Guapo is a blend of Tempranillo, Cabernet Sauvignon, and Garnacha that has a good tannin structure with full ripe fruit.

When you talk to Jim about his wines, it quickly becomes apparent that Sangiovese holds a special place in his heart. His 2000 Sangiovese is a blend of that grape with Cabernet Sauvignon, Syrah, and Malvasia to create a spicy, fruity wine on the order of a Pinot Noir style. The 2000 Sangiovese Reserva is a blend that has been barrel aged for two years to produce a Chianti style wine. Finally, the 2001 Sangiovese uses the grapes of Cherokee Creek Vineyards to create a wine with bright cherry and cola flavors.

Alamosa Wine Cellars wines are available in Austin, Dallas, Houston, and San Antonio. Jim wants the winery to remain small, focusing on specialty wines based on his unique selection of grapes. But don't let his humble demeanor fool you; we expect a long line of creative, fabulous wines coming from this small patch of earth, just west of Bend, Texas.

DIRECTIONS: FROM ALAMOSA WINE CELLARS, WE HEAD BACK TO LAMPASAS ON FR 580, THEN SOUTH ON FM 1478 TO VISIT PILLAR BLUFF VINEYARDS.

♣Pillar Bluff Vineyards

www.pillarbluff.com

300 County Road 111
Lampasas, Texas 76550
Phone: (512) 556-4078

> **OPEN: SATURDAYS**
> **12:00 P.M.–5:00 P.M.**

Many of you may not associate the Lampasas area as synonomous with wine country, but Gill Bledsoe owner and winemaker at Pillar Bluff Vineyards, like his neighbor Jim Johnson in Bend, knows

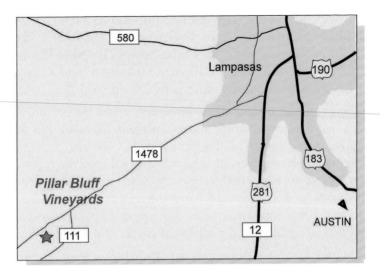

580

Lampasas

190

1478

183

Pillar Bluff
Vineyards

281

AUSTIN

12

111

PILLAR BLUFF VINEYARDS

a secret: grapes will thrive in this area. Gill should know; he's had a thriving vineyard on the rich alluvial plains of Pillar Bluff Creek along the northernmost edge of the Llano uplift, just 3.2 miles southwest of Lampasas. The winery takes its name from the wet weather creek, Pillar Bluff Creek, which forms the southernmost border of the vineyard.

Sitting in the northern corner of the Hill Country Viticultural Appellation, his two-acre vineyard, contains Merlot, Chardonnay, Chenin Blanc, and Ruby Cabernet. Then, after fortifying his years of experience as a grape grower and amateur winemaker with enology courses at the T. V. Munson Center at Grayson County College, Gill made the decision to open the winery.

In June 1999, Pillar Bluff Vineyards officially opened for business. Gill explained that since his total 1999 production was only eighty cases, distribution through retail outlets was out of the question. Most of his wine has been sold though cooperation with the Hill Country Wineries Association, a group of sixteen wineries in the Hill Country that have formed an alliance and sponsor a series of events during the year. This all fits well into Gill's philosophy toward the winery, which he describes as a "Go Slow" approach. His patience has served him well; the 1999 vintages of his Chenin Blanc and Blush quickly sold out.

THE WINES

Gill believes that the more memorable wines are those that possess the complexity gained through blending. To that end, the vineyard was planted with the intention of fermenting and aging a portion of the fruit through a slow, cold process to bring out the characteristics of the fruit and then blend it with American and French oak aged wines.

White wines from Pillar Bluff Vineyards include Chardonnay and Chenin Blanc. The Chardonnay features nuances of apple, pear, and citrus, which burst from the glass, with only a hint of oak to allow the wine to be light and spritzy on the palate. The Chenin Blanc is done with 100 percent stainless steel cold fermentation, offering a crisp white wine with a full-mouth finish.

For red wine lovers, Gill offers a Cabernet Sauvignon, a Merlot, and a unique White Merlot. The 2001 Cabernet Sauvignon, made available in late 2002, was carefully barrel aged, producing a wine that is alive with currants and black berries with a hint of tobacco. The Merlot, which took a silver medal in the Wines of the South Competition, was made with one year of aging in French and American oak, resulting in a black cherry nose and soft chewy tannins. The White Merlot, now a Christmas classic, is a blend of Merlot and Chenin Blanc featuring a ruby hue, fruity nose, and a slight sweetness.

A new wine, the Estate Blush, first available in early 2003, is a blend of 85 percent Chenin Blanc and 15 percent Merlot. Featuring a crisp, light taste, this European-style rosé is perfect for sipping on a hot summer day. As Gill patiently completes his vineyard plan, we can look for more delicious and creative wines with greater availability. Until then, savor these wines if you are lucky enough to find a bottle or two.

DIRECTIONS: FROM PILLAR BLUFF VINEYARDS, WE BACKTRACK ALONG FM 1478 TO LAMPASAS AND HEAD SOUTH ON SH 281, TURNING EAST ON SH 71 TO VISIT SPICEWOOD VINEYARDS IN THE TOWN OF SPICEWOOD.

❧Spicewood Vineyards

www.spicewoodvineyards.com

1423 Country Road 409
Spicewood, Texas 78669

Phone: (830) 693-5328
Fax: (830) 693-5940

> OPEN: WEDNESDAY–FRIDAY
> 12:00 P.M.–5:00 P.M.
> SATURDAY
> 10:00 A.M.–5:00 P.M.
> SUNDAY
> 12:00 P.M.–5:00 P.M.

Now this is Texas! Located thirty-five miles north of Austin, Spicewood Vineyards is a bit of a challenge to find. Heading south along SH 71, if you pass the Exxon station at the intersection of SH 71 and SH 191, well pardner, you've gone too far! There is no "Winery" sign to mark the turn onto Route 408, a small two-lane highway. Your only landmark is Cypress Creek, which flows under SH 71. Once on Route 408, you follow a twisting road for a mile or two to Route 409. The "Spicewood Vineyards" sign nailed to an oak tree tells you where Route 409 is before the highway sign may be visible. Turn here and the fun begins. After driving along a ranch road for a mile or so, a sign greets you, saying, "Livestock on the road ahead." Sure enough, a few turns later, horses and cows are feeding along the roadway and look up momentarily, unimpressed as you drive past them. A cluster of buildings can be seen on the right, and there on the left, the winery appears between the trees.

The vineyard is located on an ancient bed of the Colorado River on the edge of the Llano Uplift. The topsoil is complex, ranging from red clay loam to the Trinity Sands over a limestone bedrock. The vines grow on a hillside with a peak elevation of 900 feet and utilize a vertical shoot positioned trellis on close spacing to convert the maximum amount of Texas sun into fine

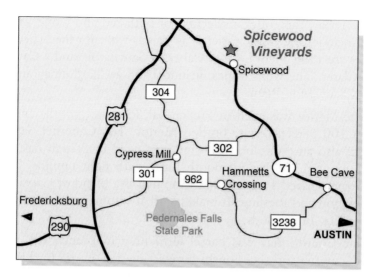

SPICEWOOD VINEYARDS

wine. The first 1.5 acres of vines were planted in 1992, then gradually expanded to a total of 175 acres in production in 1998. Major varietals include Cabernet Sauvignon, Merlot, Chardonnay, Sauvignon Blanc, Zinfandel, Semillon, Muscat Blanc, Cabernet Franc, and Johannisberg Riesling.

Built on a hillside, the winery is a beautiful architectural combination of strength and design. A new winery facility adjacent to the original building was completed in 1999. The winery building is approximately 5,000 square feet on two levels. The upper level has a large tasting and special events room, suitable for catered dinners, weddings, receptions, and other special events. There is an outdoor pavillion with a water feature and shaded area for sipping wine, picnicking, and viewing the vineyard and the Texas Hill Country. Wine is made on the lower level of the winery building that includes an area for stainless steel tanks with a fermenting and storage capacity of more than 10,000 gallons of wine. The lower level also has an underground barrel room capable of holding more than 400 barrels.

THE WINES

Bonded in 1995, Spicewood Vineyards released its first wine— a Holiday Blush—that same year and sold out in the first nine days. Today, they offer a selection of both red and white wines that includes the classic varietals as well as a blush wine. The red wines are 1998 Merlot, 1998 Cabernet Sauvignon, and a Cabernet Claret. The white wines include 1998 a Chardonnay and a 1998 Sauvignon Blanc.

The Merlot was aged in French oak for nine months and is from 100 percent estate-bottled Merlot. The Cabernet Sauvignon, also an estate-bottled wine, was aged in French oak for nine months and has a smooth finish with light tannins. The Cabernet Claret is a sweet red wine that is a blend of Cabernet Sauvignon and Riesling. It makes a great summer wine to enjoy with spicy Texas foods.

The Chardonnay was barrel fermented in French oak and aged *sur lies* for six months, imparting flavors of hazlenut, vanilla, and butterscotch into this complex wine. The Sauvignon Blanc was produced entirely in stainless steel tanks and blended with Muscat and Semillon. With flavors of tropical fruit and spices, this wine has won silver medals at the Los Angeles County Fair, the Eastern Wine Competition, and Best of Class at the Lone Star Wine Competition. The Bluebonnet Blush is a lighter, sweet wine with the floral notes of a Riesling.

Dedicated to producing quality Hill Country wines, the Manigolds look forward to the future as their vineyard continues to mature, improving the fruit quality. As producers of hand-crafted wines, the Manigolds understand the importance of the relationship between quality grapes and quality wines. They are hands-on owners who participate in every stage of the process, including planting and tending the vineyards, picking the grapes, making the wine and personally bottling it.

Spicewood wines are available across the state in fine wine retail establishments.

DIRECTIONS: WE LEAVE THE AROMATIC SPICE BUSHES GROWING ALONG CYPRESS CREEK NEXT TO SPICEWOOD VINEYARDS FOR A TRIP DOWN SH 71 TO HAMILTON POOL ROAD (RR 3238), THEN TURN RIGHT ON FM 962, AND RIGHT AGAIN ON FM 304 (SHOVEL MOUNTAIN ROAD) TO VISIT ONE OF THE MORE UNIQUE WINERIES, MCREYNOLDS WINERY NEAR CYPRESS MILL.

McReynolds Winery

www.mcreynoldswines.com

706 Shovel Mountain Road
Cypress Mill, Texas 78654

Phone: (830) 825-3544

> OPEN: SATURDAY–SUNDAY
> 12:00–5:00 P.M.
>
> OTHER TIMES BY APPOINTMENT
>
> RETAIL SALES

The antilock braking system was straining to slow us down, my sweaty palms gripping the wheel tightly as I wrestled the car into the hairpin turn, our tires squealing ever so slightly. My wife sat silently next to me; we both knew I misjudged our speed coming into this turn. As we reached the midpoint of the turn, I strained to maneuver the car into the center of the narrow road. Items inside were catapulted across the backseat as the G-forces tried to throw us over the cliff, and I prayed the traction

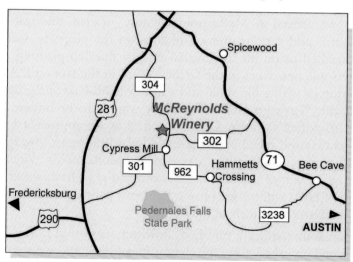

McReynolds Winery

sensors would do what they were designed to do. Quickly down-shifting, I felt the rear tires lose traction momentarily as we slid off the pavement onto the shoulder, gravel spraying up behind us. My wife nervously looked at the edge of the cliff perilously close to her window. I breathed a sigh of relief as I felt the tires grab on the edge of the pavement once again. My wife was, shall we say, not amused. A half-mile later, the road snapped back around like an angry rattlesnake in two back-to-back hairpin turns. This time I was ready. This time I obeyed the speed limit signs.

Are we driving through the mountains of Southern California or a road rally in the Pacific Northwest? Neither. We are on the road to McReynolds Winery, heading along FM 962 toward the town of Cypress Mill. This road is great fun to drive; offering scenic views along each turn. Just be careful.

Gerald McReynolds, a jovial man with a heart as big as Texas, had been around wineries for a long time when he bought the property near Cypress Mill in the mid-1990s. As early as 1969, Gerald assisted wineries in the United States by creating a de-vice that would submerge the cap that formed on the top of fer-menting wine, allowing the winemakers to pump wine over the cap, generating a deeper color and enhancing the flavor of the wine.

As we arrived at McReynolds Winery, nestled amongst the vineyards and various utility buildings on the property, Gerald approached us on his tractor, having just finished planting and tying some new vines in the farthest point in the vineyard. After greeting us with a big smile and a hearty handshake, he grinned and said, "Let's go taste some of my wine!" To be honest, we have to admit we were a little skeptical as we approached the moderate-sized metal building Gerald was leading us toward. A small sign leaning against a tree read "McReynolds Winery." The metal skin of the building was old and gray, having seen its share of Hill Country seasons—a light rust patina created a mot-tled pattern over much of the exterior.

Our doubts quickly vanished, however, as Gerald ("Mac" to his friends) pushed aside the sliding metal door and we stepped into the inviting environment that he has created. Welcome to Mac's world, where the entire building has been chilled to around 65 degrees! On one side of the building, the walls are lined with hundreds of wine bottles, stored in handmade wine cubes. A simple table and chairs sit under a single bare-bulb light fixture, exuding a charm that just makes you want to sit down. The other side of the building holds racks of oak barrels and stainless steel fermentation tanks in the process of assembly. After one sip of his wine though, you know Mac is no amateur. This is wine made at a very personal, almost private, level. We were glad he invited us into his world.

THE WINES

McReynolds Winery is a small boutique winery, having produced less than 300 gallons in 1999. The five-acre vineyard includes Chardonnay, Chenin Blanc, Cabernet Sauvignon, Syrah, Zinfandel, Barbera, Viognier, and Sangiovese. McReynolds Winery currently offers a Sauvignon Blanc and a 1998 Cabernet Sauvignon; the 1999 Cabernet Sauvignon was still in the barrel at the time of our visit. At this time, all wines are aged in oak barrels, while work is underway to complete the stainless steel fermentation tanks. After tasting the Sauvignon Blanc, we might suggest staying with the current technique, which produces a fruity, slightly peppery wine with a wonderful after taste; perhaps the most unique elaboration of a Sauvignon Blanc we have ever sampled.

Mac's style of winemaking is fashioned after winemakers in Australia, where he and his wife have traveled frequently over the last twenty years. McReynolds Winery will expand their selection of wines in the coming harvests. Mac told us he might even produce another Shiraz, a personal favorite from his experiences in Australia. We sampled a 1995 Shiraz that captured a medal at the Lone Star Wine Competition as well as a 1996 Shiraz that was blended with 30 percent Cabernet Sauvignon. If these wonderful wines are any indication, look for some great vintages from McReynolds Winery in the future.

This is our last winery along the Highland Trail. We hope you have enjoyed your trip, and we welcome you to continue your tour of the Hill Country wineries with the Balcones Trail.

ALONG THE TRAIL

Austin, Travis, LBJ, Buchanan—no, not a list of statesmen—these names, along with Inks and Marble Falls, identify the six Highland Lakes that dominate the landscape along this trail. Water. Water everywhere, be it the cool, clear, spring-fed streams or the deep blue beauty of these lakes, serves as a backdrop for life in this part of the Hill Country.

The Highland Lakes are popular during the summer, and visitors to the area can choose from fishing, hunting, boating, and even innertube rides down the rivers. Holidays can be crowded, so make plans in advance if you'll be visiting during one of the summer holiday weekends. This area is also a mecca for bravely going where none have gone before along winding two-lane roads through breathtaking scenes of the Hill Country. While always beautiful, Springtime is perhaps the most scenic.

The Highland Trail actually circles the Highland Lakes area. On the northern leg, you travel along well-paved, winding roads just made for a convertible and pass through a series of scenic and historic communities such as Jonestown and Marble Falls. The quarries around Marble Falls supplied the marble for the construction of the state capitol building in Austin. The town of Kingsland, located at the confluence of the Llano and Colorado rivers, is a popular fishing spot—and has been for centuries.

TEXAS WINERIES OFTEN SCATTER VINEYARDS ACROSS THE STATE TO MINIMIZE HAIL DAMAGE. (COURTESY OF GRAPE CREEK VINEYARDS)

ENJOYING THE ROMANTIC SETTING OF A TEXAS TOWN ALONG THE WINE TRAIL. (COURTESY OF AUSTIN CONVENTION AND VISITORS BUREAU)

The southern leg of the trail is a more casual drive along SH 71. A straighter shot, the trip between Spicewood Vineyards and Bee Cave will be less twisting and not as steep as you make your way back toward Austin. The city of Austin often feels like a big small-town. As the state capital and host to prominent universities, Austin offers the charm of a college town combined with the sophistication of a state capital. While the town has grown dramatically over the past ten years, it still manages to retain its smalltown atmosphere that drew so many over the years.

Billing itself as the "Live Music Capital of the World," Austin has it all: blues, country/western, jazz, Tejano, and rock. The popular Sixth Street area is home to much of this entertainment along with a great selection of eateries.

Austin is also host to the Hill Country Wine and Food Festival every April. A major event that attracts Texas and California wineries, the event is a collage of dinners, luncheons, early morning and afternoon wine tastings, and desserts and foods from some of the finest restaurants in Texas. The festival also includes musical guests, charitable auctions, and a black-tie extravaganza with a gourmet dinner and dancing into the night. A particular favorite of ours is the Lunch with the Vintners. Festival attendees are given a list of restaurants. They are asked to pick one and attend a luncheon there with mystery vintners. The mystery is the attendees do not know which winery or wineries will be represented until they arrive. We had the pleasure of sitting with vintners from Spicewood Vineyards and Becker Vineyards for a truly enjoyable lunch that once again confirmed our opinion that folks in the wine industry have to be some of the nicest people we have ever met.

If you are interested in this event, you can contact the festival's management at Texas Hill Country Wine and Food Festival, 1006 Mopac Circle, Ste. 102, Austin, Texas 78746. The phone number is (512) 329-0770.

THE BALCONES TRAIL

The Balcones Fault slashes across this area of Texas from southwest to northeast, creating a fascinating array of geological

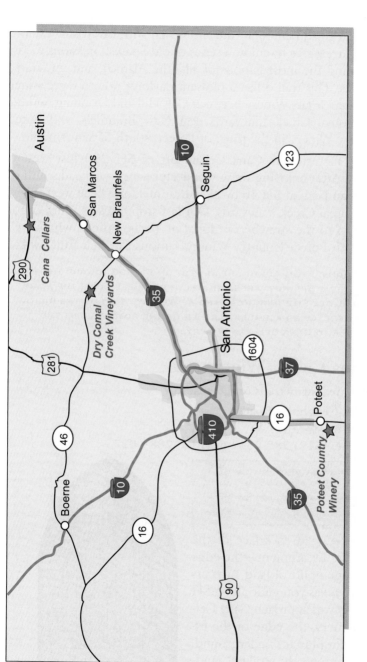

THE BALCONES TRAIL WINERIES

wonders to be enjoyed by scientists and tourists alike. The area between Austin and San Antonio is rich with caverns to explore, aquatic treasures to enjoy, a series of old Spanish missions to visit (including the most famous of all—the Alamo), and, of course, wineries. This trail offers a pleasant daylong ride to three wineries: Cana Cellars Winery between Oak Hill and Dripping Springs, Dry Comal Creek Vineyards near New Braunfels, and Poteet Country Winery in the town of Poteet, south of San Antonio.

Our first stop is Cana Cellars off of SH 290 just west of Austin. After enjoying these wonderful wines, we head south on IH 35 and exit at SH 46 by New Braunfels and head west to visit Dry Comal Creek Vineyards. Our last stop takes us south of San Antonio to the strawberry capital of Texas, Poteet, where we'll visit with Poteet Country Winery, famous for their fruit wines.

DIRECTIONS: FROM AUSTIN, HEAD WEST ON SH 290 TOWARD THE TOWN OF DRIPPING SPRINGS. APPROXIMATELY FIVE MILES DOWN THE ROAD, YOU WILL SEE FITZHUGH ROAD AND A "WINERY" SIGN ON THE RIGHT. TURN HERE. ONE-HALF MILE FARTHER UP THE ROAD WILL BE THE ENTRANCE TO CANA CELLARS WINERY.

&Cana Cellars Winery

www.texaswinetrails.com/cana.htm

11217 Fitzhugh Road
Austin, Texas 78736
Phone: (512) 288-2582 or (512) 288-6027

OPEN SATURDAY—SUNDAY
12:00 P.M.—5:00 P.M.
OTHER TIMES BY APPOINTMENT
TOURS, TASTING, AND RETAIL SALES

The rugged rock-face of the Balcones Escarpment—the edge of a large uplift of land—towers above you as you glide along SH 290. As you approach Cana Cellars Winery, the edge of the escarpment plunges underground, leaving only the rolling landscape between Oak Hill and Dripping Springs.

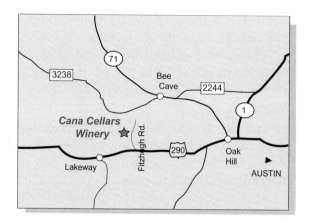

CANA CELLARS WINERY

Joe and Deena Turner, owners of Cana Cellars Winery, are blessed to be landowners in this picturesque area, where a chaotic geological past has given way to dramatic landscapes. As you pull into their farm off Fitzhugh Road, you are welcomed by the sight of longhorn steer casually grazing along the roadside. As you make your way up the curving one-lane blacktop leading up to the winery itself, a sign warns you: "Loose Livestock."

The winery is truly a cellar, having been built into the basement of a home already on the property when Joe purchased the land. As a lover of wine and a visitor to a friend's vineyard/winery in Italy over the years, the first thing Joe did was plant a two-and-a-half acre vineyard. Today the vineyard plays host to Cabernet Sauvignon, Sauvignon Blanc, Merlot, and Chardonnay grapes for the Cana Cellars wines.

The vineyard was in its fifth year when Joe and Deena married. As an incredibly romantic gesture, the Turners decided to release their first wine for their wedding. Although, as Deena told us, bottling hundreds of bottles of wine hours before five hundred wedding guests were to arrive wasn't exactly a romantic experience. The wine was a success however, and both newlyweds proudly showed off the first release of Cana Cellars wines.

The winery, housed in the basement of their ranch home, is a charming combination of handcrafting and efficient use of space. Entering through massive rounded oak doors, you step directly into the barrel room/production facility of the winery. Another warmly lit room off to one side houses the tasting room. Here, beneath the low ceilings, the walls are handsomely lined with wine racks, storing all the wines available from Cana Cellars. Music fills the air as Joe or Deena proudly take you on a tasting tour of their wines. While there was no gift shop available during our visit, Deena explained that they will be expanding their offerings soon.

The Turners enlisted Enrique Ferro as their wine consultant. Enrique has a long history of experience in the Texas vineyards and is a consultant for a number of wineries around the state. Using the grapes of the Turner vineyard, along with grapes purchased from around the state, Cana Cellars produced approximately two-thousand cases of wine in its first year. Deena told us that while they don't plan to expand their production capability for a number of years, they will be expanding their selection.

Cana Cellars Winery offers a Fumè Blanc, Chardonnay, Muscat Canelli, Merlot, Cabernet Sauvignon, and a Cabernet Rosè. The Cabernet Rosè won the People's Choice Award at the 1997 Grapefest and the Muscat Canelli—made in the traditional Italian style—took the silver at two separate national competitions.

DIRECTIONS: FROM CANA CELLARS, WE TURN BACK TOWARD AUSTIN AND SOUTH ON IH 35 TO SH 46 AT NEW BRAUNFELS. FOR THOSE OF YOU LOOKING FOR SHOPPING, THE OUTLET MALLS AROUND SAN MARCOS ARE ALWAYS A HIT. FOR FAMILIES, THE SAN MARCOS AREA OFFERS AQUARENA SPRINGS, WONDER WORLD, AND TUBING/RAFTING ALONG THE GUADALUPE RIVER. ONCE ON SH 46, DRY COMAL CREEK VINEYARDS IS ABOUT TWELVE MILES AHEAD ON YOUR LEFT.

&Dry Comal Creek Vineyards

www.drycomalcreek.com

1741 Herbelin Road
New Braunfels, Texas 78132

Phone: (830) 885-4121
Fax: (830) 885-4124

> OPEN: WEDNESDAY–SUNDAY
> 12:00 P.M.–5:00 P.M.
> TOURS, TASTING, AND RETAIL SALES

We stopped by to visit Franklin Houser in mid-1999, a few weeks before his winery was officially

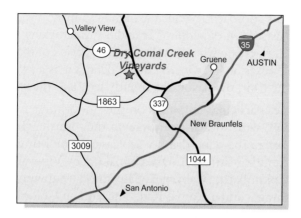

DRY COMAL CREEK VINEYARDS

open, though you would never have known they were not open for business by the warm response we received. With the main winery building under construction, we were escorted into what is now the tasting room, but back then doubled as winery and tasting room. For the grand opening, Franklin had a delicious French Columbard, a buttery Chardonnay, and a blend of red wines still in the barrel. The barrel tasting he offered gave us an opportunity to taste a great wine in the making.

Franklin, a native of San Antonio, jokingly refers to himself as a "recovering lawyer." With this humor and outgoing personality, Franklin had been gladly allowing folks who got word of his winery to drop in weeks before his scheduled grand opening. Today, Dry Comal Creek Vineyards is a sheer pleasure to visit. The winery building is finished, and the tasting room/gift shop has been tastefully remodeled. In addition to the charming proprietor/winemaker, the winery is a beautiful example of custom stonework that has been incorporated in both the facilities and walls that surround the property to visually balance structure with the beautiful patterns of the lush foliage in the vineyard.

THE WINES

Set at the foot of the Balcones Escarpment, Franklin told us the five-acre vineyard and winery grew from the pleasure of growing grapes. Like many winemakers, Franklin has a love for the land and farming. His approach to winemaking is "to make a nice wine for a large cross-section of people." Franklin's winemaking philosophy has led him to create what he calls a "Texas Style" of making wine. What is a "Texas Style" wine? Franklin defines it as a style that emphasizes the fruit, the flavor, the mouth–feel, and the smoothness.

He places particular emphasis on the smoothness from beginning to end, with special attention on the "finish." In this way, Franklin offers the wine drinker a pleasant, smooth experience, not a challenging situation. Dry Comal Creek Vineyards offers a French Columbard, Cabernet Sauvignon, Sauvignon Blanc, White Veritage, and a Comal Red. The French Colombard, a favorite with visitors, won a Bronze Medal in the 1999 Lone Star Wine Competition, as did the 1998 Chardonnay, which is fermented in French oak for a more "buttery" flavor.

For those hot Texas summers, Franklin has invented the "Dry Comal Creek Margarita," which is a combination of his French Colombard poured into a frozen glass, topped off with a slice of lime floated on top. We tried it, and it is very tasty!

DIRECTIONS: AFTER SAMPLING DRY COMAL CREEK VINEYARDS WINES AND MAKING PLANS TO CREATE YOUR BATCH OF THEIR MARGARITA, WE HEAD BACK DOWN SOUTH ON IH 35 TO SAN ANTONIO. YOU MIGHT WANT TO STOP IN SAN ANTONIO FOR LUNCH ALONG THE RIVER WALK TO ENJOY SOME OF THE SIGHTS AND SOUNDS OF THIS FANTASTIC TOWN. AFTER LUNCH, WE HEAD SOUTH ON HIGHWAY 16, TURN RIGHT ON HIGHWAY 476, THEN LEFT ON FM 2146, AND RIGHT ON TANK HOLLOW ROAD TO VISIT POTEET COUNTRY WINERY.

⚘Poteet Country Winery

www.poteetwine.com

**400 Tank Hollow Road,
Poteet, Texas 78065**

Phone: (830) 276-8084

OPEN FRIDAY–SUNDAY
12:00 P.M.–6:00 P.M.
WEEKDAYS BY APPOINTMENT
TASTINGS, RETAIL SALES, AND GIFTS

Strawberries have made Poteet famous. This town, which is the birthplace of country music legend, George Strait, has been home to the Poteet Strawberry Festival, the largest agricultural festival in Texas, for over fifty years.

It was only natural that Jim Collums, a strawberry grower and picker, partnered with Bob Denson, a winemaker with twenty-six years of experience, to create Poteet Country Winery. The result is a winery surrounded with a relaxed country atmosphere in which folks can sample wine, enjoy a picnic, or attend one of the many hayrides, cook-offs, or music events held during the year.

Poteet Country Winery believes that progress does not preclude preserving what was best about the past—even if it was only a rustic charm. Located in an old dairy barn, the production facility and the General Store, where the tasting room is located, reflect that belief in every detail, from the rough-hewn tasting counter to the racks and shelves of products. The decor is pre-Prohibition period, and the products displayed and sold are all handmade, handcrafted, or hand-decorated. Quality, craftsmanship, and nostalgia are the hallmarks of the winery, and the General Store is the heart of it all.

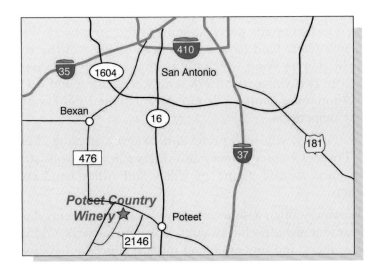

POTEET COUNTRY WINERY

The winery was started in 1997 and opened its doors on July 4, 1998. Demand for their fruit wines has outpaced production ever since. To keep up with the rising demand, Bob Denson told us that he was in the process of adding nine 500-liter and two, 2,000-liter stainless steel tanks to augment the existing production facilities.

THE WINES

The well-drained sandy loam soils of the nearby Atascosa River Valley create a perfect environment for growing berries and fruit, supplying Poteet Country Winery with an abundant supply for their wines. Winemaker Bob Denson creates an enjoyable selection of fruit wines that include Strawberry, Blackberry, Peach, and Pear wines. He also produces what he believes are the only wines made in Texas from the Mustang grape: a White Mustang table wine, which is similar to White Zinfandel, and a red Mustang table wine with characteristics of a Cabernet Sauvignon.

All of Poteet's wines are aged in stainless steel tanks; no oak is used at the winery. To maintain a rich color in their Strawberry wine, Bob uses a "reserve method," which involves adding in strawberry juice saved from the initial crush. The juice deepens the red color, which is what he believes people look for in his wines. He also avoids heavy filtering of the Strawberry Wines, since fine filters tend to remove a large amount of the color. Their Blackberry Wine, which has a rich deep burgundy color, is offered in two vintages: a 1998 semisweet version and a 1999 dry version that captured a Bronze Medal in the 1999 Lone Star Wine Competition.

For those of you who prefer not to drink alcoholic beverages, Poteet Country Winery also offers a nonalcoholic strawberry juice as well a line of jellies and other handcrafted products.

The winery offers visitors an active calendar of events during the year that includes chuckwagon cook-offs, hayrides, Old West get-togethers, and foot-stomping musical concerts. Groups are always welcome, and you can call to inquire about organizing your own event.

Directions: This is our last stop along the Balcones Trail. We hope you have enjoyed the unique environments created by these three boutique wineries in this part of the Hill Country.

Along the Trail

The Balcones Trail offers the wine tourist a smorgasbord of cultures as you travel south from Austin to San Antonio. The German heritage that dominates the Enchanted and Highland Trails begins to merge with the Spanish heritage of old San Antonio.

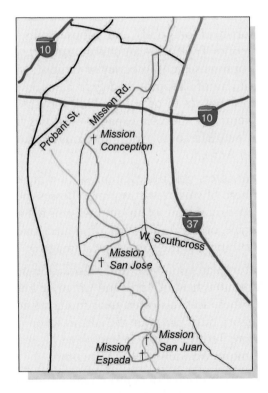

San Antonio Missions

Remnants of the influence of eighteenth-century Spanish Missionaries can be seen in the five San Antonio missions: Alamo, San Jose, San Juan, Concepcion, and Espada. The last four missions continue to operate as active parishes of the Catholic Church, and all are open to the public. In and around modern day San Antonio, the influence of Mexico's culture can be seen in the architecture, cuisine, and music.

This blending of history, cultures, and beautiful countryside helps create a playland for both adults and children. Lakes and springs abound here, providing cool relief in the summer, whether your preference is boating, fishing, or just floating down the Guadalupe River on an innertube. The many caves and caverns that permeate this area provide exciting trips into the Earth with dramatic soaring chambers, rock formations, and cool subterranean streams.

A rich assortment of goods and shops awaits the shopper along the Balcones Trail. You can choose from the quaint shopping districts of towns like Wimberley or Gruene, where you can spend a casual day of shopping and grab a snack at one of the numerous cafés. For those of you looking for a more challenging environment, try the vast expanse of stores in the outlet malls around San Marcos or the numerous markets and retail districts in San Antonio.

San Antonio offers you the excitement of a big city wrapped in an atmosphere of small town warmth. Possessing neither the twenty-first-century skyline of an oil town nor the tumbleweed-strewn landscape of the Wild West, this attractive and festive town looks nothing like the stereotypical image of Texas.

If you want to plan your wine tour to coincide with a festival, Fiesta San Antonio is held in April, and Cinco de Mayo is in early May. Both of these festivals offer great food, music, and entertainment. History buffs can tour the Alamo, drop in for a drink at the bar where Teddy Roosevelt assembled his roughriders, or stop by the unique Wooden Nickel Museum.

A major attraction that offers more restaurants than you can possibly eat at in one trip is the River Walk in downtown San

Antonio. Triggered by drastic flooding in the 1920s, a sensitive WPA program revitalized what is now one of the city's prettiest sites: the River Walk is a gorgeous promenade strung out below street level, along the turquoise San Antonio River—reached by steps and crossed by humpbacked stone bridges. For the kids, there's the San Antonio Zoo, undoubtedly one of the best in the country, and Six Flags Fiesta, a major theme park in Texas.

With this diversity of towns, events, and attractions, the Balcones Trail is one that you will want to travel time after time.

BED AND BREAKFASTS ALONG THE ENCHANTED TRAIL

Boerne

BOERNE LAKE LODGE BED AND BREAKFAST RESORT

Hosts: Leah Glast and Alan Schuminsky, 310 Lakeview Drive, Boerne 78006, (210) 816-6060 or (800) 809-5050. Also listed with Bed and Breakfast Hosts of San Antonio (800) 356-1605. 3 separate accommodations, continental and full breakfast, $$$$, no credit cards.

OLDFATHER INN BED AND BREAKFAST

Host: Valerie Oldfather, 120 Old San Antonio Road, Boerne 78009, (210) 249-8908. Also listed with Bed and Breakfast Hosts of San Antonio (800) 356-1605. 2 cottages, OYO full breakfast, $$$–$$$$, no pets, smoking in designated areas, children 10 and over, MC, V, AE, DC.

Comfort

BRINKMANN HOUSE BED AND BREAKFAST

Hosts: Melinda and John McCurdy, 714 Main Street, Comfort 78013, (210) 995-3141. 2 cottages with private baths, gourmet breakfast, $$, no pets, no children (with exceptions), smoking in restricted areas, phone in house, no credit cards.

COMFORT COMMON

Hosts: Jim Lord and Bobby Dent, P.O. Box 539, Comfort 78013, (210) 995-3030. 5 rooms (ask about baths), 2 suites, 2 cottages (one a log cabin), unique breakfast arrangements, $$–$$$, TV in rooms, no children, smoking in restricted areas, all credit cards.

THE MEYER BED AND BREAKFAST ON CYPRESS CREEK

Innkeeper: Dorcas Mussett, , 845 High Street, P.O. Box 1117, Comfort 78013, (800) 364-2138 or (210) 995-2304. 9 suites with private baths, full breakfast, $$, cable TV, smoking outside, no pets, AE, MC, V.

IDLEWILDE LODGE

Hosts: Hank and Connie Engle, 115 Texas Hwy., 473, Comfort 78013, (210) 995-3844. 2 cabins, full breakfast, $$, smoking in restricted areas, pets allowed, no credit cards.

Dripping Springs

DABNEY HOUSE

Hosts: Jack and Patti Dabney, Autumn Lane, Dripping Springs, Wimberley Lodging Reservations, (800) 460-3909. Room with king-sized bed and cottage suite with queen-sized bed, $$–$$$, smoking in restricted area, children accepted, no pets.

SHORT MAMA'S HOUSE B&B

Host: Keely Peel, Manager, 101 College, Dripping Springs, (512) 858-5668. 4 bedrooms with baths (1 bedroom has an extra room with a twin bed), continental breakfast, $$–$$$, no smoking, no children, no pets, credit cards.

Fredericksburg

ADMIRAL NIMITZ BIRTHPLACE AND COUNTRY COTTAGE INN

Hosts: Michael and Jean Sudderth, 249 E. Main, Fredericksburg 78624, (210) 997-8549. 9 suites, gourmet breakfast, $$$–$$$$, no pets, no smoking, MC, V.

AUSTIN STREET RETREAT

Unhosted: Contact Gastehaus Schmidt, (210) 997-5612. 5 separate quarters, OYO continental breakfast, $$$, no pets, children allowed, no smoking, all credit cards.

BAETHGE-BEHREND HAUS

Unhosted: Contact Gastehaus Schmidt, (210) 997-5612. Guest house with 2 bedrooms sleeps 6, 2 baths, OYO continental breakfast, $$$, children welcome, no pets, smoking outside only, all credit cards.

BED AND BREW

Hosts: Richard Estenson and John Davies, The Fredericksburg Brewing Company, 245 E. Main, Fredericksburg 78624, (210) 997-1646. 12 rooms with private baths, brew in lieu of breakfast, $$–$$$, no pets, no children, smoking outside only, AE, V, MC.

THE DELFORGE PLACE

Hosts: George and Betsy Delforge, Contact Gastehaus Schmidt, (210) 997-5612. 3 rooms, 3 baths, 1 suite, gourmet breakfast, $$–$$$, no pets, no children, no smoking, D, MC, V.

FREDERICKSBURG BAKERY BED & BREAKFAST

Hosts: Mike and Patsy Penick, Contact Gastehaus Schmidt, (210) 997-5612. 3 suites, continental plus breakfast, $$$, no pets, no children, no smoking, D, MC, V.

HILL COUNTRY GUESTHOUSE AND GARDEN

Unhosted: Contact Gastehaus Schmidt, (210) 997-5612. 2 suites, full breakfast or continental plus, $$$, no pets, no children, smoking outside in designated areas.

HOTOPP HOUSE

Unhosted: Contact Gastehaus Schmidt, (210) 997-5612. 2 separate suites or entire house available, OYO continental plus, $$$$, children welcome, no pets, no smoking, all credit cards.

MAGNOLIA HOUSE

Hostess: Joyce Kennard, 101 East Hackberry, Fredericksburg 78624, (210) 997-0306, fax (210) 997-0766. 4 rooms, 4 baths, 2 suites, full breakfast, $$–$$$, no pets, no children, smoking in common areas only, MC, V, AE.

SCHMIDT BARN

Hostess: Loretta Schmidt. Contact Gastehaus Schmidt, (210) 997-5612. 1-bedroom barn, continental plus breakfast, $$, no restrictions, D, MC, V.

THE YELLOW HOUSE AND THE KEEPSAKE KOTTAGE

Unhosted: Contact Gastehaus Schmidt, (210) 997-5612. Both have queen-sized beds, OYO continental breakfast, $$–$$$, infants and children 12 and over, no pets, no smoking, all credit cards.

WATKINS HILL GUEST HOUSE

Host: Edgar Watkins, 608 East Creek Street, Fredericksburg 78624, (800) 899-1672, (210) 997-6739. 2 suites, 2 log guest rooms, all with private baths, gourmet breakfast, $$$$, no pets, infants, or children over 12, smoking outside in designated areas, MC, V.

Stonewall

HOME ON THE RANGE B&B

Hosts: Don and Velna Jackson (known locally as The Stonewall Jackson), Route 2721, Stonewall, (888) 458 BEVO, (800) 460-2380, (210) 644-2380, or contact Hill Country Accommodations (512) 847-5388. 1 cottage (sleeps 6), full breakfast in refrigerator, $$, 11 stocked ponds, Longhorn lean beef, 2 barbecue pits, no pets, restricted smoking, credit cards.

RESTAURANTS ALONG THE ENCHANTED TRAIL

Boerne

BEAR MOON BAKERY AND CAFE

401 S. Main Street, Boerne, (830) 816-2327. Soup/Sandwiches, Breakfast Buffet, Open Tuesday–Sunday for breakfast and lunch only, $.

COUNTRY SPIRIT

707 S. Main Street, Boerne, (830) 249-3607. Homestyle cooking, Beer and wine, Texas wines. Open Wednesday–Monday, $.

FAMILY KORNER RESTAURANT

Highway 46, Boerne, (830) 249-3054. Homestyle cooking. Bar open Monday–Sunday, $$.

MARGARITA'S PATIO

1361 S. Main Street, Boerne, (830) 249-9846. Mexican. Bar open daily, $$.

PEACH TREE KOUNTRY KITCHEN

448 S. Main Street, Boerne, (830) 249-8583. Homestyle cooking. Open Thursday–Saturday for lunch only, $.

PO-PO FAMILY RESTAURANT

435 NE IH 10 Access Road, Boerne, (830) 537-4194. American. Beer and wine, Texas wines. Open Thursday–Sunday, $$.

SCUZZI'S ITALIANO RISTORANTE

128 W. Blanco Road, Boerne, (830) 249-8886. Italian. Bar, Texas wines. Open daily, $$–$$$.

SUNSET GRILL

430 W. Bandera Road, Boerne, (830) 816-2663. American. Beer and wine. Open daily, $$.

Comfort

DOUBLE D CAFE

SH 27, west of the bridge, (830) 995-2001. American. Beer only, Monday–Saturday for breakfast, lunch, and dinner, breakfast only on Sunday, $.

CYPRESS CREEK INN

400 block of SH 27, (830) 995-3977. American. Beer and Ste. Genevieve wines, lunch and dinner Tuesday–Saturday, lunch only on Sunday, $.

Dripping Springs

See Austin.

Fredericksburg

ALTDORF RESTAURANT

301 W. Main, Fredericksburg, (830) 997-7774. American-Mexican-German. Beer and wine, lunch and dinner Wednesday–Monday, closed Tuesday and the month of January, $–$$.

ANDY'S DINER

413 S. Washington/US 87, Fredericksburg, (830) 997-3744. American-German. Breakfast, lunch, dinner Tuesday–Saturday, breakfast and lunch only Sunday–Monday, $.

ENGEL'S DELI

320 E. Main, Fredericksburg, (830) 997-3176. Salads, soups, sandwiches, pastries. Breakfast and lunch Monday–Saturday, $.

GEORGE'S OLD GERMAN BAKERY AND RESTAURANT

225 W. Main, Fredericksburg, (830) 997-9084. Salads, sandwiches, pastries. Breakfast, lunch, and dinner Thursday–Monday, $.

Stonewall

See Austin.

BED AND BREAKFASTS ALONG
THE HIGHLAND TRAIL

Austin

AUSTIN'S WILDFLOWER INN

Host: Kay Jackson, 1200 W. 22½ Street, Austin 78705, (512) 477-9639, fax (512) 474-4188. 4 guest rooms, 3 baths, full breakfast, $–$$, children welcome, but no smoking inside or pets, MC, V, AE.

BREMOND HOUSE

Host: Connie Burton, 404 W. 7th, Austin 78701, (512) 482-0411, fax (512) 479-0789. 4 rooms, 2 private baths, 1 shared, gourmet breakfast, $$–$$$, no pets, smoking on porch or grounds only, MC, V.

THE BROOK HOUSE

Host: Barbara Love, 609 W. 33rd, Austin 78705, (512) 459-0534. 6 guest rooms, 6 baths, full breakfast, $–$$, smoking on porches and grounds, all credit cards.

CARRINGTON'S BLUFF AND THE GOVERNOR'S INN

Hosts: Lisa and Ed Mugford, 1900 David Street, Austin 78705, (512) 479-0638 or (800) 871-8908, fax (512) 476-4769. 8 rooms, 7 private baths, 1 shared, the Writers' Cottage, full breakfast, $–$$, children and (well-behaved) pets are welcome, but smoking outside only, all credit cards.

CASA LOMA

Hosts: Ron and Sharon Hillhouse, 5512 Cuesta Verde, Austin 78746, (800) 222-0248 or (512) 327-7189, fax (512) 327-9150. 1 suite, 2 guest rooms, all private baths, full breakfast, $$$–$$$$, no children, pets, or smoking, all credit cards.

CHEQUERED SHADE (LAKE AUSTIN)

Host: Millie Scott, 2530 Pearce Road, Austin 78730, (800) 577-5786 or (512) 346-8318. 3 rooms, 2 baths, full breakfast, $$, no pets or children under 12, smoking outside only, MC, V, AE.

CITIVIEW

Host: Carol Hayden, 1405 E. Riverside Drive, Austin 78741, (512) 441-2606 or (800) BST-VIEW, fax (512) 441-2949. 3 rooms, 3 baths, full breakfast, $$$, no smoking indoors, MC, V, AE.

FAIRVIEW

Hosts: Duke and Nancy
Waggoner, 1304 Newning
Avenue, Austin 78704,
(512) 444-4746 or
(800) 310-4746. 4 rooms,
4 baths, 2 suites in the
Carriage House, full breakfast,
$$–$$$$, no pets or smoking,
children in Carriage House
only, all credit cards.

THE GARDENS ON DUVAL

Host: Dorothy Sloan, 3210 Duval, Austin 78705, (512) 477-9200,
fax (512) 477-4220. 2 suites, full breakfast, $$, no children under 12,
pets, or indoor smoking, MC, V.

THE INN AT PEARL STREET

Host: Jill Bickford, 809 West Martin Luther King at Pearl Street,
Austin 78701, (800) 494-2203 or (512) 477-2233,
fax (512) 795-0592. 5 guest rooms, private baths, continental
breakfasts OYO weekdays, full on Saturday, champagne brunch on
Sunday, $$$–$$$$, no children, pets, or smoking, all credit cards.

LAKE TRAVIS BED AND BREAKFAST

Hosts: Judy and Vic Dwyer,
4446 Eck Lane, Austin
78734, (512) 266-3386.
3 bedrooms, 3 baths, full
breakfast, $$$$, no city hotel
tax, no children, pets, or
smoking inside, MC, V, AE.

McCALLUM HOUSE

Hosts: Nancy and Roger
Danley, 613 W. 32nd,
Austin 78705, phone/fax
(512) 451-6744. 3 guest
rooms, 3 baths, 2 suites in
Garden Apartment, full
breakfast, $–$$$, no pets,
children over 11 are welcome,
smoking on porches or
grounds, MC, V.

SOUTHARD-HOUSE

Hosts: Jerry and Rejina Southard, 908 Blanco, Austin 78703, (512) 474-4731. 4 rooms, 4 baths, 1 suite, 2 cottages, continental breakfast weekdays, full breakfast weekends with 3 seatings, $$–$$$, no pets, children, or smoking, all credit cards.

WOODBURN HOUSE

Hosts: Herb and Sandra Dickson, 4401 Avenue D, Austin 78751, (512) 458-4335. 4 rooms, 4 baths, full breakfast, $$, children 9 and up, smoking on porches only, no pets, MC, V, AE.

ZILLER HOUSE

Hosts: Sam and Wendy Kindred, 800 Edgecliff Terrace, Austin 78704, (800) 949-5446 or (512) 462-0100, fax (512) 462-9166. 3 rooms, private baths, 1 suite, Carriage House, full or continental breakfast OYO, $$–$$$, children welcome with prior approval, no pets, smoking on terraces only, MC, V, AE.

Georgetown

CLAIBOURNE HOUSE

Host: Clare Easley, 912 Forest Street, Georgetown 78626, (512) 930-3934 and (512) 913-2272. 4 bedrooms, each with private bath (although 1 is on a separate floor), expansive continental breakfast, $$$, smoking in restricted areas, children with prior arrangement, accommodates pets.

THE HARPER-CHESSHER HISTORIC INN

Hosts: Leight Sumner Marcus; Manager: Kathy Frye, 1309 College Street, Georgetown 78628, (512) 863-4057. 4 rooms, 4 baths, buffet continental breakfast and noon high tea, $$$, no pets, no smoking, AE, MC, V.

RIGHT AT HOME B&B

Host: Barbara Shepley, 1208 Main Street, Georgetown 78626-6727, (512) 930-3409 or (800) 651-0021. 4 rooms (2 with shared bath), full breakfast, dinners by request, $$, well-behaved children accepted, smoking outside, no TV in rooms (by design), MC, V.

Lake Travis

CHANTICLEER LOG CABIN (SPICEWOOD)

Hosts: Ceaser and Mallonee Mellenger, P.O. Box 232, Spicewood 78669, (210) 693-4269 or ph/fax (512) 346-8814. 1 guest room, 1 bath, full breakfast, $$$, no pets, no children, smoking only on porch, no credit cards.

TRAILS END

Hosts: JoAnn and Tom Patty, 12223 Trails End Rd. #7, Leander 78641, (512) 267-2901. (800) 850-2901. 2 guest rooms, 2 baths, 1 guest house, full breakfast, $–$$$, no pets, no smoking, MC, V.

Luckenbach

LUCKENBACH INN B&B

Hosts: Capt. Matthew Carinhas and Eva Carinhas, HC 13, Box #9, Luckenbach 78624, (800) 997-1124, (210) 997-2205. 6 rooms, 2 with Jacuzzis and fireplaces, 1 with shared bath downstairs, gourmet breakfast, $$$, no TV/phones in rooms, accepts children and pets (with pet carriers), smoking in designated areas, Saturday night dinners by reservation. wine cellar, http://www.ccsi/ ~elyons/luckenbach.html

RESTAURANTS ALONG THE HIGHLAND TRAIL

Austin

BARBARA ELLEN'S

13129 SH 71 W. at RR 620, Austin, (512) 263-2385. American. Bar, Texas wines, lunch and dinner daily. $–$$.

BASIL'S

900 W. 10th and Lamar, Austin, (512) 477-5576. Italian. Beer and wine, Texas wines, open daily, dinner only. $$$.

CARMELO'S

504 E. 5th, Austin, (512) 477-7497. Italian. Bar, Texas wines, open daily, lunch and dinner. $$–$$$.

CITY GRILL

401 Sabine, Austin, (512) 479-0817. Mesquite-grilled steak and seafood, pasta, Bar, Texas wines, dinner daily. $$.

DAN MCKLUSKY'S

301 E. 6th, (512) 473-8924, or 10000 Research at the Arboretum, Austin. (512) 346-0780. Steak, bar, Texas wines, dinner daily, lunch Monday–Friday on 6th St.; lunch daily at the Arboretum. $–$$.

PEACOCKS ROAM THE WELL-MANICURED LAWNS WHILE GUESTS ENJOY VINTAGE SOUTHERN CUISINE AT GREEN PASTURES.

GREEN PASTURES

811 W. Live Oak, Austin, (512) 444-4747. American-Southern. Bar, Texas wines, lunch and dinner Monday–Saturday, brunch and dinner Sunday. $$–$$$$.

HOT AND CRUNCHY TROUT IS A FAVORITE WITH DINERS AT HUDSON'S ON THE BEND.

HUDSON'S ON THE BEND

3509 RR 620, 1.5 miles southwest of Mansfield Dam, Austin, (512) 266-1369. Eclectic. Bar, Texas wines, dinner daily. Reservations recommended. $$$.

JEAN-PIERRE UPSTAIRS

3500 Jefferson at 35th, Austin, (512) 454-4811. Continental. Bar, Texas wines, dinner Monday–Saturday, lunch Monday–Friday. $$–$$$.

THE WINE CELLAR AT JEFFREY'S HAS EARNED WINE SPECTATOR MAGAZINE'S AWARD OF EXCELLENCE EACH YEAR SINCE 1991. IT'S A FINE COMPLIMENT TO CHEF DAVID GARRIDO'S AWARD-WINNING TEXAS CUISINE.

JEFFREY'S

1204 W. Lynn, Austin, (512) 477-5584. Continental-Southwestern. Bar, Texas wines, dinner Monday–Saturday. No reservations taken. $$–$$$.

LA PALAPA

6640 US 290 East, Austin, (512) 459-8729. Tex-Mex. Bar, Texas wines, open daily, lunch and dinner. $–$$.

LOUIE'S 106

106 E. 6th, Austin, (512) 476-2010. Continental. Bar, Texas wines, dinner daily, lunch Monday–Friday. $–$$.

OLD PECAN STREET CAFÉ

310 E. 6th, Austin, (512) 478-2491. Continental. Bar, Texas wines, lunch and dinner daily. $–$$.

SHORELINE GRILL

98 San Jacinto in San Jacinto Center overlooking Town Lake, Austin, (512) 477-3300. Continental. Bar, Texas wines, dinner daily, lunch Monday–Friday. $$–$$$.

THREADGILL'S

6416 N. Lamar, Austin, (512) 451-5440. American. Bar, Texas wines, open daily, lunch and dinner. $.

WEST LYNN CAFÉ

1110 West Lynn, (512) 482-0950. Continental. Beer and wine, Texas wines, lunch and dinner daily. $.

Z TEJAS GRILL

1110 W. 6th, (512) 346-3506 or 9400 Arboretum, Austin, (512) 478-5355. Southwestern. Bar, Texas wines, breakfast, lunch, and dinner daily, Bar, Texas wines. $–$$.

ENJOY GOOD WINE **AND** GOOD FOOD ALONG THESE WINE TRAILS.
(COURTESY OF AUSTIN CONVENTION AND VISITORS BUREAU)

Georgetown

CROSETTI'S

119 West 7th, Georgetown, (512) 863-0596. American and Italian. Beer and wine, Texas wines. $–$$.

Lake Travis

See Austin.

Luckenbach

See Austin.

BED AND BREAKFASTS ALONG THE BALCONES TRAIL

Boerne

YE KENDALL INN

128 W. Blanco Road, Boerne 78006, (800) 364-2138. $$$$.

Gruene

GRUENE MANSION INN

1275 Gruene Road, New Braunfels 78130, (512) 629-2641.

New Braunfels

THE PRINCE SOLMS INN

295 E. San Antonio, New Braunfels 78130, (512) 625-9169.

THE FAUST HOTEL

240 S. Seguin Ave., New Braunfels 78130, (512) 625-7791.

San Marcos

CRYSTAL RIVER INN

326 W. Hopkins Street, San Marcos 78666, (512) 326-3739. $$.

RESTAURANTS ALONG THE BALCONES TRAIL

Bee Cave

BARBARA ELLEN'S

13129 SH 71 W. at RR 620, Bee Cave, (512) 263-2385. Open daily, lunch and dinner. $–$$.

Gruene

GUADALUPE SMOKED MEAT COMPANY

1299 Gruene Road, Gruene, (512) 629-6121. Open daily, lunch and dinner. $.

GRISTMILL RESTAURANT

Behind Gruene Hall, Gruene, (512) 625-0684. Memorial Day through Labor Day: open daily; rest of year: closed Monday. $–$$.

GRUENE HALL

Gruene, (512) 606-1281. Open daily.

New Braunfels

BAVARIAN VILLAGE

212 W. Austin Street, New Braunfels, (512) 625-0815. Memorial Day through Labor Day: dinner, Monday through Friday, and lunch and dinner, Saturday and Sunday; rest of year: dinner, Friday, and lunch and dinner, Saturday and Sunday. $–$$.

EUROPA FINE FOODS

1162 Eikel Street, New Braunfels, (512) 606-1086. Open Monday through Saturday. $.

KRAUSE'S CAFÉ

148 S. Castell Ave., New Braunfels, (512) 625-7581. Monday through Saturday, 6:30–8:30; closed Sunday; breakfast, lunch, and dinner. $.

WOLFGANG'S KELLER

295 E. San Antonio in the Prince Solms Inn, New Braunfels, (512) 625-9169. Open Tuesday through Sunday. $$–$$$.

San Marcos

CAFÉ ON THE SQUARE & BREW PUB

126 N. LBJ Dr., San Marcos, (512) 353-9289. Open daily, breakfast, lunch, and dinner. $–$$.

FUSCHAK'S PITT BAR-B-Q

920 SH 80, east of I 35, San Marcos, (512) 353-2712. Open daily, lunch and dinner. $.

JOE'S CRAB SHACK

100 Sessoms Dr. at the dam below Spring Lake, San Marcos, (512) 396-5255. Open daily, lunch and dinner. $–$$.

Chapter 4

SOUTHEASTERN WINERIES

THE BRAZOS TRAIL

*I*f you decide to travel along SH 290 out of Houston on a sunny afternoon in mid-April to check out the annual display of bluebonnets, you will not be disappointed. As you near the town of Brenham, all along the road and up the hillsides you will see an explosion of blues, reds, and muted yellows, compliments of the Texas bluebonnet and Indian paintbrush wildflowers. Brenham has always been a treat for travelers, offering rolling hills, happy cows, and the Blue Bell Ice Cream factory—a personal favorite. Now, Brenham even has a winery, and we are on our way to start the Brazos Trail.

The Brazos Trail, named for the Brazos River that dominates the area, will introduce you to seven wineries: Haak Vineyards, Pleasant Hill Winery, Messina Hof Wine Cellars, Wimberley Valley Winery, Red River Winery, Piney Woods Country Wines, and Bruno and George Wines, Inc. The Brazos Valley is an area as rich in history as the Brazos River is long, so leave enough time to do some sightseeing if you are a history buff.

◄ **CHARDONNAY AND CABERNET SAUVIGNON DOMINATE THE VINEYARDS IN TEXAS. (COURTESY OF THE TEXAS DEPARTMENT OF AGRICULTURE)**

143

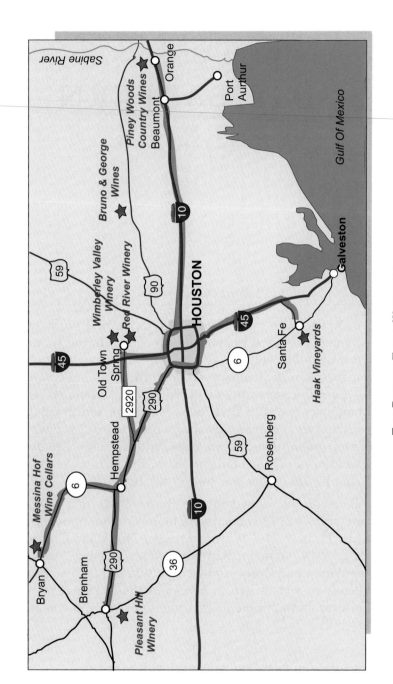

THE BRAZOS TRAIL WINERIES

THE BRAZOS TRAIL

     🍂 Haak Vineyards   🍂 Red River Winery

     🍂 Pleasant Hill Winery   🍂 Piney Woods Country Wines

     🍂 Messina Hof Wine Cellars   🍂 Bruno and George Wines, Inc.

     🍂 Wimberley Valley Winery

This trail is ideal for a pleasant Saturday or weekend trip. You will pass through the towns of Brenham, Bryan, Old Town Spring, Santa Fe, Orange, and Sour Lake. These towns offer the weary traveler a wonderful selection of shops and restaurants to satisfy all of your urges.

Using Houston as our base, we head south on IH 45 toward Galveston and turn west on SH 502 to visit the recently opened Haak Vineyards in Santa Fe. After sampling the wines and enjoying the warm ocean breezes, we head north again on IH 45 to Beltway 8 and head west around Houston to SH 290 to Brenham, about two hours away. Turn left on SH 36 and within a mile you

PAUL BONNARIGO, OWNER/WINEMAKER OF MESSINA HOF WINE CELLARS, PROUDLY DISPLAYS HIS AWARD-WINNING WINE.

will spot a winery sign on the right side of the road, directing you to Pleasant Hill Winery on Salem Road. After enjoying the wine and hospitality of Bob and Jeanne Cottle, head back toward Houston on SH 290 for about twenty-two miles. Turn left (north) on SH 6 to the town of Bryan, and get ready to experience the ambiance of Old World Italy at Messina Hof Wine Cellars.

From Messina Hof Wine Cellars, head back toward Houston, turning off SH 290 onto FM 2920, which will take you into Old Town Spring to Visit Wimberley Valley Winery and Red River Winery. Each of these wineries fits well into Old Town Spring's exciting retail and dining atmosphere. After sampling the wines and stopping for a bite to eat, head south on IH 45 to IH 10 and eastward toward the city of Orange on the Texas-Louisiana border and a stop at Piney Woods Country Winery. From there we head eastward on Route 105 to the town of Sour Lake, self-proclaimed gateway to the Big Thicket, to visit Bruno and George Wines, Inc.

Now off to Haak Vineyards!

♠Haak Vineyards

www.haakwine.com
6310 Ave T / P.O. Box Drawer F
Santa Fe, Texas 77510
Phone: (409) 925-8627
Fax: (409) 925-0276

OPEN: SUMMERTIME:
MONDAY–FRIDAY
11:00 A.M.–6:00 P.M.
SATURDAY
11:00 A.M.–7:00 P.M.
SUNDAY
12:00 P.M.–6:00 P.M.
WINTERTIME:
MONDAY–SATURDAY
11:00 A.M.–5:00 P.M.
SUNDAY
12:00 P.M.–5:00 P.M.
TOURS, TASTINGS, RETAIL
SALES, AND GIFTS

A winery on the Texas Coast!

Raymond Haak, owner/winemaker at Haak Vineyards, has the only winery in Texas located on the Gulf of Mexico—at least one within twelve miles of the coast. We have to admit that we never thought of this area, known for NASA, Kemah, boating, and fishing, to be home to a vineyard and winery. Boy, were we wrong! Raymond has been successfully growing grapes on his Santa Fe property for over nineteen years.

When we first visited Haak Vineyards and Winery, the 4,000-square-foot facility was in its infancy—lots of concrete, mud, and structural steel reaching toward the sky. Eight months later, Haak Vineyards officially opened for business; what a difference a few months can make! This winery is a beautiful Spanish-style structure, complete with a copper dome above the entry tower.

The friendly, knowledgeable staff greet visitors in the spacious tasting room, furnished with a magnificent marble-topped bar that was handmade for the winery. Raymond's attention to detail is apparent everywhere you look, from the 350-pound cast-iron chandelier to the strategically placed windows allowing visitors views of the vineyard outside and of the gleaming stainless steel of the production facility—all with just a turn of the head.

HAAK VINEYARDS

THE WINES

As we walk through his vineyard, Raymond, normally a soft-spoken man, becomes animated as he explains the years of work and research he has done with a variety of grapes. The vineyard currently contains Black Spanish and Blanc du Bois grapes, known for being hardy enough to tolerate the highly humid conditions found this close to the coast. As we examined the newly budding grape clusters, we caught a hint of the ocean on the prevailing breeze.

In a small vineyard separated from the rest of the grapes, Raymond is experimenting with grape varietals from Portugal that he feels will do well in these conditions. Not far from this experimental vineyard, another experimental patch of land acts as an incubator for an orchard of baby olive trees. While he admits to not knowing much about growing olives, he feels that they are a natural compliment to wine and plans to sell them in his gift shop.

Haak Vineyards white wines include Blanc du Bois, Sauvignon Blanc, and Chardonnay. The Blanc du Bois is a lively semi-dry wine with wonderful floral and fruit aromas. The only problem with this wine is keeping enough in stock! The Sauvignon Blanc is cold-fermented in stainless steel tanks, imparting a crisp, clean taste with hints of pear, grapefruit, and figs. Served cold or over ice, it is a fantastic summer wine for south Texas.

Raymond offers two Chardonnays: one aged in stainless steel and one aged in oak barrels, each style having a dedicated following among his customers. Using 1,500-gallon stainless steel fermentation tanks, the wine is fermented at 55° F to retain the fruit and floral characteristics of the grape. This method imparts a lighter, crisp flavor, allowing the fullness of the grape to be expressed in the wine.

The oak-aged Chardonnay sits at the other end of the flavor spectrum. It is briefly held in stainless steel and then placed in oak barrels to complete the fermentation. Raymond then uses malolactic fermentation to soften the wine and add that buttery, creamy flavor produced from converting the malic acid into lactic acid. Judging by the barrel sample we tried in midsummer of 2001, this wine promises to be fantastic.

Haak Vineyards red wines include Cabernet Sauvignon, Zinfandel, and a Vintage Port. For the Cabernet Sauvignon, Raymond crushed, cold-soaked and then fermented the grapes on their skins at 85° F to extract the maximum color and flavor. The resulting wine was then placed in American oak for aging. Released in 2001, this wine captured a gold medal at the Spring Fest Media Choice Competition.

The Zinfandel was created in a similar fashion to the Cabernet Sauvignon, with the exception of being oak-aged for only four months. This wonderful, full-mouthed wine has just a hint of pepper as it explodes on the palate. We had to buy a few extra bottles to share with friends. Lastly, the Vintage Port is made from the Black Spanish grape harvested from Haak vineyard and vineyards across Texas. Raymond slowly ferments the juice with a special yeast that produces 19 to 20 percent alcohol levels, in situ. The wine is then aged in oak to develop the characteristic flavors and aromas of true Vintage Ports.

During your visit, you just might be able to talk Raymond into a tour of one of the few fully functional wine cellars in Texas. Due to the close proximity to the coast, he took great care in designing a robust drainage and pumping system to keep his cellar dry. Besides being a magical environment, it is a technological masterpiece.

All of the oak aging at Haak Vineyards is performed deep below the tasting room in the subterranean barrel cellar. This cellar is a testament to technological skill and sheer determination. Great care was taken in the design and construction of the drainage and pumping systems required to keep this cellar dry in the high water table typical so close to the coastline.

Why go through all this trouble? For the same reason that Raymond created a wonderful patio area alongside the vineyard—to create an environment where people want to linger. After many years of involvement in the wine business as an amateur winemaker, Raymond knew that opening a winery to make wine was only half the battle; he knew he was also entering the entertainment business. Haak Vineyards maintains a full calendar of events throughout the year for holiday celebrations, wine and cheese pairings, and his ever-popular "jazz-in-the-vineyard" events, which now draw over 300 people.

DIRECTIONS: FROM THE OCEAN BREEZES OF HAAK VINEYARDS, WE HEAD WEST ON HIGHWAY 6 TO SH 288, AND TURN TOWARD HOUSTON, THEN HEADING WEST ON BELTWAY 8 TO SH 290. HEAD WEST ON SH 290 TO THE TOWN OF BRENHAM, TURNING LEFT ON SH 36 TO SALEM ROAD, WHERE WE WILL VISIT PLEASANT HILL WINERY.

Pleasant Hill Winery

www.pleasanthillwinery.com

1441 Salem Road
Brenham, Texas 77833

Phone: (979) 830-VINE or -8463
Fax: (979) 277-9218

OPEN: SATURDAY
11:00 A.M.–6:00 P.M.
SUNDAY
12:00 P.M.–5:00 P.M.
TOURS, TASTINGS, RETAIL
SALES, AND GIFTS

After enjoying the ride in the country—perhaps even waving at a few of the happy Brenham cows, turn into the driveway of Pleasant Hill Winery, situated on forty acres of lushly covered rolling hills. The winery, built into the side of one of these rolling hills, was constructed from wood salvaged from the original structures that were there when Bob and Jeanne Cottle bought the property. A sturdy, rustic-looking structure, the hillside location allowed the Cottles to create a handsome cellar on the lower side to house the winemaking and fermentation facilities. But this is, after all, only phase one of their master plan.

Bob and Jeanne, both from Italian families with a long history of winemakers, have a vision. The Cottles describe a plan that includes another structure capable of holding up to 100,000 gallons, a maze of tunnels to pipe wine between buildings, a lake to picnic alongside, and the largest crushing pad in Texas at 10,000

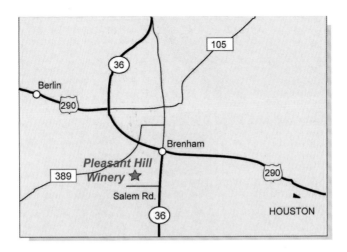

PLEASANT HILL WINERY

THE RUSTIC LOOK OF PLEASANT HILL WINERY IN BRENHAM.

square feet. Quite a leap in scale for a couple who have been making only 200 gallons of wine in their Spring home.

As amateur winemakers since moving to Texas in the 1970s, the Cottles have been very active in amateur winemaking organizations in Texas—sharing what they have learned. In 1989 the

STEP THROUGH THESE DOORS FOR A TEXAS WINE ADVENTURE.

couple decided to turn their passion into a way of life for their family. After making the decision to become a professional winemaker, Bob obtained his degree in oenology from Grayson County College in Denison, Texas, traveling over 300 miles each weekend for three years to earn the degree. When asked how the education will change the winemaking style he has used as a home winemaker, Bob said, "It has given me a much better technical understanding of the chemistry of wine." He feels it has vastly improved his winemaking techniques.

The one-acre experimental vineyard at the winery contains Black Spanish and Herbemont grapes, both of which are known to do well in the environments, east of IH 35, which approximates the humidity line in Texas. Other rows include Cynthiana, Blanc du Bois, Lake Emerald, and Favorite, a grape native to the Brenham area. The Favorite grape, once grown by the Niderauer Winery that existed in the Brenham area from the late 1880s to the 1950s, is a hybrid of Black Spanish and Herbemont grapes.

In addition to the vineyard at the winery, Bob is using grapes from a number of grape growers within a hundred-mile radius and from his newly acquired Delores Mountain vineyard near

Fort Davis in west Texas. Located at an elevation of 5,200 feet, on the east-facing slope of a mountain, Bob currently has roughly half of this six-acre vineyard in production with Cabernet Sauvignon and Sauvignon Blanc.

THE WINES

The increased access to local grapes and the addition of the Delores Mountain vineyard have dramatically increased the style and variety of wines that Pleasant Hill Winery will be able to create. From the grapes within a hundred-mile radius of the winery, Bob told us that he will "continue to produce light, crisp, refreshing wines that reflect the best qualities of the local grapes." These wines are typified in his very popular Collina Rossa and Collina Bianca, which won bronze medals at the Lone Star Wine Competition and the Old Town Spring Wine Competition.

The grapes from his west Texas vineyard will allow Bob to create a premium Cabernet Sauvignon that, as he explains, "will truly show what great wines can be made from European vinifera grown in Texas soils." The quality of that fruit makes life easier for winemakers, according to Bob, requiring very little manipulation of the grape must and juice during fermentation. Basically, he has to start the process, step back, and get out of its way. Other wines available from Pleasant Hill Winery include a Sauvignon Blanc, which captured a bronze medal in the Old Town Spring Wine Competition, and a 1998 Port, released in 2000 in a limited edition of only 600 bottles.

The winery has a well-stocked gift shop offering wine accessories and gifts. Outside of the tasting room is a balcony that offers a fantastic view of this undulating property. In combining the passion this family has for winemaking, with the quality fruit it will work with in the near future, we can continue to expect great wine from Pleasant Hill Winery for years to come.

DIRECTIONS: FROM PLEASANT HILL WINERY RETURN TO SH 290, AND HEAD EAST BACK TOWARD HOUSTON TO SH 6, WHICH IS ABOUT TWENTY-TWO MILES AWAY. TURN NORTH ONTO SH 6 TOWARD THE CITY OF BRYAN,

USUALLY REFERRED TO AS BRYAN-COLLEGE STATION BECAUSE THE TWO TOWNS MERGE TOGETHER AND HAVE TEXAS A&M UNIVERSITY AS THEIR ANCHOR. MESSINA HOF WINE CELLARS IS THE NEXT STOP ON OUR TOUR—ONE THAT IS GOING TO BE A REAL TREAT FOR WINE AND FOOD LOVERS ALIKE.

☙Messina Hof Wine Cellars

www.messinahof.com
**4545 Old Reliance Road
Bryan, Texas 77808**
Phone: (979) 778-9463
Fax: (979) 778-1729

OPEN: MONDAY–FRIDAY 8:30 A.M.–5:30 P.M.
SATURDAY 10:00 A.M.–5:00 P.M.
SUNDAY 12:00 P.M.–4:00 P.M.
TOURS, TASTINGS, RETAIL SALES, GIFTS, BED AND BREAKFAST, AND RESTAURANT

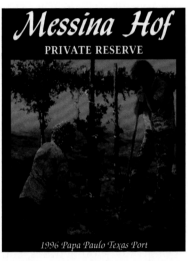

Messina Hof
PRIVATE RESERVE

1996 Papa Paulo Texas Port

Family, tradition, and romance—three fundamental elements that have shaped Paul and Merrill Bonarrigo's approach to winemaking in Texas. Located in the town of Bryan, the Messina Hof Wine Cellars is an award-winning winery, enjoying recognition in the United States, Europe, and Japan.

A visit to the Messina Hof winery (only ninety miles from Houston) is a pleasant two-and-a-half hour drive on SH 6. In the spring the traveler is treated to vistas of rolling hills covered with bluebonnets and Indian paintbrushes. In the fall, the landscape is cloaked in the autumn colors of the hardwood trees. You can plan a trip with just the winery tour in mind, or visit the winery and enjoy a picnic with the wine you purchase. With the variety of sights and activities available in the valley, the only thing difficult about this short jaunt will be deciding what to do.

Paul's winemaking skills are a combination of the Old World traditions taught to him by his grandmother and his ed-

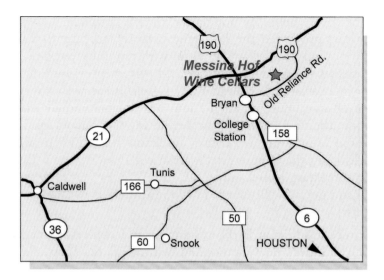

MESSINA HOF WINE CELLARS

ucation from the Napa Wine School at the University of California at Davis. Here he learned that when his grandmother taught him to use his senses to determine tartness and sweetness, he was actually evaluating the acidity and sugar in the wine.

The winery's name, Messina Hof, combines the name of the European towns that were the origins of Paul's and Merrill's families—Messina, Sicily, and Hof, Germany. Their tradition of winemaking goes back two hundred years, when Paul's grandfather made wine for the people in his village. That tradition continued when the Bonarrigos moved to New York's Little Italy in 1927. In the Bonarrigo family, the first son is always named Paul and is given the responsibility of being the winemaker for his generation. The Messina Hof vintner, Paul V, is the first Bonarrigo to produce and sell wine commercially in the United States.

The tasting room, a romantic country affair with a warming fireplace when a chill reaches the Bryan area, offers a splendid collection of gifts, accessories, and foods, including cheeses. During pleasant weather, the Bonnarigos encourage folks to take a hunk of cheese along with one of their bottles of wine out to the deck overlooking their small lake.

The overwhelming popularity of the original Bed and Breakfast prompted the Bonarrigo's to replace it with a new facility called The Villa. The Villa, with ten unique rooms, offers guests the kind of romance and privacy previously found only in exclusive European resorts. Furnished with antiques from all over Europe, each room has been designed with a unique theme in mind, whether it be the flavors of Italy or France or even a Thomas Jefferson room. With patios overlooking the winery estate, fresh cut flowers, and a European breakfast buffet, the Villa offers guests a sumptuous weekend getaway. Book ahead though, there is usually a waiting list.

A recent addition is the restaurant and conference center, which has become very popular with local residents. Paul's chef prepares a wonderful selection of foods for evening dinner and for special occasions such as weddings in the comfortable restaurant with the look and feel of a wine cellar. Don't be surprised to see the master vintner walking around this premier restaurant to greet his guests on any given evening.

MESSINA HOF WINE CELLARS IN BRYAN.

**THE WELL-APPOINTED TASTING ROOM AT
MESSINA HOF WINE CELLARS.**

THE WINES

Paul and Merrill took a cautious approach to expanding their vineyard, working the land personally until the winery's vineyard reached thirty acres. Messina Hof recently expanded its facilities, and now harvests grapes from an additional 200 acres in Texas. Paul prefers to produce his reds in the Bordeaux style, while he admires the German winemaking techniques for his white wines. In 1997, Paul introduced the concept of double-barrel fermentation for his wines. After the normal barrel fermenting Messina Hof has always used, Paul removes the wine and places it into a fresh oak barrel to extract that little extra something that make his wines so distinctive.

Messina Hof Wine Cellars now produces almost thirty wines, ranging from their Traditions label for table wines to their Private Reserve line featuring premium varietals. The dry white wines include Private Reserve Chardonnay, Barrel Reserve Chardonnay, Traditions Chardonnay, Barrel Reserve Sauvignon Blanc, Semillon, and a Champagne. The semi-dry white wines and blush wines include Muscat Canelli, Gewurztraminer, Johannisberg Riesling, Chenin Blanc, White Zinfandel, and Traditions Blush.

The red wines include Private Reserve Cabernet Sauvignon, Barrel Reserve Cabernet Sauvignon, Traditions Cabernet Sauvignon, Private Reserve Merlot, Barrel Reserve Merlot, Barrel Reserve Pinot Noir, and Gamay Beaujolais. The popular dessert wines include Private Reserve Papa Paulo Port; Barrel Reserve Papa Paulo Port; Angel, a late harvest Riesling; Glory, a late harvest Muscat Canelli; and Grace, a late harvest Semillon.

Paul's experiment with Pinot Grigio and Shiraz in 1999 has been a huge success, winning medals in both the 2001 and 2002 Lone Star Wine Competition. The Pinot Grigio is a crisp, clean wine with floral and citrus aromas and flavors. The Shiraz is a full-bodied red that is robust yet well balanced.

The Messina Hof Winery has an active calendar of special events planned throughout the year. There are harvest weekends in which you can join their "Picker's Club" and participate in the picking of the grapes and in grape stomping. A tour of the after-harvest process and a sampling of wines produced from the previous harvest make the day complete. Other events include demonstration of vine grafting and a special dinner centered around fine meals with complementing Messina Hof wines.

Call for the latest planned events and schedules. Messina Hof has one of the most active events schedules in the state.

DIRECTIONS: FROM YOUR ENJOYABLE STAY AT MESSINA HOF, HEAD BACK TO THE HOUSTON AREA TO VISIT TWO UNIQUE WINERIES. YOU WILL RETRACE YOUR STEPS DOWN SH 6 TO SH 290, HEADING SOUTH TOWARD HOUSTON. NEAR HOUSTON, TURN EAST ON FM 2920, WHICH WILL TAKE YOU THROUGH THE TOWN OF TOMBALL ON YOUR WAY TO OLD TOWN SPRING. THE CITY OF TOMBALL HAS GROWN FROM A QUAINT TEXAS TOWN TO A THRIVING METROPOLIS IN THE SHADOW OF HOUSTON. KNOWN FOR ITS ANTIQUE STORES, IT OFFERS A VARIETY OF PLACES TO GRAB A LUNCH BEFORE HEADING OFF TO OLD TOWN SPRING, WHICH IS APPROXIMATELY A HALF-HOUR AWAY. OUR FIRST STOP IN OLD TOWN SPRING WILL BE WIMBERLEY VALLEY WINERY. UPON ENTERING OLD TOWN SPRING, STAY LEFT AT THE FORK IN THE ROAD.

❧Wimberley Valley Winery

www.wimberleyvalleywinery.com
206 Main Street
Old Town Spring, Texas 77373
Phone: (281) 350-8801

> **OPEN: TUESDAY–SATURDAY**
> **11:00 A.M.–5:00 P.M.**
> **SUNDAY**
> **12:00 P.M.–5:00 P.M.**
> **TASTINGS, RETAIL SALES,**
> **AND GIFTS**

WIMBERLEY VALLEY WINES

Christmas Cuvée
WHITE WINE
TEXAS
ALC 12.0% BY VOL • 750 ML

Main Street in Old Town Spring is alive with music, restaurants, and people. Folks from all over come here to shop, enjoy a meal, people-watch, and sample Texas wines. Located right in the center of this exciting environment is Wimberley Valley Winery's tasting room on Main Street. The large, boldly colored sign outside beckons you to come in and sample a wide variety of premium wines.

The winery itself—completed in 1983—is located in Hays County, between the towns of Wimberley and Driftwood. Hays County is a dry county, which until recently prohibited the sale of wine at the winery. When winery cofounders decided to open a tasting room offering tastings and retail sales, the casual, fun-loving atmosphere of Old Town Spring was seen as a natural location.

"Life is too short to drink bad wine"—a phrase that captures the sentiment expressed by both Dean Valentine, cofounder and winemaker, and Howard Pitman, CEO of the winery. Both men share a passion for wine and strive to offer wine tourists a unique tasting experience, along with sharing their knowledge about wine in general. Questions are encouraged at the Wimberley Valley

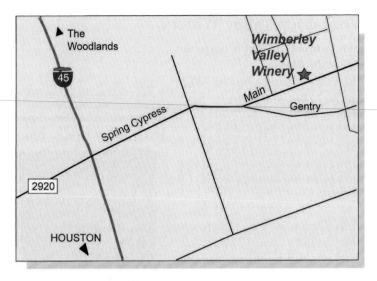

WIMBERLEY VALLEY WINERY

Winery tasting room, so don't be afraid to ask—every wine question is considered a good one by the staff.

THE WINES

Using grapes picked from vineyards located in west Texas, Dean utilizes imaginative practices combined with traditional winemaking techniques to give his wines a distinctive style. This style has won the winery numerous awards over the years and created a dedicated following of wine drinkers. The winery produces wines under two labels: Cellar Select and Texas Country Cellars. A few unique wines are also released on individual label designs.

The Cellar Select label is reserved for premium varietals and blended wines, while the Texas Country Cellars label is used for semi-sweet and sweet wines. With the creation of the Texas Country Cellars line, Dean realized he had discovered an untapped market of wine consumers. The wines were an instant success, and each year demand continues to grow. The winery consistently sells all the wine it can produce, so if you like something, buy it! It may be gone the next time you visit the tasting room or your local liquor store. As Howard Pitman told us, "A lot of Texans talk dry, but drink sweet," to explain the surprising popularity of these wines.

The Sweet Red is low in tannins, with a light body and a clean fruity taste. The Sweet Blush is perfect for the wine drinker who wants a little more body than a white wine, but still wants the sweetness usually not available in a red wine. The Sweet White is a straightforward, uncomplicated wine designed for the hot Texas summers and is best served chilled.

GRAPES AFTER HARVEST—JUICY, PLUMP, AND READY FOR THE PRESS. (COURTESY OF THE TEXAS DEPARTMENT OF AGRICULTURE)

The Texas Country Cellars label also includes Sangria, a Spiced wine, and a Mulled wine. Three unique wines offered under individual labels are the Christmas Cuvee, with a semi-dry, crisp finish, and an Apple Wine and Spiced Apple Wine.

In addition to their own line of wines, Wimberley Valley Winery has broken with tradition and offers wines from a handful of small California wineries. These wines, which are generally available outside of California, are offered at the tasting room to allow the wine consumer to expand their knowledge of wines in general and experience a number of winemaking styles.

Look for Wimberley Valley Winery to continue to produce a selection of unique wines in the twenty-first century. A visit to their tasting room, which shares a building with a Christmas collectibles store owned by Dean's wife, is pleasurable for wine drinkers and Christmas lovers alike.

DIRECTIONS: AFTER SAMPLING THESE FINE WINES, YOU MAY WISH TO CONTINUE YOUR STAY IN OLD TOWN SPRING, WHERE YOU CAN DO SOME SHOPPING OR GRAB A BITE TO EAT FROM ONE OF THE QUAINT RESTAURANTS. AFTER ALL, OUR NEXT WINERY, RED RIVER WINERY, IS JUST A FEW BLOCKS AWAY.

❧Red River Winery

www.redriverwinery.com

421 Gentry Street, #204
Old Town Spring, Texas 77373

Phone: (281) 288-WINE

OPEN: TUESDAY–SATURDAY
10:00 A.M.–5:00 P.M.

SUNDAY
12:00 P.M.–5:00 P.M.

TASTINGS, RETAIL SALES,
AND GIFTS

1995

Red River

Texas
Cabernet Sauvignon
Cellared and Bottled by Red River Winery
Spring, Texas

Contains Sulfites   750ml   Alcohol 12% By Volume

You won't find a vineyard around the Red River Winery in Old Town Spring, at least not yet. What you will find are the smiling faces of Mark and Tina Woolington welcoming you into their establishment. Red River's tasting room and gift shop is housed in a unique octagonal-shaped tower, giving the winery a distinctive character from the other retail shops in this cluster of buildings. It is a spacious place with a soaring ceiling, and its many windows fill the central area with sunshine to produce a bright, cheerful atmosphere. If you thought wineries had to be dark and damp, you are in for a pleasant surprise.

The Woolingtons' path to becoming winery owners took them on a route that involved leaving mainland United States for an island adventure. After establishing themselves as players in the banking and real estate industries in Hawaii, Mark and Tina decided to move back to the mainland to be closer to family. Having come from a winemaking family, Mark saw Old Town Spring as a great environment to establish a small boutique winery. The rest, as they say, is history.

Bonded in 1995, Red River Winery opened its doors in October of that year and offered a selection of gifts, handmade wine accessories, and, initially, only wines from other Texas wineries. Before their first anniversary, however, Mark and Tina were pro-

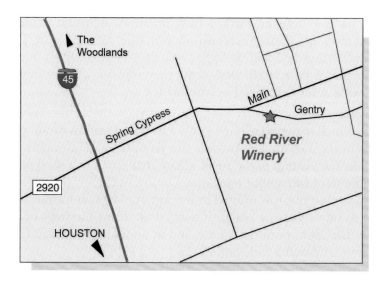

RED RIVER WINERY

ducing small quantities of their own wines. To date, Mark and Tina have released an assortment of wines that include Sauvignon Blanc, Cabernet Sauvignon, Chardonnay, and Pinot Noir. Each vintage is usually limited to 500 gallons, so if you enjoy what you taste on your visit, you should buy it right then; it will probably be gone the next time you visit.

Mark, an easygoing man with a quick smile, was quite demur when we asked him about his winemaking technique. "I'm really still learning the craft of winemaking," he said. His early attempts at winemaking belie his genuine humility, however. The Sauvignon Blanc we tasted was a delightful surprise, exhibiting characteristics of the smokey, buttery tastes of a Chardonnay that had undergone secondary barrel fermentation. A recent Cabernet Sauvignon was also a grand surprise, with complex flavors of oak, spices, and berries. As Mark poured a sample of this wine, he simply offered, "We're fairly proud of this one." As indeed they should be.

Red River offers customers specialized labels on their wine. Customers can walk in, order a custom label, do some shopping around Old Town Spring, and pick up their customized wine afterward. Whenever Mark is busy in the background working his label magic, Tina greets customers in their tasting room. Tina offers tastings and will be happy to help you select from one of the many wine-related food items they offer or explain one of the wine accessories she has handmade.

Future plans call for continued expansion of the production area, which may necessitate opening a second tasting room, perhaps in the Kemah area or near the Woodlands. The winery offers outside seating in the small square that serves as a focal point for numerous neighboring shops. During weekends throughout the year, live music is offered in the square. Mark and Tina invite you to buy a glass or bottle of wine, walk down the steps of the deck that opens onto the square, and sit under a tree-shaded table to enjoy the sights and sounds.

DIRECTIONS: FROM OLD TOWN SPRING YOU HAVE A CHOICE: THE FAST UNSCENIC WAY ALONG IH 10 OR THE SLOWER, SCENIC ROUTE ALONG FM 1960, WHICH BECOMES SH 90 AS IT NEARS THE CITY OF BEAUMONT. EITHER WAY, THE CITY OF ORANGE, TEXAS, IS APPROXIMATELY 100 MILES TO THE EAST.

♣Piney Woods Country Wines

www.texaswinetrails.com/piney.htm

3408 Willow Drive
Orange, Texas 77632

Phone: (409) 883-5408
Fax: (409) 883-5483

OPEN: MONDAY–SATURDAY
9:00 A.M.–5:00 P.M.
SUNDAY
12:30 P.M.–4:00 P.M.
TOURS BY APPOINTMENT ONLY
TASTINGS, RETAIL SALES,
AND GIFTS

As you approach the city of Beaumont, the grand pines of Big Thicket National Preserve loom to the north and the damp organic scent of the

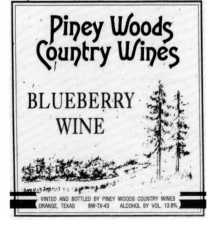

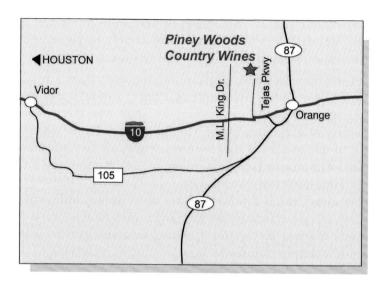

PINEY WOODS COUNTRY WINES

forest can be detected as you drive along to the border town of Orange. Orange, the last stop along IH 10 in east Texas, is a portal to the southern states and home to Piney Woods Country Wines.

Alfred Flies, owner and winemaker, is having good results from an experimental vineyard with a half-acre each of Black Spanish and Blanc du Bois and plans to expand this crop for production of his popular Port wines.

What started out as a hobby after retirement from interior design has become a big business over the past twelve years. Business has doubled recently, providing the catalyst for the latest round of expansions to the facility, vineyards, and orchards. Piney Woods grows all its own plums for it's popular Plum Wine, and uses local fruit for its Blueberry and Strawberry wines.

THE WINES

The style of wines Alfred produces is controlled primarily by his location in the state. His winery is too far east and south to grow vinifera or transport grapes or juice in from the rest of the state. Besides, as Alfred explains, he prefers to produce wines that reflect the local community and resources.

From his three-acre muscadine vineyard, Alfred produces six or seven wines, including two reds, a blush, and a white table wine. Depending on the harvest in any given year, the quantity of grapes and fruit will determine exactly what selection of wines he will make. In one particularly good harvest, Alfred had an excess of muscadine juice that he turned into his now famous Pecan Mocha Wine. Not exactly a dessert wine, nor a mead, it has a flavor unique unto itself. Oddly enough, the wine has become so popular over the past few years, Piney Woods has had to expand its muscadine vineyard to assure a plentiful supply of juice to keep producing this wine.

Piney Woods offers two Port wines—a light Ruby Port and a light White Port, plus a lower alcohol version of the Ruby Port, which has proved to be a strong seller over the years. With only 14 percent alcohol content, this Port can be sold by grocery stores.

The Piney Woods Country Wines product line is rounded out with a popular selection of sparkling wines. To compliment the award-winning Muscadine Champagne and Champear—a sparkling pear wine—a sparkling orange wine called Texas Breakfast Sparkling Orange Wine is now available.

What's in store for the future? According to Alfred, more of the same. As he puts it, "I'm going to leave the Cabs and the Chardonnays to my neighbors to the west." Alfred is happy to concentrate on his specialty wines that are unique in the Texas wine industry.

Directions: From Piney Woods Country Wines, we head back to Houston along IH 10, changing to Highway 90 in Beaumont. Head east to Nome (about fifteen miles outside of Beaumont), and turn north on Highway 326 to Old Beaumont Highway and turn right. Turn right on Nevada Street, and follow it to Bruno and George Wines, Inc., in the historic town of Sour Lake.

❧Bruno and George Wines, Inc.

www.texaswinetrails.com/bruno.htm

400 Massena Road
Sour Lake, Texas 77659
Phone: (409) 898-2829 or (409) 755-6944

OPEN BY APPOINTMENT ONLY

The gateway to the Big Thicket! That's how the town of Sour Lake likes to promote itself. This small country town in east Texas is home to around 1,500 residents and Bruno and George Wines, Inc.

For those of you not familiar with Sour Lake, its name is taken from the small nearby lake—Sour Lake. In revolutionary days, the surface of the lake was covered with floating splotches of oil and gas, and the water was sour to the taste. Local Indians believed that the King of Fire lived in the lake and the constant bubbling from outgasing was his breath. Early settlers thought the water contained medicinal benefits and soon a booming industry was built on shipping the water to folks in Houston and Galveston. Then in the early twentieth century, oil was discovered near the lake and the oil boom swept over this town.

It is in this somewhat surrealistic pioneer town that Shawn Bruno and Gary George decided to build their winery. The idea for the winery started in 1996 when Shawn and Gary began learning how to make wine in the Bruno family tradition from Shawn's Uncle Joe. Uncle Joe learned how to make wine from his father, Salvatore Bruno, who had made wine all his life in Salaparuta, Sicily, before coming to America. His favorite wine was the traditional Sicilian wine made from raisins.

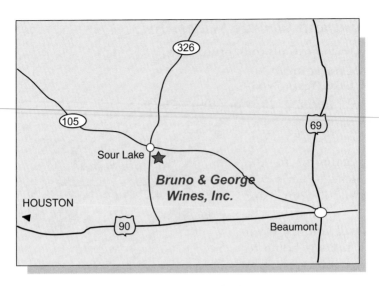

BRUNO AND GEORGE WINES, INC.

THE WINES

With Uncle Joe's guidance, Shawn and Gary learned how to make a number of different wines, including Salvatore's raisin wine—which they were excited about making in Texas. As they formalized their plans for the winery, however, they discovered that it was illegal in the state of Texas to make wine from dried fruit or raisins with the intent to resell. Shawn and his brother then set out to change the law, allowing them to offer their grandfather's wine. After over a year of hard work, they succeeded in changing the law during the seventy-sixth Texas Legislature.

Bruno and George Wines, Inc., focuses on producing wines from fruit and raisins. Their wines include White Orchard Pear, Strawberry, Holiday Blueberry, Raisin, and Other Than Raisin Wine. The Raisin Wine, made in the family tradition, is a popular seller. The Other Than Raisin Wine is a big bold fortified wine with 16.5 percent alcohol. Current Federal law prohibits the winery from using the term "fortified raisin wine," so they chose "other than." It has turned out to be a popular wine and a great marketing ploy. Most folks familiar with the wine simply ask for the *OTR-wine*!

Bruno and George Wines, Inc., selection of wines can be found in restaurants, liquor stores, and nightclubs across southeast Texas. Be sure to stop by the tasting room and hear their story regarding the legislative fight to make raisin wine.

ALONG THE TRAIL

For travelers planning one-day trips, a tour of the wineries near Brenham can be combined with a stopover at the Antique Rose Emporium near the town of Independence on FM 50, just south of the intersection with FM 390. If you have a love for roses, this is a must see. The Emporium has created an English garden with many species of antique roses, native shrubs, and perennials. Its Fall Festival of Roses (usually planned for the first weekend in November) is filled with seminars and lectures on collecting and growing roses. There is a gift shop area with one-of-a-kind garden gifts and books. Ask them about their Republic of Texas Collection representing a collection of roses known to have grown when Texas was a republic. Also, their orphaned roses (roses that have lost their tags) usually come in grabbags at a great price. You can contact them at 409-836-9051 to request a mail-order catalog to browse before you visit.

Texas history can be seen at Washington on the Brazos State Park. Within this park you will also be able to visit the Star of Republic Museum, Independence Hall, and the Anson Jones House. All of these exhibits show early Texas life in one of the state's most picturesque parks and features picnic areas amidst rolling acres and live oaks. This is the site of the signing of the Texas Declaration of Independence. It wouldn't be hard to find a perfect spot for a romantic picnic in this park. A blanket, a crust of bread, a bottle of wine along the banks of the Brazos just could be the reason Sam Houston fought so hard for Texas.

Closer to Houston, the city of Tomball offers shopping and refreshments and a quaint cluster of antique stores to browse in along FM 2920. Further along the trail, Old Town Spring is a pure delight for adults and children, with restaurants, shops, shade trees to rest under with a cool drink, and even a Christmas store that is open all year. Old Town Spring is also well-known for its popular festivals held during the year, including the Crawfish Festival that features music, food, and fun, and the extremely popular Home for the Holidays Festival held every weekend in November and December.

For those wine tourists who venture out to Piney Woods Country Winery, the city of Orange is the easternmost city on the Sabine River boundary with Louisiana. Orange was established in 1836, the year of Texas Independence and was named after the wild orange groves on the banks of the Sabine. Downtown Orange offers marvelous walking tours and opportunities to sit and rest a spell with a cool drink before heading home.

BED AND BREAKFASTS ALONG THE BRAZOS TRAIL

Brenham

ANT STREET INN
BED AND BREAKFAST

Hosts: Tommy and Pam Traylor,
107 West Commerce, Brenham 77833,
(800) 481-1951, (409) 836-7393,
fax (409) 836-7595. 14 rooms
with private baths, gourmet breakfast,
$$$–$$$$, children over 12 welcome,
no pets, smoking in designated areas only,
most credit cards.

CAPTAIN TACITUS T. CLAY
HOUSE

Hosts: Thelma M. Zwiener,
Fieldstone Farm, 9445 FM 390
E. Independence, Brenham 77833,
(409) 836-1916. 5 guest rooms,
4 baths, full breakfast, $–$$,
children welcome, no pets, smoking
in designated areas, no credit cards.

FAR VIEW—
A BED AND BREAKFAST

Hosts: David and Tonya Meyer,
1804 South Park Street, Brenham 77833,
(409) 836-1672. 5 bedrooms, 4 with private
baths, gourmet breakfast, $$$–$$$$,
children over 12 welcome, no pets, smoking
permitted in designated areas, MC, V, AE.

SCHUERENBERG HOUSE

Host: Kay Gregory, 503 West Alamo, Brenham 77833,
(409) 830-7054, (800) 321-6234. 3 bedrooms (2 with private baths),
1 double suite, third-floor grand attic suite with private bath, gourmet
breakfast, $$$–$$$$, children over 12 welcome, no pets, smoking
permitted in designated areas, MC, V.

JAMES WALKER HOMESTEAD

Hosts: John & Jane Barnhill, Route 7, Box 7176, Brenham 77833,
(409) 836-6717, fax (409) 836-6922. 1 bedroom, 1 loft, 1 daybed,
1 bath, full breakfast, $$$$, OYO, no pets, no children, no smoking,
no credit cards.

Bryan-College Station

ANGELSGATE
BED AND BREAKFAST

Hosts: Gary and Beth Goyen, 615
East 29th Street, Bryan 77803,
(409) 779-1231 or (888) 779-1231.
2 suites with private baths, gourmet
breakfast, $$$–$$$$, children 10 and
over welcome, no pets, smoking
permitted outside only, MC, V.

BONNIE GAMBREL (BRYAN)

Hosts: Blocker and Dorothy
Trant, 600 East 27th Street,
Bryan 77803, (409) 779-1022,
fax (409) 779-1040. 1 suite
with private bath, 2 guest rooms,
1 bath, gourmet breakfast or
brunch, $$$–$$$$, children 12
and over (facilities for one infant),
no pets, smoking permitted in
designated areas, MC, V, D.

MESSINA HOF VINEYARD/VINTNER'S LOFT BED & BREAKFAST (BRYAN)

Hosts: Paul & Merrill Bonarrigo,
4545 Old Reliance Road, Bryan 77802,
(409) 778-9463, fax (409) 778-1729.
1 bedroom, 1 bath, continental breakfast,
$$$, no pets, no children, no smoking,
MC, V, AE.

THE FLIPPEN PLACE (COLLEGE STATION)

Hosts: Flip and Susan Flippen,
1199 Haywood Drive,
College Station 77845,
(409) 693-7660,
fax (409) 693-8458.
3 guest rooms, 3 private baths,
gourmet breakfast, $$$–$$$$,
no children, no pets, no
smoking, MC, V, AE.

Chappell Hill

BROWNING PLANTATION

Hosts: Richard and Mildred Ganchan, Route 1, Box 8, Chappell Hill
77426, (409) 836-6144, (713) 661-6761. 4 guest bedrooms, 2 private
baths, 2 shared half baths, gourmet breakfast, $$$$, no pets, no
children, no smoking, no credit cards.

THE MULBERRY HOUSE

Host: Katie Cron, P.O. Box 5,
Chappell Hill 77426,
(409) 830-1311. 5 bedrooms,
5 baths, gourmet breakfast,
$$–$$$, no pets, no children,
no smoking, no credit cards.

THE STAGECOACH INN

Hosts: Mr. and Mrs. H. Moore, Main at Chestnut, P.O. Box 339,
Chappell Hill 77426, (409) 836-9515. 6 bedrooms, 4 baths,
gourmet breakfast, $$$–$$$$, no pets, no children, no smoking,
no credit cards.

Houston

ANGEL ARBOR BED AND BREAKFAST INN

Host; Marguerite Swanson, 848 Heights Blvd., Houston 77007, (713) 868-4654, fax (713) 861-3189. 3 guest rooms, 1 suite, private baths, full breakfast, $$$$, no children, no pets, no smoking, MC, V, DC, AE.

SARA'S BED AND BREAKFAST

Host: Donna and Tillman Arledge, 941 Heights Blvd., Houston 77008, (800) 593-1130, (713) 868-1130, fax (713) 868-1160. 10 bedrooms, 9½ baths, continental, $–$$, no pets, children in carriage house, smoking designated areas, all credit cards.

Old Town Spring

McLACHLAN FARM BED AND BREAKFAST

Hosts: Jim & Joycelyn McLachlan Clairmonte, 24907 Hardy Road, (mailing address) P.O. Box 538, Spring 77383, (800) 382-3988, (713) 350-2400. 3 bedrooms, 2 baths, gourmet breakfast, $$–$$$$, no pets, no children, no smoking, no alcoholic beverages, please, no credit cards.

RESTAURANTS ALONG THE BRAZOS TRAIL

Brenham

THE GREAT ANT STREET RESTAURANT

205 S. Baylor, Brenham, (409) 830-9060. American. Bar. $–$$.

K & G STEAKHOUSE

2209 S. Market near Becker Drive, Brenham, (409) 836-7950. Breakfast, lunch, and dinner Tuesday–Sunday, dinner only Monday. Steak, seafood, chicken, bar. $–$$.

Bryan-College Station

BLACK FOREST INN

On TX 30 approx. 21 miles east of College Station, Bryan, (409) 874-2407. American-German. Beer and wine, Texas wines, dinner Wednesday–Saturday. Reservations required. $$.

THE KAFFEE KLATSCH

106 North Avenue, Bryan, (409) 846-4360. American. Lunch Monday–Saturday. $.

THE TEXAN

3204 S. College, Bryan, (409) 822-3588. Continental. Bar, Texas wines, dinner Monday–Saturday. Reservations suggested. $$–$$$$.

Chappell Hill

See Bryan-College Station.

Houston

BABA YEGA

2607 Grant, Houston, (713) 522-0042. American. Bar, Texas wines, lunch and dinner daily, breakfast Saturday–Sunday. $.

BISTRO LANCASTER

701 Texas, Houston, (713) 228-9502. Steak, seafood, pasta, bar, Texas wines. Reservations recommended. $$$$.

BISTRO LANCASTER, LOCATED INSIDE THE LUXURIOUS LANCASTER HOTEL, IS AN EXCELLENT SPOT TO ENJOY A PRE-THEATER DINNER.

BRENNAN'S

3300 Smith, Houston, (713) 522-9711. French-Creole-Southwestern. Bar, Texas wines, lunch and dinner Monday–Friday, brunch and dinner Saturday-Sunday. Reservations required. $$$–$$$$.

CHEF ROBERT DEL GRANDE'S FLAVOR-CHARGED DISHES SUCH AS BEEF FILET WITH MOLE SAUCE AND LOBSTER ENCHILADAS MAKE CAFÉ ANNIE A BENCHMARK FOR QUALITY SOUTHWESTERN CUISINE.

CAFÉ ANNIE

5860 Westheimer, Houston, (713) 840-1111. Southwestern. lunch and dinner Tuesday–Friday, dinner only Saturday. Reservations suggested. $$$–$$$$.

CLIVE'S

517 Louisiana, Houston, (713) 224-4438. Steak, seafood, grilled specialties, bar, extensive Texas wine list, lunch and dinner Monday–Saturday. Reservations required. $$$$.

CONFEDERATE HOUSE

2925 Weslayan, Houston, (713) 622-1936. American. Bar, Texas wines, lunch and dinner Monday–Saturday. Reservations required. $$–$$$.

DE VILLE

1300 Lamar in the Four Seasons Hotel, Houston, (713) 650-1300. Continental. Breakfast, lunch, and dinner Monday–Saturday, Sunday brunch only. Bar, Texas wines. Reservations suggested. $$$.

LA RESERVE

4 Riverway in the Omni Hotel, Houston, (713) 871-8177. French.
Bar, Texas wines, lunch and dinner Monday–Saturday. Reservations
required. $$$$.

LA TOUR D'ARGENT SERVES TOP-
SHELF FRENCH CUISINE THAT
SHOWCASES SEVERAL EXCELLENT
VEAL ENTREES ALONG WITH QUAIL,
DUCK, AND OTHER DELECTABLE
DISHES.

LA TOUR D'ARGENT

2011 Ella Blvd., Houston,
(713) 864-9864. French. Bar,
Texas wines, lunch and dinner
Monday–Saturday. Reservations
required. $$$$.

RAINBOW LODGE

1 Birdsall Street (off Memorial), Houston, (713) 861-8666.
Continental. Bar, Texas wines, lunch and dinner Monday–Friday, dinner
only Saturday. Reservations suggested. $$$.

ROBERT DEL GRANDE,
CHEF AT THE UPSCALE
CAFÉ ANNIE, GETS A
CHANCE TO SHOW-OFF HIS
SKILL WITH DOWN-HOME
TEXAS FOOD, SUCH AS
XYZ, AT RIO RANCH.

RIO RANCH

9999 Westheimer, inside the Hilton Hotel, Houston, (713) 952-5000.
Southwestern. Bar, Texas wines, breakfast, lunch, and dinner daily,
Reservations for large or private parties. $$–$$$.

RITZ-CARLTON HOTEL

1919 Briar Oaks Lane, Houston, (713) 840-7600. Continental. Bar,
Texas wines, lunch and dinner daily. $$$$.

THE STUFFED DOVER SOLE, A 14-OZ. VEAL CHOP, AND TABLESIDE
FLAMBÉS MAKE A DRAMATIC IMPRESSION AT THE RIVOLI, AS DOES THE
EXTENSIVE WINE LIST.

RIVOLI

5636 Richmond, Houston, (713) 789-1900. Continental. Bar, Texas
wines, lunch and dinner Monday–Friday, dinner only Saturday.
Reservations required. $$$–$$$$.

ROTISSERIE FOR BEEF AND BIRD

2200 Wilcrest, Houston,
(713) 977-9524. Steak,
seafood, grilled specialties.
Bar, extensive Texas wine list,
lunch and dinner
Monday–Friday, dinner only
Saturday. Reservations
required. $$$-$$$$.

Old Town Spring

PUFFABELLY'S

100 Main, Old Town Spring, 281-350-3376. Burgers, sandwiches,
chicken fried steak. Beer and wine, house wine is Red River label. Open
daily. $$.

Chapter 5

WEST TEXAS
WINERIES

*V*ast prairies covered with seas of undulating grasses;
fractured mountains with mesquite bushes; a sky that
goes on forever, interrupted only by a distant thun-
derhead cloud floating like a jellyfish above with its tentacles
of rain dragging across the earth—this is wine country? You
bet! This is wine country—West Texas style. In fact, most of
the original experimental work done with grapevines in the
early 1970s was done in this area. It was here that folks such
as Clint McPhearson and Robert Reed, professors at Texas
Tech University, and Bobby Smith from La Buena Vida Winery proved that Texas was capable of competing in the wine
marketplace.

THE TRAILS

For the sake of our wine trails, West Texas means everything
west of the town of Fredericksburg and includes the Panhandle,
the High Plains, Trans-Pecos Country, and Big Bend Country.
It is a vast area with few people. It is an area where, if you travel down the right road, fences, phone lines, and the arteries of
the national power grid disappear. It is also, as some say, going

◀ **THE LONGER GRAPES REMAIN ON THE VINE, THE SWEETER THEY
BECOME. (COURTESY OF THE TEXAS DEPARTMENT OF AGRICULTURE)**

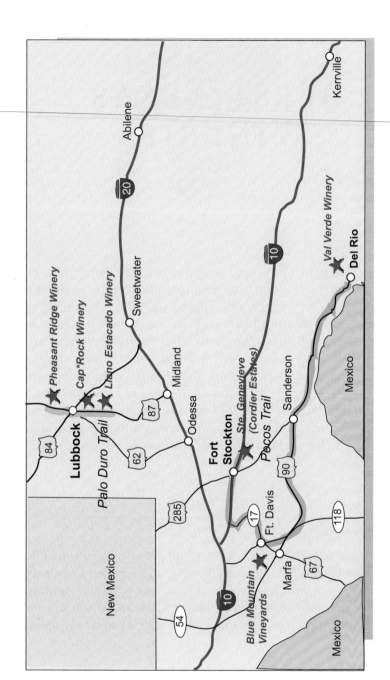

THE WEST TEXAS WINERIES

PALO DURO TRAIL	PECOS TRAIL
❧ Pheasant Ridge Winery	❧ Blue Mountain Vineyard
❧ Llano Estacado Winery	❧ Ste. Genevieve Winery
❧ Cap*Rock Winery	❧ Val Verde Winery

to be the savior of the Texas wine industry. Farmlands around the Lubbock and Fort Stockton areas offer some of the best conditions for growing wine-quality grapes. This area is also isolated from Pierce's disease, which is slowly destroying the vineyards of the Hill Country.

The western half of Texas is home to only six wineries and a multitude of vineyards that supply roughly eighty percent of all the grapes and wine in Texas. The large distances between grape-growing areas and the often rugged landscape prompts us to divide these wineries into two trails. The Palo Duo Trail links the wineries around the Lubbock area, and The Pecos Trail connects the wineries near the Pecos River with Val Verde Winery in Del Rio.

Tours at some of these wineries are by appointment only and may be restricted to certain times of the year. Call ahead before planning your journey along these trails.

We start our travels in the Lubbock area with a visit to Pheasant Ridge Winery, just north of town.

THE PALO DURO TRAIL

The cloudless, crystal clear sky seems to glimmer as we arrive in Lubbock. Having left the busy metropolitan areas of the great techno-cities of eastern Texas, we step into the vast, fertile fields of the Panhandle. Here atop the escarpment that forms the High Plains, you're tempted to believe that if you squint hard enough, you could see all the way to Canada.

The Palo Duro Trail, named for the magnificent Palo Duro Canyon, just north of the Lubbock area, consists of three

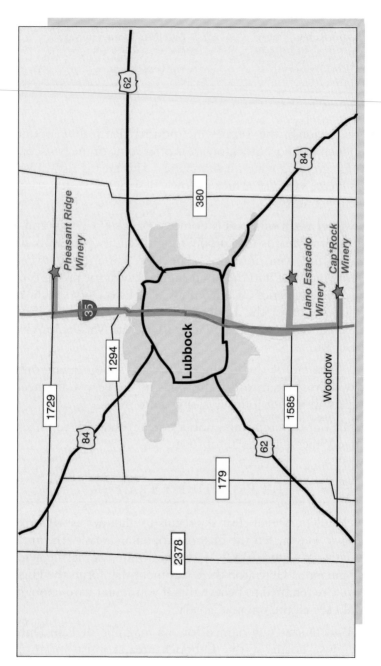

THE PALO DURO TRAIL WINERIES

wineries: Pheasant Ridge Winery, Llano Estacado Winery, and Cap*Rock Winery. Of the three, Pheasant Ridge requires appointments for tours and tastings, and no retail sales are available at the winery itself.

Our first winery on this trail is Pheasant Ridge just north of town, off of SH 87/27. Take the highway to the town of New Deal and right (east) on FM 1729. Pheasant Ridge Winery is approximately three miles from the intersection.

❧Pheasant Ridge Winery

www.pheasantridgewinery.com

Route 3, Box 191
Lubbock, Texas 79401

Phone: (806) 746-6033, (806) 746-6750

OPEN: FRIDAY–SATURDAY
10:00 A.M.–5:00 P.M.
SUNDAY
12:00 P.M.–5:00 P.M.
TOURS, TASTINGS, AND SALES

PHEASANT RIDGE

CABERNET SAUVIGNON
TEXAS HIGH PLAINS
1994

PRODUCED & BOTTLED BY PHEASANT RIDGE WINERY, LUBBOCK, TEXAS ALC. 13.2% BY VOL.

When owner Bobby Cox and his wife Jennifer went on their first visit to the California wine country in the early 1970s, they returned to Texas disenchanted. The wineries they saw were magnificent complexes of vast vineyards, high-tech equipment and well-tuned marketing organizations. In short, something way beyond their financial horizons. Though they desperately wanted to start a winery in Texas, the California trip made them think they needed that vast scale and technology they saw in California to be able to make a comparable wine.

A trip to France in 1977 for a tour of the wine regions there changed their minds about winemaking. In the most famous

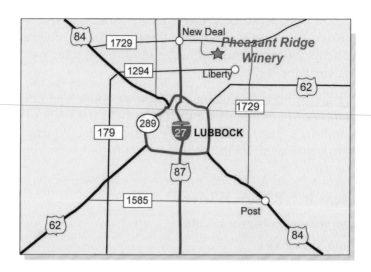

PHEASANT RIDGE WINERY

French wineries, wine was made in quite primitive conditions, by California standards. It was in France that the Coxes realized that fine wine is not made by stainless steel and glycol coolers—it is made in the vineyard!

Encouraged by what they saw, the Cox family vineyard was planted in 1979. Pheasant Ridge Winery offered its first commercial release in 1984 to wide acclaim. Bobby described Pheasant Ridge as a very small European-style winery, that used the philosophies and techniques he observed in France. All Pheasant Ridge wines are made in blended styles, and except for the Blush, all are aged in French oak.

As the 1990s drew closer for Bobby and Jennifer, the popularity of their wines continued to increase, as did the number of awards they collected. Based on this early success, the couple incorporated and brought in investors in order to improve the capabilities of the winery. Pheasant Ridge is now owned by the Texas Corporation and day-to-day tasks are managed by officers of the company.

THE WINES

Like numerous other winemakers, Bobby believed that wine is made in the vineyard first. Quality grapes are necessary for quality wine, though he does admit that a good winemaker could make a good wine from lower quality grapes. Much of the success of these wines can be attributed to the unique conditions enjoyed by the vineyards of the High Plains in Texas. With well-drained soils at 3,400 feet above sea level, the days are warm and the nights cool and dry. In this environment, grapes develop intense flavors in a growing season that runs from April to August.

The wines produced from Pheasant Ridge Winery's fifty-acre vineyard have been recognized for their excellence since their first releases in 1983. Their red wines include Proprietor's Reserve, Cabernet Sauvignon, Pinot Noir, and Merlot. The Proprietor's Reserve is made in the Bordeaux style and is a blend of Cabernet Sauvignon, Merlot, and Cabernet Franc. The Cabernet Sauvignon is a typical Bordeaux-style red wine consisting of 80 percent Cabernet Sauvignon, 10 percent Merlot, and 10 percent Cabernet Franc. Aged for two years in oak, this full-bodied wine consistently wins awards and praises from wine critics across the country. The Pinot Noir, aged in French oak, is a classic Burgundian-style wine with a smooth, silky texture. While drinkable now, this wine has potential for aging.

The white wines offered by Pheasant Ridge include Dry Chenin Blanc, Barrel Fermented Chardonnay, and Proprietor's White. The Chenin Blanc is light and dry with hints of peaches and citrus. The Barrel Fermented Chardonnay was aged in both French and American oak, giving the wine a mellow, clean character with light toasty oak flavors. The Proprietor's White is a soft, fruity estate-grown and -bottled blend of Semillon and Chardonnay. It's a great summer wine with an elegant finish.

DIRECTIONS: HEAD SOUTH ON SH 87 THROUGH LUBBOCK AND BEYOND LOOP 289 TO FM 1585. TURN EAST AND YOU ARE JUST A FEW MILES FROM THE NEXT STOP—LLANO ESTACADO WINERY.

❧Llano Estacado Winery

www.llanowine.com
P.O. Box 3487
Lubbock, Texas 79452
Phone: (806) 745-2258
Fax: (806) 748-1674

OPEN: MONDAY–SATURDAY
10:00 A.M.–5:00 P.M.
SUNDAY
12:00 P.M.–5:00 P.M.

TOURS, TASTINGS, RETAIL SALES,
AND GIFTS

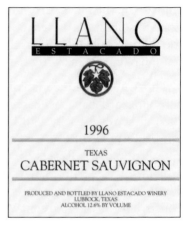

LLANO
E S T A C A D O

1996

TEXAS
CABERNET SAUVIGNON

PRODUCED AND BOTTLED BY LLANO ESTACADO WINERY
LUBBOCK, TEXAS
ALCOHOL 12.6% BY VOLUME

From its humble beginnings as a casual project on the patio of a Texas horticulturist in the mid-1970s, Llano Estacado has grown to be the largest producer of premium wines in the High Plains Appellation. The first wines were released in 1977 under the Staked Plains label, which is still used today for some of Llano's wines. Since those

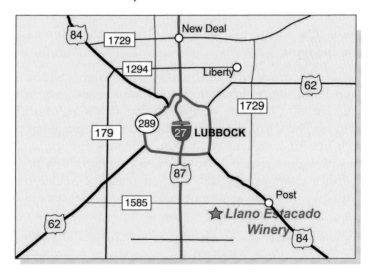

LLANO ESTACADO WINERY

VIEW OF LLANO ESTACADO WINERY FROM THE ROADWAY.

early days of producing only 1,300 cases, the winery embarked on an ambitious expansion project in 1997 to accommodate production of 125,000 cases. Current capacity ranges from 70,000 to 100,000 cases annually, depending on availability and quality of fruit.

The management of Llano Estacado Inc. has undertaken an effort to increase their share of the American wine market, as well as to raise the level of quality of their wines. As part of that effort, the company hired veteran California winemaker Greg Bruni in 1993. Mr. Bruni's winemaking experience dates back to 1977 when he graduated from the University of California, Davis. He also comes from a family with three generations of winemaking experience. Working for a variety of successful wineries in California, Greg was rewarded for his efforts with an impressive array of medals and honors.

Walter Haimman, president of Llano Estacado Winery, said "Greg brings an entirely new and higher level of experience to the Texas wine industry and certainly to Llano Estacado." Mr. Haimman feels that Llano Estacado could not undertake current efforts to increase the winery's visibility and quality of its products without Greg on board.

The quality of Llano Estacado wines is confirmed by the innumerable awards it has collected recently. Highly respected in America, these wines enjoy national as well as international distribution throughout Europe. Interestingly, the popularity of these wines has spilled over into the political arena as well. Llano Estacado wines were served by President Reagan in the White House, at the Houston Economic Summit, and at the Bush-Gorbachev Summit. Queen Elizabeth was served Llano Estacado wine during her visit to the United States.

THE WINES

For a grape, Llano Estacado Winery must seem like a paradise. The winery has great growing conditions in the High Plains viticulture area with warm days and cool nights, plenty of water, and some of the best equipment to squeeze out the juices without bruising and damaging the fruit.

Greg Bruni shares winemaker Dean Valentine's belief that the High Plains area of Texas has great potential for world-class grape production—they just have to perfect their techniques. What works in California or Europe may not be the best practice in the High Plains. Part of the experimentation at Llano includes the use of mechanical harvesters and the purchase of low-pressure bladder presses to slowly extract the juice without damaging the fruit and releasing unwanted chemical compounds into the juice.

With over 100 acres of their own and more than 300 acres under long-term contract, Llano Estacado is producing a well-rounded collection of quality wines. Their red wines include Zinfandel, Merlot, Cellar Select Merlot, Cabernet Sauvignon, Cellar Select Cabernet Sauvignon, and Signature Red Meritage. The Zinfandel was originally produced in a "claret style," carrying a medium to light body. Since 1997, however, it has been made as a hearty, full-bodied wine. The Merlot was aged for three months in French and American oak, taking on the aromas and flavors of vanilla and cedar. The Cellar Select Merlot has a small amount of Carignane blended in to enhance the flavor and body of the wine with hints of currant and plum flavors.

The Cabernet Sauvignon received over a year of aging in French and American oak, producing a wine with intense fruit and light tannins. The Cellar Select Cabernet Sauvignon, a blend of Cabernet Sauvignon and Merlot, is aged for fifteen to twenty months in small oak barrels, producing a rich full-bodied wine. The Signature Red Meritage is a blend of traditional Bordeaux Varietals: Cabernet Sauvignon, Merlot, and Cabernet Franc. This deep-colored wine with vibrant fruity flavors was the first non-California wine to be accepted to the prestigious Meritage Association.

Llano Estacado Winery's white wines include Sauvignon Blanc, Chardonnay, Cellar Select Chardonnay, Signature White, Chenin Blanc, Johannisberg Riesling, and Gewurztraminer. The Sauvignon Blanc received no oak aging to be crafted as a dry wine, preserving the fruit flavors.

All of their Chardonnays are left *sur lie* for ninety days after fermentation, then barrel aged in French and American oak. The Chardonnay underwent 40 percent malolactic fermentation, while the Cellar Select Chardonnay was allowed to complete 100 percent malolactic fermentation. Believing that Chardonnay is a white wine that benefits from bottle aging, the winemaker allowed both of the Chardonnays to bottle age for six months prior to release.

The Signature White is a blend of Sauvignon Blanc, Chenin Blanc, and Chardonnay and fermented in Stainless steels tanks in the cold-fermentation, fruity style. The Chenin Blanc has received numerous gold medals over the years. Also made in the cold-fermented style, this wine offers pineapple and honeydew flavors with a fresh acidic finish. The Riesling and Gewurztraminer possess ample residual sugar to pair well with spicy foods.

Llano Estacado Winery offers two dessert wines: Muscat Canelli and a Port. The Muscat Canelli is a fruity, sweet wine that is low in alcohol. The Port, aged in oak for two years, has been fortified to 19 percent alcohol level.

DIRECTIONS: AFTER ENJOYING YOUR STAY WITH LLANO ESTACADO, HEAD BACK TO SH 87 AND CONTINUE SOUTH TO WOODROW ROAD AND TURN EASTWARD TO THE MAGNIFICENT CAP*ROCK WINERY.

❧Cap*Rock Winery

www.caprockwinery.com

Route 6, Box 713K
Lubbock, Texas 79423

Phone: (806) 863-2704
Fax: (806) 863-2712

> OPEN MONDAY–SATURDAY
> 10:00 A.M.–5:00 P.M.
> SUNDAY
> 12:00 P.M.–5:00 P.M.
> TOURS, TASTINGS, RETAIL SALES,
> AND GIFTS SHOP

Cap*Rock is possibly the most attractive of all the existing Texas wineries, an architectural jewel set in the High Plains. Originally built for Teysha Wine Cellars, this $5 million facility was purchased by the Plains Capital

THE MAGNIFICENT ARCHITECTURE OF CAP*ROCK WINERY.

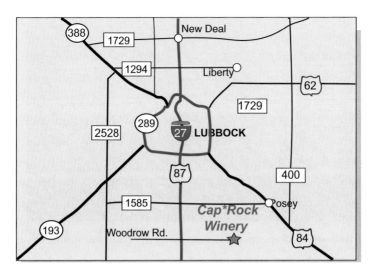

CAP*ROCK WINERY

Corporation in 1990. As a magnificent example of Southwestern architecture, the well-appointed visitors' center/tasting room beckons visitors in to relax, tour the facilities, and sample some exceptional wines.

The winery's name is derived from the geological formation it sits on, which extends from the High Plains up into the northern part of the Texas Panhandle. In geological terms, a caprock is an impenetrable layer of sediment set down during a single geological period. The Cap*Rock label is a creative depiction of this geological formation. The subtle technique of the minimalist design allows for varied interpretation of the Cap*Rock label. Some see a geological formation, while others see an abstract painting, and the romantics among us, see an embrace.

Ninety-eight of the 119 acres at this facility are cultivated as vineyards, and yet, you will not find the Estate Bottled designation on any of the labels shown here. Even with this amount of vines planted, additional grapes must be purchased from area growers to support this modern facility, capable of storing 139,000 gallons of wine. Of course without a strong commitment to quality and a vintner with a firm hand on the

THE WELL-APPOINTED TASTING ROOM AT CAP*ROCK WINERY.

winemaking process, even the most modern of wineries would not produce premium quality wines. For this reason the owners hired Kim McPhearson as Cap*Rock's winemaker.

Kim's internship in the Napa Valley wine industry is enhanced by years of expertise in the Texas wine industry and by association with several successful wineries. His efforts in Texas over the years have produced wines that have won more than 300 medals at tasting events throughout the United States. By using a combination of stainless-steel tanks with American and French oak barrels, Kim keeps fermentation lots small to allow the wine to develop to its full potential.

THE WINES

Cap*Rock Winery currently produces fourteen wines in three price groups, called tiers. Tier I is used for their reserve wines and includes Reserve Cabernet Sauvignon, Reserve Toscano Rosso, Reserve Merlot, Reserve Orange Muscat, and Cap*Rock Sparkling. Tier II offers varietal wines: Cabernet Sauvignon, Chardonnay, and Merlot. Tier III includes proprietary wines: Cabernet Royale, Topaz Royale, Vintner's Red, Vintner's White, and a Blush.

Tier I wines are Cap*Rock's premium labels. The Sparkling Brut is a blend of Chardonnay and Pinot Noir, produced in the classic French *Methode Champenoise*. The Cabernet Sauvignon is a full-bodied wine with rich color and oak-aged highlights. The winemaker feels that this wine will continue to age well in the bottle for at least five years.

Tier II wines have been briefly aged in oak to enhance the character of the grape with just a hint of oak flavor. These wines have been crafted by the winemaker to be very approachable in their youth. Tier III represents Cap*Rock Winery's table wine selection, featuring some of the most ambitious blending done by Kim McPhearson. The Topaz Royale, for example, is an off-dry blend of Chenin Blanc, Riesling, and Muscat Canelli, resulting in a fruity, sweeter wine.

The wines offered by Cap*Rock Winery, which are the largest exported of the Texas wines, have received over 350 medals since first introduced in 1992. Of special note is the Reserve Toscano Rosso, which is a Tuscan-style blend of Sangiovese, Barbera, and Cabernet Sauvignon. In a recent blind tasting by restaurant owners, this wine was identified as an Italian-made wine. In recent years, it has captured Silver and Gold medals in

AN INSPIRING DISPLAY OF WINES.

A BARREL "NURSERY" FOR MATURING WINES.

American competitions. The Reserve Orange Muscat—a fortified dessert wine—also captured a Silver medal at the Los Angeles County Fair Wine Competition.

Plans are in place to expand production, fermentation, and vineyard capabilities. As part of that plan, in 1999 Cap*Rock Winery opened a tasting room in the town of Grapevine. You can read more about that tasting room on the Munson Trail.

ALONG THE TRAIL

The High Plains of Texas are filled with great western wilderness, pioneer spirit, and numerous historical sites. Near Canyon, just south of Amarillo, off IH 27 is perhaps the largest attraction in this area—Palo Duro Canyon. Named for the hardwoods that grow here, the Palo Duro Canyon State Park covers more than 15,000 acres of this geological area. This canyon was carved out of the plateau by a branch of the Red River, exposing rock formations and beautiful vistas that are now accessible via paved roads.

The musical drama *Texas* draws international crowds annually to this region. Performed against the rugged canyon wall, this musical lets the audience experience the pioneer story in song and dance. The state park is open year round with a small admission charge per vehicle. The musical is performed in the summer months, nightly except Sunday. Tickets are under $15 per person, and reservations are necessary. Call (806) 655-2181 for information and reservations. And remember—dress warm, the evenings can get a bit cool in these parts.

The town of Plainview lies between Canyon and Lubbock and offers antique shopping in the historical downtown district. The Llano Estacado Museum exhibits pioneer life collections and archeological site remains of prehistoric mammoths and armadillos that grew up to six feet long! A small admission fee is requested.

The Lubbock area offers a unique combination of history and entertainment. The Buddy Holly Statue and the Walk of Fame feature numerous contributions by many West Texas natives, with of course, a special salute to Mr. Holly. The historic district offers a nightlife of fine restaurants and a wide selection of live music guaranteed to provide a good time for all. Scenic drives south of this area are a yearly favorite for many travelers to this area. Pack a picnic basket and take in the breathtaking views of the canyons in the Texas High Plains.

THE PECOS TRAIL

The Pecos River Valley is an almost uninhabited river basin. In the distance loom the rugged Davis Mountains, announcing a remote land that once boasted being home to desperadoes who fled to the "bad lands." Fortunately, you won't have to go quite that far into the area—unless, of course, you like backcountry expeditions. The Pecos Trail, named for the Pecos River with its "West of the Pecos" history, begins approximately 200 miles south and east of Lubbock, in the foothills of the Davis Mountains.

The longest wine trail in the state, at approximately 300 miles end to end, this trail is best approached as a long weekend trip, allowing for an overnight stay along the way. From the Davis Mountains, which serve as home to Blue Mountain Winery, Ste. Genevieve Winery, and the McDonald Observatory, you will swoop down along SH 90 and close in on the Rio Grande River as

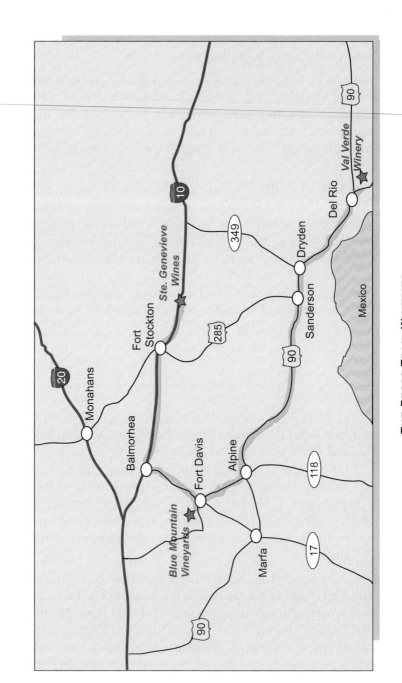

THE PECOS TRAIL WINERIES

you near Del Rio to visit Texas' oldest operating winery, Val Verde Winery. You will pass through mountain towns like Balmorhea, Fort Davis, and Alpine, and see dramatic views of some of the highest peaks in Texas, such as Timber Mountain, Mt. Livermore, and Cathedral Mountain. Take plenty of film with you on this trip.

Leaving Fort Stockton, you will notice the land continues to rise before you as you travel west along SH 10 to SH 17 and south for approximately forty miles to the town of Fort Davis, home of Blue Mountain Vineyards.

☙Blue Mountain Vineyards

www.texaswinetrails.com/blue.htm

HCR 74, Box 7
Fort Davis, Texas 79734

Phone: (915) 426-3763
Fax: (915) 426-3763

> TOURS AND TASTINGS BY
> APPOINTMENT

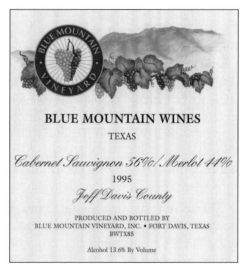

Life in the mountains is different somehow. Brilliant sun-filled days warm the mountainsides, allowing plants and animals to flourish in this steeply sloped world. Nightfall brings cool, crisp evening and a night sky packed with stars. Rainfall, temperatures, and the tempo of life itself are all controlled by the mountains. Patience, hailed as a virtue by the civilized world, is a necessity for living and thriving in this mountain environment. Patrick Johnson, winemaker at Blue Mountain Vineyards, understands the importance of such patience, as does owner Nell Weisbach.

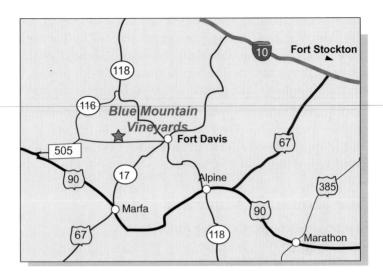

BLUE MOUNTAIN VINEYARDS

Set at 5,300 feet above sea level in the dramatic beauty of the Davis Mountains, Blue Mountain Vineyards has been producing red and white grapes of superior quality for over a decade for vintners around the state. Patrick, who was educated at University of California at Davis and apprenticed at one of the largest wineries in California, patiently waited for Nell to have the winery bonded to produce wines. In the interim, he studied the unique characteristics of the Fort Davis area and applied his winemaking skills to nurturing his grapes to produce great wines. Bonded in 1994, Blue Mountain Vineyards has been producing award-wining wines ever since.

The scenic vineyard snuggled into the side of Blue Mountain contains fifty-five acres of Cabernet Sauvignon, Merlot, Sauvignon Blanc, and Chenin Blanc. Patrick uses these grapes exclusively to produce Cabernet Sauvignon, a Cabernet Sauvignon/Merlot blend, made in the Bordeaux style, a Sauvignon Blanc, and a white table wine made from Chenin Blanc and Sauvignon Blanc. He uses all his own grapes and does not bring grapes in from other vineyards in order to produce wines that can be classified as Estate Bottled. The word "estate" on a wine label signifies that the wine was made at the winery from grapes grown at the winery's vineyard.

THE WINES

During our conversation, Patrick used a term to describe himself that we have not often heard. He referred to himself as a winegrower, instead of a winemaker. As he explains it, "Wine is made in the field. You can't have a quality wine without first having quality grapes." At an elevation of 5,300 feet, Blue Mountain Vineyards is blessed with cool nights even in the months of July and August, which allow the grapes to ripen slowly on the vine. By stretching out the crucial ripening phase to seven or eight weeks, the vinter allows the vines time to work their magic on the grapes to metabolize a multitude of components into the fruit.

As a result, the wines produced by Blue Mountain Vineyards are fruity, full-mouthed wines of a remarkably rich color. Patrick also has the advantage of being able to crush the grapes within hours of being picked, something he feels adds greatly to the final flavor of the wine. Using oak sparingly, he tries to age his reds for at least a year. Like many vinters, Patrick prefers to produce red wines that are a blend of French and American oak aging: "a blending of the two is really nice, in my opinion."

With around 1,000 cases a year, Blue Mountain Vineyards wines are not available all across Texas. Outside of the winery, you can find them in the Midland/Odessa, El Paso, and Dallas areas. Patrick is working on expanding the list of locations, but as with everything else, it takes time. It's good he is a patient man!

DIRECTIONS: FROM BLUE MOUNTAIN VINEYARDS DOUBLE BACK ALONG SH 17 TO SH 10 TO RETURN TO FORT STOCKTON TO VISIT STE. GENEVIEVE WINERY. IF YOU WOULD LIKE A MORE SCENIC ROUTE, TAKE SH 118 SOUTH TO SH 67 AND TURN LEFT (NORTHEAST) FOR A SIXTY-SEVEN MILE TRIP THROUGH THE GLASS MOUNTAINS.

♣Ste. Genevieve Winery (Cordier Estates)

www.texaswinetrails.com/gen.htm

P.O. Box 697
Fort Stockton, Texas 79735

Phone: (915) 395-2417
Fax: (915) 395-2431

> **Tours and tastings
> arranged
> by Chamber of
> Commerce**
>
> **(915) 336-2264 or
> (800) 336-2166**

Ste. Genevieve Winery is located just outside of Ft. Stockton on land owned by the University of Texas and leased to Cordier Estates Winery. Out here, everything is BIG. The vineyard covers more than 1,000 acres, making it the largest in Texas. Matching the scale of the vineyard is the winery's fermenting capacity at 1.2 million gallons! Yes, this is big country. The vines stretch out into the shadow of the Skyscraper Mesa that dominates the visual horizon here. The word *mesa* is taken from the Spanish word for table, which aptly describes these stark monolithics set against the vast West Texas sky.

The vineyard is unique in many ways. It is supplied with an ample supply of water from an underground aquifer and uses drip irrigation to conserve water usage in this arid area. The size of the available land also allows large spacing between vines and between vine rows, making the use of mechanical harvesters quite easy. Though somewhat lower in altitude than the Lubbock area wineries, Ste. Genevieve enjoys similar soil conditions and temperature ranges to promote juicy, healthy fruit. The Escondido Valley in which the vineyard is located is surrounded by expanses of desert, which effectively isolates the vineyard from other horticultural areas. The result is a virtually pest-free environment—a big plus considering recent outbreaks of Pierce's disease around the state.

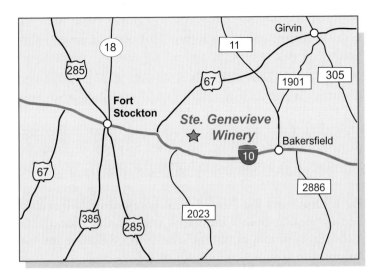

STE. GENEVIEVE WINERY

THE WINES

The name Ste. Genevieve was taken from Genevieve, the patron saint of Paris, who is credited with saving the city and its vineyards by turning away Attila the Hun's troops. With such a rich tradition and a owner like Domaines Cordier—the largest vineyard owner in France—it's not surprising to see a French influence in the winemaking.

Mark Penna oversees the winemaking process at what is the largest winery in Texas. Under his guidance, the winery now produces wines under four labels: Ste. Genevieve, Escondido Valley, L'Orval, and Big River. The wines under the Ste. Genevieve and Escondido Valley labels are created from grapes grown primarily in the Escondido viticultural area. This vineyard contains Cabernet Franc, Merlot, Barbera, Zinfandel, Pinot Noir, Cabernet Sauvignon, Ruby Cabernet, Chenin Blanc, Chardonnay, Sauvignon Blanc, Muscat Canelli, and French Columbard.

The Ste. Genevieve label is used to market a line of table wines produced in 750 ML. and 1.5 L. sized bottles. These include

White Zinfandel, Merlot, Chardonnay, Gamay, Pinot Noir, Texas Red, Texas White, and Texas Blush. This popular group of wines is usually available at grocery and liquor stores across the state.

The Escondido Valley label is reserved for a line of more upscale wines. As winemaker, Mark Penna explained, the creation of this label resulted from the desire to produce estate-bottled varietals that have more oak introduction and longer aging. These wines include Merlot, Cabernet Sauvignon, Pinot Noir, Chardonnay, and Syrah. Look for the Escondido line in liquor stores across the state.

The L'Orval and Big River labels represent the winery's venture in importing bulk wines from outside the United States. Spot shortages of grapes through the 1990s forced many wineries around the country to look for grapes or juice from sources beyond our borders. The L'Orval label is used to market wines made from bulk wine brought in from France. These include Cabernet Sauvignon, Chardonnay, Merlot, and Syrah.

Based on the success of these efforts, the Big River label was created to market wines made from bulk wine brought in from Australia. Both the L'Orval and Big River wines are distributed almost exclusively outside Texas. The Ste. Genevieve and Escondido Valley wines are distributed primarily within Texas.

A brief note on touring this winery. Ste. Genevieve does not host tours and tastings. Tours are available, however, through the Fort Stockton Chamber of Commerce, which holds vineyard and winery tours and tastings on Wednesday and Saturday mornings. You can contact the Fort Stockton Chamber of Commerce at (915)-336-2264 or (800)-336-2166. Wines are also available for sale at the end of the tour. Remember though, don't just show up at the winery. You won't be admitted unless you are part of the Chamber of Commerce tour group.

DIRECTIONS: FROM STE. GENEVIEVE IT IS APPROXIMATELY A 200 MILE JOURNEY TO DEL RIO TO VISIT VAL VERDE WINERY. TRAVEL SOUTH ON SH 285 TO THE TOWN OF SANDERSON. TURN SOUTH ONTO SH 90 AND CONTINUE ON TO DEL RIO, PASSING OVER THE AMISTAD RESERVOIR. IF YOU PLAN TO DRIVE THIS LEG OF THE TRAIL, GIVE YOURSELF PLENTY OF TIME.

❧Val Verde Winery

www.texaswinetrails.com/val.htm

100 Qualia Drive
Del Rio, Texas 78840

Phone: (830) 775-9714

OPEN: MONDAY–SATURDAY
9:00 A.M.–5:00 P.M.

TOURS, TASTINGS, RETAIL SALES,
AND GIFT SHOP

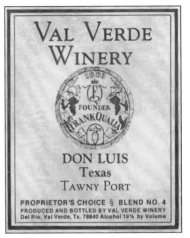

VAL VERDE
WINERY

1883

FOUNDER
FRANK QUALIA

DON LUIS
Texas
TAWNY PORT

PROPRIETOR'S CHOICE § BLEND NO. 4
PRODUCED AND BOTTLED BY VAL VERDE WINERY
Del Rio, Val Verde, Tx. 78840 Alcohol 19% by Volume

Tucked into this hot, dry corner of South Texas you will find an oasis called Del Rio, nicknamed Queen of the Rio Grande. Del Rio sits atop the cool, refreshing waters of the San Felipe Springs, which pours out over 90 million gallons of crystal clear water daily. When Frank Qualia purchased his land in Del Rio in 1882 to become a farmer, a number of Lenoir grapevines were already growing. The abundance of water and the obvious health of the grapevines prompted Frank to start his vineyard more than 100 years ago.

Val Verde Winery is the oldest in Texas, and the only one to survive Prohibition. Unlike most other winemakers, the Qualia family tended to their vineyard during Prohibition and used the grapes to produce jellies, sacramental wines, and also shipped grapes to cities such as Houston and Galveston for fruit consumption. Following the repeal of Prohibition, second-generation winemaker Louis Qualia planned the resumption of commercial winemaking and introduced the Herbemont grape to the vineyard for diversification and increased production.

Tom Qualia, third-generation winemaker, assumed care of the winery in 1973. Although he originally planned to become a

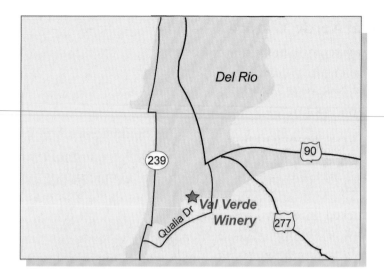

VAL VERDE WINERY

rancher, his love of winemaking and its place in family tradition made him totally dedicated to what his family had accomplished. After a concentrated effort to modernize and improve the facilities during the 1970s and 1980s, Val Verde still concentrates on the production of Lenoir and Herbemont grapes, which are well-suited to the environment. Tom replaced all but two of his father's original 2,350-gallon concrete tanks with new stainless-steel tanks. He continues his father's commitment to making "a few good bottles of wine."

THE WINES

Val Verde Winery produces an impressive selection of wines that includes Sauvignon Blanc, Muscat Canelli, Ruby Cabernet, Lenoir, and a newcomer—Ehrenfelser, a fruity white with a German heritage. Last, but perhaps the most well-known and most-awarded Val Verde wine is their exceptional Tawny Port Don Luis, produced in honor of Tom's father.

Val Verde produces approximately 3,000 cases of wine annually, and the majority of its sales is at the winery itself. A limited selection of its wine can be found around the state, particularly in the larger cities such as Austin, Houston, and Dallas/Ft. Worth.

ALONG THE TRAIL

The sun doesn't just set in this part of Texas, it crashes into the desert around you, as the evening sky goes from pale rose to blood red before being swallowed in inky blackness. The Pecos Trail travels through some of the most remote areas of Texas, where tumbleweed and sagebrush are king. On the west end of the trail, the McDonald Observatory sits majestically atop the Davis Mountains, while the lush beauty of the Amistad Reservior waits for you on the east end of the trail.

This is, of course, a trail for wine lovers, but it is also much more. It is a trail for reflection and contemplation. It is a journey that may show travelers something of themselves in addition to Texas wines. The wide-open spaces and the star-filled evenings are perfect for thinking about the past and considering the potential of the future. As the sun sinks behind the mountains, there is a moment, just before the stars invade the night, when time seems to stand still and everything is possible.

Just south of Fort Davis are the towns of Marfa and Alpine. Though only about twenty-six miles apart, these towns seem to be separated by half a century in time. Marfa is a town that has changed little over the years, and has become popular with artists and sculptors. By contrast, Alpine, which is on the route for tourists heading down to the Big Bend National Park, is a modern-day fast-food wonderland.

Leaving these towns behind, you pass Marathon on SH 90 and leave the last of the mountain ranges behind you, as you enter Hell's Half Acre—not exactly a popular resort acre. Keep plenty to drink on hand, gas up the car, and cruise for the Pecos River. The town of Langtry, which lies ahead of you, was home to Judge Roy Bean, known as the "Law West of the Pecos." Where the Pecos joins the Rio Grande River, the land changes from parched desert to lush greenery as you enter the Amistad National Recreation Area. The sleepy town of Del Rio lies just beyond the reservoir.

BED AND BREAKFAST
ALONG THE PALO DURO TRAIL

Canyon

COUNTRY HOME BED AND BREAKFAST AND MOM'S PLACE

Host: Tammy Money-Brooks, Rt. 1, Box 447, Canyon 79015, (800) 664-7636 or (806) 655-7636. 4 rooms, 3½ baths, 1 guest house, full breakfast, $–$$$, no pets, no smoking, MC, V, AE, D.

THE HUDSPETH HOUSE

Hosts: Mark and Mary Clark, 1905 4th Ave., Canyon 79015, (800) 655-9809, (806) 655-9800, fax (806) 655-7457. 8 guest rooms, 8 baths, full breakfast, $–$$$, MC, V, AE, D.

Lubbock

WOODROW HOUSE

Hosts: Dawn and David Fleming, 2629 19th St., Lubbock 79410, (806) 793-3330, fax (806) 793-7676. 7 guest rooms, 7 private baths, breakfast buffet, $$, children welcome, no pets, no smoking, MC, V, AE.

VIRGINIA'S BED AND BREAKFAST

Host: Virginia Baker, 310 Breckenridge, Albany 76430, (915) 762-2013. 3 guest rooms, 3 baths, 1 suite, 1 guest house, country or continental breakfast, $$, no pets, smoking, no alcohol, no credit cards.

RESTAURANTS
ALONG THE PALO DURO TRAIL

Canyon

COPE'S CONEY ISLAND

2201 Fourth Ave., Canyon, (806) 655-1184. Homestyle fried chicken, fried fish, club steak, homemade pies. Breakfast, lunch, and dinner Monday-Saturday. $.

Lubbock

COUNTY LINE

FM 2641 west of IH-27 N., Lubbock, (806) 763-6001. Barbecue. Bar, Texas wines, dinner daily. $–$$.

STUBB'S BAR-B-Q

620 Nineteenth St., Lubbock, (806) 747-4777. Barbecue. Bar, Texas wines, lunch and dinner daily. $.

BED AND BREAKFASTS
ALONG THE PECOS TRAIL

Alpine

HOLLAND HOTEL

Host: Carla McFarland, 209 W. Holland Ave., Alpine 79830, (915) 837-3844 or (800) 535-8040. 10 guest rooms, 10 baths, penthouse, continental plus breakfast OYO, children welcome, pets okay by prior arrangement, smoking in two guest rooms. $–$$, MC, V, AE.

THE CORNER HOUSE

Host: Jim Glendinning, 801 East Ave. E., Alpine 79830, (800) 585-7795 or (915) 837-7161, fax (915) 837-3638. 6 guest rooms, 4 private baths, 1 shared bath, country or continental breakfast, $, smoking only on porch, MC, V, AE, D.

THE WHITE HOUSE INN

Host: Anita Bradney, 2003 Fort Davis Hwy., Alpine 79830, (888) 774-7171 or (915) 837-1401, fax (915) 837-2197. 6 guest rooms, 6 baths, 1 guest house, gourmet breakfast, $$, children over 12 welcome, no pets, no smoking, MC, V, D.

Del Rio

THE 1890 HOUSE

Hosts: Alberto and Laura Galvan, 609 Griner Street, Del Rio 78840, (800) 282-1360 or (210) 775-8061, fax (210) 775-4667. 3 rooms, 1 suite, gourmet breakfast, $$–$$$$, no pets, MC, V.

Fort Davis

NEILL MUSEUM B&B

Host: Shirley Neill Vickers, P.O. Box 1034, Fort Davis 79734, (915) 426-3838 or (915) 426-3969. 2 rooms, 2 baths, continental breakfast OYO, $–$$$, no children, pets, or smoking, no credit cards.

THE VERANDA
COUNTRY INN

Hosts: Kathie and Paul Woods, 210 Court Avenue, Fort Davis 79734, (888) 383-2847. 3 guest rooms, 5 suites, 1 guest house, private baths, full breakfast, $–$$$$, no pets, no smoking, MC, V, D.

Marathon

CAPTAIN SHEPARD'S INN

Co-managers: Bill and Laurie Stevens, P.O. Box 46, Marathon 79842, (800) 884-4243. fax (915) 386-4510, 5 guest rooms, 6 baths, full breakfast, $$$, children welcome, but no pets, smoking in one sitting room, all credit cards.

RESTAURANTS ALONG
THE PECOS TRAIL

Alpine

CORNER HOUSE CAFÉ

801 E. Ave. E, Alpine, (915) 837-7161. Breakfast and lunch
Tuesday–Saturday. $.

LITTLE MEXICO CAFÉ

204 W. Murphy Ave., Alpine, (915) 837-2855. Mexican. Beer, lunch
and dinner Monday–Saturday. $.

PONDEROSA INN RESTAURANT

East Hwy. 90, Alpine, (915) 837-3321. American. Breakfast, lunch, and
dinner daily. $.

Del Rio

CRIPPLE CREEK SALOON

US 90 about one mile west of the "Y" with US 277/377, Del Rio,
(830) 775-0153. Steak and seafood. Bar, Texas wines, dinner
Monday–Saturday. $$.

MEMO'S

804 E. Losoya, Del Rio, (830) 775-8104. American and Tex-Mex. Bar,
lunch and dinner Monday–Saturday, dinner only Sunday. $–$$.

Fort Davis

BLACK BEAR RESTAURANT AT THE INDIAN LODGE

Davis Mountains State Park, 4 miles northwest of Fort Davis via
SH-118, Fort Davis, (915) 426-3254. American. Open daily. $.

THE DRUGSTORE RESTAURANT

At the Old Texas Inn, Fort Davis, (915) 426-3118. American and
Tex-Mex. Soda Fountain fare such as floats, malts, sundaes, and
phosphates. Breakfast and lunch, closed Wednesday. $.

HIGHWAY 118 CAFÉ

Hwy. 118 south of Fort Davis, (915) 426-3934. American and Tex-Mex. Open 6:30 A.M.–8:30 P.M. Tuesday–Sunday, closed 2:30 P.M.–5:30 P.M. $.

HOTEL LIMPIA DINING ROOM

Main Street at the Town Square, Fort Davis, (915) 426-3241. American. Bar, including Texas wines. In The Bandana Room bar ($3 membership fee for non-hotel guests required by state law in this "dry" county). Dinner daily, breakfast and lunch Saturday–Sunday. $–$$.

Marathon

GLASS MOUNTAIN BAR AND GRILL

Inside the Gage Hotel, Marathon, (915) 386-4205. Southwestern. Bar, Texas wines. Breakfast, lunch, and dinner daily. $–$$.

Chapter 6

FESTIVALS AND SPECIAL EVENTS

*W*hen Texans like something, they celebrate it in a big way, and their pride in Texas wines is no exception. Festivals and special events sponsored by wineries and organizations are held around the state throughout the year. As you plan your tours along the Texas wine trails, keep these events in mind. Every festival brings out the best of the food, music, and wine of each sponsoring locale. Many wine-related festivals are now annual events that are held about the same time each year, which makes it convenient to plan yearly trips. Individual winery events may change each year, so it is best to contact the wineries ahead of time. Some of the wineries will even place your name on their mailing list of upcoming events and new wine releases.

Listed below are the major wine-related festivals in Texas that are open to the public during the spring, summer, and fall seasons. It is worth noting that while wine events occur throughout the year, the months of April and October are particularly busy times for festivals, and festival-goers can enjoy some of the most colorful scenes in Texas during these months. April is bluebonnet time, when the roadsides are awash in violet blues and the orange hues of the Indian paintbrush blossoms. In October, fall colors sneak into Texas where you'd least expect them. The

◀ A VARIETAL WINE MUST CONTAIN **75** PERCENT BY VOLUME OF THE
GRAPE MENTIONED ON THE LABEL. (COURTESY OF THE TEXAS DEPARTMENT OF
AGRICULTURE)

days are sunny and comfortable and the evenings crisp and clear—perfect weather for attending the festivals.

SPRING EVENTS

Denison Arts and Wine Festival

Old Katy Depot in Denison, Texas
(817) 424-0570
March; call for dates

One of the newest wine festivals in Texas, this well-organized event drew large enthusiatic crowds at its premier. It is a celebration of Texas wine and the visual and musical arts of local artists around Denison. Bring the family to enjoy the live entertainment and food from local Denison restaurants.

Lubbock Cork and Fork Affair

Lubbock, Texas
(806) 742-3077
March; call for dates

Held in the Lubbock Memorial Civic Center, the Cork and Fork Affair is a wondrous mix of food and wine, with more than thirty restaurants and over a dozen Texas wineries offerings tastings of their products. For the price of the entry ticket (around $25), you get to eat and drink as much as you want. Besides the good food and wine, guests may enjoy live music and meet people from restaurants and wineries across the state. A sell-out each year, be sure to book ahead. Tickets are available at the door or from the Lubbock Chamber of Commerce.

Springfest, in Old Town Spring, Texas

Phone: (877) 978-9463
March; call for dates

Springfest is a two-day event in Old Town Spring, Texas, and is one of the largest wine festivals held in the Houston area. Activities include a Vintner Dinner, wine tasting booths around

Old Town Spring, and the popular Annual Media Choice Texas Wine Competition and Awards Ceremony.

Texas Hill Country Wine and Food Festival

Four Seasons Hotel, Austin
(512) 329-0770
April; call for dates

This festival is a must for adults who love sampling good wine and food in one of America's most elegant and charming hotels. The Four Seasons Hotel is the backdrop for this four-day event that includes wine-tasting sessions of both Texas and California wines, seminars and tastings of the creations of some of this country's finest chefs, and a fabulous dinner and dance. A particular favorite event of this festival is the Winemaker's Luncheon in which attendees select from one of five great Austin restaurants to break bread with winemakers. Each day is packed full of events and all are priced separately, so call for details.

New Vintage Festival

Grapevine, Texas
(800) 457-6338
April; call for dates

The newest releases of Texas wines are celebrated during this three-day event. The festival includes the traditional Blessing of the Vines ceremony, seminars on winemaking and on food and wine pairings, and the popular Taste and Toast of Texas during which the public tastes Texas wines in downtown Grapevine.

Texas Hill Country Wildflowers and Wine Trail

Participating Wineries in the Hill Country
(817) 424-0570
April; call for dates

It doesn't get any better than this—the beauty of wildflowers in the Hill Country and the enjoyment of delicious local wines. All the wineries along the Enchanted and Highland Wine Trails participate in this extremely popular event. The event features tours, tastings, food, music, and fun for all. For details of activities, contact the wineries along the Enchanted and Highland Wine Trails.

Texas Wine and Brew Festival

San Angelo, Texas
(915) 653-6793
April; call for dates

This weekend festival kicks off on Friday with a Gourmet Dinner, a six-course meal presented each year by a well-known Texas chef. Reservations are required and seating is limited, so be sure to call ahead. On Saturday morning, cooking classes are followed by the Wine, Brew, and Food Tasting, featuring Texas wineries, microbreweries, and more than a dozen of San Angelo's restaurants and caterers. Live music is also available. All events are priced separate, so call ahead for information.

Dallas Morning News Wine Awards

Fairmont Hotel
(214) 319-7000
May; call for dates

The public is invited to sample the wines from the wineries that participated in the Dallas Morning News Wine Competition which is held in March. Wineries from across the state are pouring their wines.

SUMMER EVENTS

Annual Kerrville Folk Festival

Kerrville, Texas
(800) 435-8429
May; call for dates

Enjoy great Texas music, food, and wine. Prices vary by events and weekends, so call for information.

Rockport Festival of Wines

Rockport, Texas

(512) 729-1271

June; call for dates

The picturesque town of Rockport on the Texas Gulf Coast is host to one of the most delightful wine festivals in the state. The Rockport Festival of Wines is a summer traveler's delight, offering generous tastings of Texas' finest wines and food from popular local restaurants. Plan on staying the weekend in this coastal resort town to enjoy the sights and sounds Rockport has to offer.

Pecos County Harvest Fest

Rooney Park, Ft. Stockton, Texas

(915) 336-2541

August; call for dates

This is a great festival and a great way to experience the hospitality of West Texas. This high energy festival includes a three-mile run, a bike tour to Ste. Genevieve Winery (and a winery tour), a huge car show, food and craft booths, and live music. At noon the Wine Emporium opens up featuring wines from numerous Texas wineries.

Annual Kerrville Wine and Music Festival

Kerrville, Texas

(800) 435-8429

Labor Day Weekend

This event features the best and newest works from Texas winemakers and more than two dozen Texas songwriters. Outdoor theaters host afternoon and evening concerts and food and wine stands are available throughout the festival. Prices vary and three-day passes are available. Bring lawn chairs and wear rugged clothing (jeans, boots, sun hats) for this primitive but beautiful setting.

FALL EVENTS

Grapefest

Grapevine, Texas
(800) 457-6338
September; call for dates

Grapefest is undoubtedly the biggest wine festival in Texas, with attendance at well over 100,000 folks during this three-day event. Downtown Grapevine is transformed into a huge carnival setting with rides for the kids, face painting, food, live music, and of course Texas wines. The People's Choice, an event in which the public gets to vote on the best wines, is a favorite part of this festival.

Annual Harvest Festival

Grapevine, Texas
(817) 424-0570
September; call for dates

Sponsored by the Texas Wine and Grape Growers Association, this festival brings together professionals from all facets of the Texas wine industry and provides opportunities to learn about grape growing and winemaking in the Lone Star state.

Uncorking Texas Wines Tasting

(817) 424-0570

This popular public food and wine event is usually held in conjunction with the Annual Harvest Festival. Call for additional information.

Fredericksburg Food and Wine Festival

Fredericksburg, Texas
(830) 997-7467
October; call for dates

Each year this determined community of 7,500 puts together an impressive collection of Texas wines, food, and entertainment. The admission price of $12 for adults includes five wine tastings and a souvenir wine glass. Inside the festival grounds are two large pavilions, a bandstand, picnic tables, and just a whole lot of fun. One pavilion houses more than a dozen Texas wineries offering samples of the best vintages, while the other pavilion contains dozens of exhibitors of Texas crafts and food. As you stroll between pavilions, enjoy the sounds of the Hill Country's performers playing blues, jazz, ethnic, and country tunes.

Festival attractions also include a grape stomp and the infamous Great Grape Toss, with an auction to top all auctions. The first evening of the festival a dinner with some of the vintners attending is held at one of the local restaurants and features Texas wines. The second day of the festival features a gourmet luncheon. Both of these special events are part of the festival patron program and include general admission to the festival. Tickets are usually available on a limited basis and sold in advance only.

Kristkindl Markt

Fredericksburg, Texas
(830) 997-8515
December weekend; call for dates

Soft carols, fresh-cut pine trees and booths stuffed full of Christmas ideas and gifts await shoppers attending this Christmas shopping festival each December. Held in downtown Fredericksburg's Martplatz, this event is an updated version of the seventeenth-century German Christmas market. Shoppers will be able to hear German music and other entertainment, enjoy Christmas lights, sample German foods, and enjoy tasting wine from the many wineries in the Fredericksburg area. A preview party is held on Friday evening and the tickets allow admittance to events throughout the weekend.

Chapter 7

COOKING WITH TEXAS WINES

*T*hese recipes feature one or more of the superb wines produced in the Lone Star State. All of them are my family and friends' favorites, and I hope they will also delight you and inspire you to create your own dishes using Texas wines. I've chosen a wide range of recipes including appetizers, salads, chicken, beef, and pasta entrées to let you experience a variety of delectable foods enhanced with the flavors of Texas wines.

None of these dishes are complicated, though some require an investment of considerable time, befitting my outlook on cooking. Cooking for family and friends is indeed an expression of love through the commitment of the cook's time. Over the years, I've come to understand that the most precious thing we can give one another is our time.

APPETIZERS

TEXAS CAVIAR

Preparation time: 2½ hours

This dish has been a huge success at parties over the last few years because it is easy to prepare and tasty to eat while standing around at a party. I can't recall one instance when the plate wasn't completely clean by the end of the evening.

There are numerous versions of this recipe around, but this one has a few twists.

	15-OUNCE CAN BLACK BEANS, RINSED AND DRAINED
3–4	OUNCES CAP*ROCK MUSCAT CANELLI
	4-OUNCE CAN RIPE OLIVES, DRAINED AND CHOPPED
1	MEDIUM ONION, FINELY CHOPPED
3	CLOVES GARLIC, CHOPPED
2	TABLESPOONS OLIVE OIL
3	TABLESPOONS OF LIME JUICE
3	HARD-BOILED EGGS
1	TOMATO, DICED IN SMALL PIECES
1	BOTTLE MILD PICANTE SAUCE
8	OUNCES CREAM CHEESE
	TORTILLA CHIPS OR CRACKERS

In a large bowl, soak the drained black beans in a few ounces of Cap*Rock Muscat Canelli for ½ hour. Drain and mix together with olives, onion, garlic, oil, lime juice, and a touch of black pepper, if you prefer. Cover and refrigerate for 2 hours, stirring occasionally.

Prepare the hard-boiled eggs, cool, and peel. Split only the white of the egg open and separate from the yoke. Set the yokes aside, chop the egg whites, and refrigerate both. Dice the fresh tomatoes and set aside. Remove the cream cheese from the refrigerator half an hour before using.

To serve, spread cream cheese on a plate and spoon bean mixture evenly over it. Place about a cup of diced tomatoes in the center of the plate forming a small mound. Surround the tomatoes with a ring of picante sauce, then surround the picante sauce with a ring of chopped egg whites, which should fill the plate nearly to the edge. Grate or finely chop two of the egg yokes and sprinkle around the plate. Place the third egg yoke in the center of the tomatoes. Serve immediately with tortilla chips or crackers. This appetizer goes well with whatever wine you like.

Cold Steak with Goat Cheese Sauce

Preparation time: 30 minutes

Serves: 4–6

This easy-to-make dish is quite versatile, working perfectly as an appetizer or served as a light, cool summer lunch item.

1	SMALL DIAMETER FRENCH BREAD, SLICED INTO ½″ THICK PIECES
2	DELMONICO OR RIBEYE STEAKS, TRIMMED
	FRESH BASIL LEAVES (WASHED)
	CILANTRO, CHOPPED (LEAVES ONLY)
5	OUNCES OF GOAT CHEESE
3	OUNCES OF MAYONNAISE
4	OUNCES OF HORSERADISH SAUCE
2	TEASPOONS OF LIME JUICE
1	TOMATO, CHOPPED
	PAPRIKA AND BLACK PEPPER AS GARNISH
3	CLOVES OF GARLIC, FINELY CHOPPED
6	OUNCES OF BALSAMIC VINEGAR
4	OUNCES OF PINOT NOIR (PHEASANT RIDGE WINERY OR MESSINA HOF WINE CELLARS)

1. After trimming excess fat, marinate steaks in balsamic vinegar and Texas Pinot Noir overnight.

2. The day of serving, pour a small amount of olive oil and the garlic in a skillet and brown. Add steaks and lightly brown on both sides, then add remainder of marinade, and cook steaks to desired level or until marinade is evaporated. Set steaks aside in the refrigerator until needed.

3. Goat Cheese Mix: In a bowl, mix together the goat cheese, mayonnaise, and horseradish sauce, then add lime juice and mix thoroughly. Refrigerate until needed.

Placed thinly sliced steak pieces (1–2 per) onto French bread in the center of a small plate and garnish with four basil leaves. Then add chopped tomatoes and cilantro before placing a dollop of the goat cheese sauce on the steak and bread. Finish the plate with a sprinkle of paprika and coarse black pepper for added color and serve.

Serve with a Texas Red Zinfandel

SALAD

MY SOON-TO-BE-FAMOUS FRESH BEET SALAD

Preparation time: 1½–2 hours

Serves: 6

I wish I could say I dreamed this one up but, in fact, this salad is an adaptation of one served to us at a vintner dinner in Texas. I've simplified it and added a splash of wine. For more fun, enjoy the optional Chardonnay tasting with this salad, which is included after this recipe.

1	BUNCH FRESH BEETS (4 BEETS PER BUNCH)
½	CUP DELANEY CHARDONNAY
½	RED BELL PEPPER
½	YELLOW BELL PEPPER
3	GREEN ONIONS
	CILANTRO
1	SMALL CAN CORN
1	FRESH CARROT
	OLIVE OIL
	BALSAMIC VINEGAR
	PARMESAN CHEESE

Remove stalks and boil the beets in salted water for 1 hour. Don't rush the process; the beets need at least 1 hour of boiling to become tender all the way through. Meanwhile, finely chop each bell pepper, but don't mix them together. Finely chop the green onions about halfway up the green portion of the stalk, and set aside. Tear off a small bunch (about 8–10 leaves) of cilantro, chop finely, and set aside. Drain juice from corn, place in a shallow bowl, pour in the Chardonnay, and set aside in the refrigerator. Pour yourself a glass of Chardonnay and relax while the beets finish cooking.

When the hour is up, remove the beets and let cool for five minutes, then peel. *Be careful; the beet juice will stain everything it touches.* Cut the beets into thin slices (about ⅛-inch thick, if you can), place on a large plate, pour two tablespoons balsamic vinegar over them, and set in the refrigerator to chill—a half hour should be sufficient.

Thirty minutes before dinner, arrange 3 to 4 beet slices on a salad plate. Drain the corn and sprinkle about 10–20 kernels on top of the beets—too much corn will overwhelm this small salad. Sprinkle some red and yellow pepper pieces around the plate, followed by the green onion and top off with just a little of the cilantro for color.

Finally, the carrot! Using a sharp knife, peel the carrot and scrape off shards onto a plate. Sprinkle these carrot shreds on the beets and along the perimeter of the plate. Using the respective bottle caps, pour one capful of olive oil over each salad, followed by two capfuls of balsamic vinegar. Sprinkle a little Parmesan cheese and place in the refrigerator until serving time, but don't let the salads remain in the refrigerator longer than 20 minutes.

Optional Wine Tasting

This beet salad goes especially well with a Chardonnay tasting. Try this if you have enough wineglasses; it always widens guests eyes as they enter the dinning room. Arrange three glasses in front of each place setting before your guests arrive. In advance, chill bottles of Delaney Chardonnay, Becker Chardonnay, and Pheasant Ridge Chardonnay. Before your guests are ready to be seated, cover each bottle for a blind tasting and pour a small amount of wine into their respective glasses. (Try to keep the order consistent from guest to guest; everyone gets confused when you switch the wines around.)

CEVICHE TOMAS

Preparation time: 60 minutes

Serves: 6

Rather than "cooking" the seafood in an acid-bath (lime juice and salt), I cook the fish and shrimp the old-fashioned way—with heat—and a little Texas wine of course. You chili-heads out there will notice that those spicy little peppers have been left out of this recipe, but they fit in quite nicely if you prefer that type of *heat*.

I should stress that freshness is critical for the success of this dish. Avoid frozen sea food and dried seasonings.

1	POUND OF WHITE FISH (FLOUNDER, WHITE, HALIBUT)
1	POUND OF 16-COUNT SHRIMP, UNPEELED
1	POUND OF CRABMEAT
4	TABLESPOONS OF CAPERS
4	OUNCES OF SPANISH OLIVES
2	STALKS OF CELERY-CHOPPED
1	RED (OR WHITE) ONION, CHOPPED
1	BUNCH OF CILANTRO, CHOPPED (LEAVES ONLY)
1 ½	CUPS OF LEMON JUICE
1 ½	CUPS OF LIME JUICE
½	CUP RED WINE VINEGAR
2	CUPS OF TEXAS CHENIN BLANC
1	TOMATO, CHOPPED

1. Before cooking the shrimp or fish, marinate as follows: *Fish:* chill in ½ cup of lemon and lime juice and ½ cup of Chenin Blanc wine for 30 minutes. *Shrimp:* marinate in ½ cup of red wine vinegar and ½ cup of Chenin Blanc wine for 30 minutes.

2. While these are marinating chop the celery, tomatoes, cilantro, onion, and olives; place in a large mixing bowl with

the remainder of the lemon juice, lime juice, and white wine; and chill.

3. *Cooking Shrimp:*
In a pot of boiling water add 1 teaspoon of garlic powder, a pinch of salt. and 2 tablespoons of Creole seasoning (Tony Chachere's™ or equivalent) and cook shrimp until pink. Drain, peel, de-vein, chop, and place into mixing bowl with marinating vegetables.

4. *Cooking Fish:*
Melt butter in a skillet, add a small amount of lemon juice, and cook fish without marinade. Remove from skillet and let cool before cutting into cubes.

Add fish, crabmeat, and capers to mixing bowl, stir until juices have covered all ingredients, then refrigerate until serving.

This Ceviche can be served as a formal appetizer or a casual buffet salad. For the appetizer style, place a scoop of Ceviche into a chilled martini glass and garnish with a slice of lime. To serve buffet style, offer the Ceviche with tortilla chips or crackers.

BEEF DISHES

CARNE GUISADA

Preparation time: 2½ hours

Serves: 6

This stewed (*guisada* is Spanish for stewed) beef dish is heavily influenced by the cooks of Mexico. Versions of this dish can be found in Tex-Mex and Mexican restaurants throughout Texas.

1	ROYAL CUT BEEF RUMP ROAST
2	TEASPOONS OLIVE OIL
2	CUPS WATER
2	MEDIUM POTATOES, PEELED AND CUT INTO 1-INCH PIECES
1	LARGE CAN PEELED TOMATOES

1	LARGE ONION, CHOPPED
4	CLOVES GARLIC, MINCED
6–10	BAY LEAVES
½	TEASPOON GROUND CLOVES
½	TEASPOON GROUND ALLSPICE
1	CUP BELL MOUNTAIN CABERNET SAUVIGNON
1	5-OUNCE BOTTLE SPANISH OLIVES
½	TEASPOON SALT AND PEPPER

Trim beef, cut into 1-inch cubes, and brown in olive oil. Season to taste with salt and pepper. Pour in water, add potatoes, bring to a boil, cover, and simmer for 1 hour. While the beef is cooking, liquefy the tomatoes and combine with onions, garlic, bay leaves, ground cloves, and allspice and combine in a separate saucepan. Bring to boil and simmer for 30 minutes. Combine this mixture with the beef and the Bell Mountain Cabernet Sauvignon. Cover and simmer for one hour.

Complete this dish by adding in Spanish olives and cook uncovered for another 30 to 60 minutes, or until the broth has reduced and thickened. Serve by spooning over rice or rolling in a tortilla with queso dip.

STEAK TOMAS

Preparation time: 3–4 hours

Serves: 6

The preparation time might seem a bit much to many of you, but trust me, it's worth it. This delicious dish, slow cooked in a broth and wine sauce results in a steak that melts in your mouth. It is best served with rosemary potatoes or cilantro spiced rice and a crispy steamed vegetable. Steak Tomas requires simple presentation, lots of laughter, and plenty of Messina Hof Wine Cellars Reserve Merlot.

4–5	DELMONICO STEAKS
2–3	TABLESPOON OLIVE OIL
1	CLOVE GARLIC, THINLY SLICED

3	OUNCES STE. GENEVIEVE WHITE ZINFANDEL
1½	CANS BEEF BROTH
3	OUNCES MESSINA HOF MERLOT
12	PEARL ONIONS, PEELED AND LEFT WHOLE

Topping

1	MEDIUM ONION, CHOPPED
	OLIVE OIL
1	RED BELL PEPPER, SEEDED AND THINLY SLICED LENGTHWISE
1	YELLOW BELL PEPPER, SEEDED AND THINLY SLICED LENGTHWISE
1	CLOVE GARLIC, SLICED
¼	CUP MARGARINE
1	OUNCE MESSINA HOF MERLOT
8–10	SPANISH OLIVES (WITH PIMENTOS), SLICED
	CILANTRO

Begin by trimming the excess fat off the steaks. Delmonico steaks have enough marbling to provide sufficient flavor. Heat a few tablespoons of olive oil in a frying pan and brown the steaks on each side. Reduce the heat and toss in sliced garlic to brown. Pour in White Zinfandel, cover, and let simmer until the wine has been reduced by half.

Pour in 1 can of beef broth, cover, and let simmer on low for one hour. Pour in another ½ can of beef broth and Merlot. Cover and let simmer for 90 minutes. If the stock reduces too quickly add in a little broth or White Zinfandel. The remainder of the bottle of Merlot is to be sipped by the cook during the rest of the preparation.

In the final hour, things get busy as you finish the steak and prepare the topping. Place the pearl onions in the pan. If there seems to be too much stock, leave the cover off to allow some reduction; otherwise, cover and simmer for 30 minutes. Use this time to prepare the steak topping.

Steak Topping

In a small saucepan, heat a few teaspoons of olive oil, stir in the chopped onion, bell peppers, and sliced garlic. Cover and simmer on low heat for ten minutes. Add margarine and Merlot and continue to simmer for 20 minutes.

Uncover the steak and add the sliced olives along with three or four cilantro leaves. Increase the heat to bring the stock to a low boil and reduce to thicken it. When the stock has cooked down to one-fourth of the volume, turn the heat to low—you're done! The steak can be served immediately or covered and kept warm until needed.

To serve, place the steak and sauce in a large serving platter and spoon the onion and pepper topping onto the steaks. Messina Hof Merlot will go very nicely with this dish. For the more adventurous, try serving this dish with a tasting of Cabernet Sauvignon from Messina Hof Wine Cellar, Llano Estacado Winery, and Blue Mountain Vineyards.

CHICKEN DISHES

GINGER CHICKEN

Preparation time: 1½ hours

Serves: 4

2–3	POUNDS BONELESS CHICKEN BREASTS
	OLIVE OIL
½	CUP CHICKEN BROTH
1	MEDIUM ONION, FINELY CHOPPED
2	CLOVES GARLIC
1	CUP STE. GENEVIEVE WHITE ZINFANDEL
1	CUP GRAPE CREEK CUVEE BLANC
½	TEASPOON LIME JUICE
2	TABLESPOONS MINCED GINGER
½	STICK MARGARINE
	SALT AND PEPPER, TO TASTE

Slice the chicken breasts lengthwise into ½-thick strips and brown in olive oil. Add chicken broth, onion, garlic, and White Zinfandel. Cover and simmer for 30 minutes. Uncover and add Cuvee Blanc and lime juice. Increase heat and reduce stock to half. Sip on the remaining Cuvee Blanc while watching the stock.

Lower the heat, add the minced ginger along with margarine, and simmer until the remaining stock has thickened and reduced down to just covering the bottom of the pan. If by chance, you've reduced the stock too far, add in a little more White Zinfandel and simmer again. Serve with rice and spoon reduced stock onto chicken. If you cannot find Grape Creek Cuvee Blanc, look for a Texas Chenin Blanc at your local stores.

Stuffed Chicken Breast

Preparation time: 1½ hours
Serves: 4

This easy-to-make dish goes well with either an alfredo-type sauce or a spaghetti sauce (see end of this chapter for my recipe).

2–3	POUNDS BONELESS CHICKEN BREASTS
1–2	CUPS CAP*ROCK CABERNET ROYALE
8	OUNCES SHREDDED MOZZARELLA CHEESE (SEE INSTRUCTIONS)
½	CUP PARMESAN CHEESE
1	EGG
	GARLIC POWDER, TO TASTE
	OLIVE OIL
	MARGARINE
	SALT AND PEPPER, TO TASTE

Trim chicken breasts, flatten, cover with wax paper, and beat with a meat mallet to thin. Place the chicken in a shallow dish. Cover with Cabernet Royale and refrigerate for 30 minutes.

Before using the mozzarella cheese, empty the package onto a chopping surface and finely chop the shredded cheese. I've found this helpful when rolling the mixture into the chicken. Combine the mozzarella and Parmesan cheese with egg and a pinch of garlic powder, mixing together thoroughly.

Remove and drain the chicken breasts, lay flat, and place 1 or 2 tablespoons (use your discretion based on the size of the chicken breast) of the cheese mix on each, carefully rolling the chicken around the cheese. I usually use toothpicks to hold the chicken roll together while baking. Place the chicken in a casserole dish. Brush a thin coat of olive oil on each, sprinkle with a pinch of salt and pepper, cover, and bake for 30 minutes at 350°. Uncover the chicken, place a pad of margarine on top of each chicken roll and bake until browned.

Serve this chicken as it is or with an alfredo or spaghetti sauce poured over it. I recommend either Cap*Rock Chardonnay, Hill Country Cellars Sauvignon Blanc, or Messina Hof's Chenin Blanc to accompany this dish.

TUESDAY'S CHICKEN

Preparation time: 1½ hours

Serves: 4

1	PACKAGE OF BONELESS CHICKEN BREASTS (4 BREASTS), TRIMMED
1	CUP OF CHICKEN BROTH
1	CUP OF VEGETABLE BROTH
2	TEASPOONS OF MINCED GARLIC
2	SHALLOTS, THINLY SLICED
2	TABLESPOONS OF CAPERS
3	STALKS OF FRESH ROSEMARY
1	CUP OF PHEASANT RIDGE CHARDONNAY
1	TEASPOON OF LEMON JUICE
½	STICK OF BUTTER
	SALT AND PEPPER TO TASTE
	ALL-PURPOSE FLOUR FOR DREDGING

Spread flour onto a large plate, add salt, pepper if desired, and dredge chicken breasts, shaking off excess flour.

In a large skillet, pour in chicken broth; add chicken breasts, salt, and pepper; and cover and simmer over medium heat for 30 minutes. Then add wine and half of the vegetable broth, cover, and continue to simmer for another 30 minutes.

Uncover skillet and simmer over high heat, adding a thin pad of butter on top of each chicken breast and four pads of butter into the remaining broth. Add rosemary and lemon juice, and continue to simmer until broth volume is reduced by half and starts to brown slightly.

Melt remaining butter in a small saucepan over low heat. Add shallots and simmer until softened, then add capers and simmer for three additional minutes.

To serve, arrange chicken breast on a plate with saffron rice and rosemary baby corn, spooning some of the reduced broth over the chicken. Top each chicken serving with a spoonful of the shallot-caper sauce.

FISH DISHES

CRABMEAT-TOPPED SALMON FILLET

Preparation time: salmon: 5–10 minutes; crabmeat topping: 30 minutes

Serves: 6

Salmon is delicious all by itself, but with this rich crabmeat topping, it is incredible. Use fresh salmon and real crabmeat for the best results.

2	POUNDS SALMON FILLETS
	GARLIC POWDER, TO TASTE
	WHITE PEPPER, TO TASTE
2	CUPS FALL CREEK CHARDONNAY
	LEMON AND DILL SAUCE (FROM YOUR LOCAL GROCER)
½	LEMON, CUT INTO WEDGES
1	TABLESPOON LEMON JUICE

Topping:

2	TABLESPOONS BUTTER
4–5	GREEN ONIONS
2	TABLESPOONS FLOUR

½   CUP HALF AND HALF

    SALT AND PEPPER, TO TASTE

¼   TEASPOON TABASCO SAUCE

¼   TEASPON GARLIC POWDER

¼   CUP LLANO ESTACADO SIGNATURE WHITE
    WINE

1   POUND CRABMEAT

4   OUNCES AMERICAN CHEESE, GRATED

3   OUNCES SWISS CHEESE, GRATED

Place salmon in aluminum foil inside a casserole dish. Add garlic powder, white pepper, and Chardonnay, and coat fillets with a thick layer of Lemon and Dill Sauce. Place two lemon wedges and lemon juice in the pan, cover, and bake for 8–11 minutes at 425° (or use a foil dish and cook on an outside grill). Just before serving, spoon crabmeat topping onto fillets.

Crabmeat Topping

Saute green onions in butter until tender. Add flour, stirring to prevent lumping, then add half and half, salt, pepper, Tabasco sauce, garlic powder, and wine and let simmer for five minutes. Add crabmeat and both cheeses, stirring constantly to prevent lumping or burning. Simmer on low heat for five minutes. Serve immediately on fillets. This dish is complemented by Fall Creek Cascade or Grape Creek Fumé Blanc.

SHRIMP-TO-DIE-FOR

Preparation time: 10–15 minutes

Serves: 6

To be honest, this recipe is my wife's creation, inspired from the time she spent in Louisiana. Although the instructions include steps for baking in an oven, she almost always prepares this on an outside grill. I try to stay away from outdoor grills; everything seems to develop a nice charcoal crust when I cook that way.

½   STICK LOW-FAT MARGARINE

GARLIC POWDER, TO TASTE

WHITE PEPPER, TO TASTE

½   CUP LEMON JUICE

2   POUNDS CLEANED AND DEVEINED SHRIMP

½   CUP STE. GENEVIEVE WHITE ZINFANDEL

Melt the margarine in a baking dish and stir in the garlic powder, pepper, and lemon juice and simmer for five minutes. Toss in the shrimp, pour in the White Zinfandel, and bake for 8 minutes on 375°. If you are cooking on the grill, wrap all ingredients in aluminum foil, place onto an aluminum tin, and grill until the shrimps turn pink. Serve as an appetizer or over rice with Spicewood Sauvignon Blanc.

PORK DISHES

PORK TENDERLOIN ROLL-UP

Preparation Time: 2–3 hours

Serves: 4–6

This unusual combination of pork and pesto gives this dish an unusual zesty flavor. Since the ingredients already contain plenty of salt, be cautious before adding more.

1   MEDIUM UNSEASONED TENDERLOIN

7   OUNCE CONTAINER OF PESTO SAUCE

3   OUNCES OF FRENCH'S MUSTARD

3   OUNCES OF HORSERADISH SAUCE

GARLIC POWDER

BASIL

BREAD CRUMBS

OLIVE OIL

1   OUNCE LIME JUICE

1   BOTTLE OF A TEXAS RIESLING

Marinate the tenderloin by placing in a shallow pan, and pour in 6 ounces of Texas Riesling and 1 ounce of lime juice. Place in refrigerator for approximately 2 hours before preparing.

Mustard Sauce:

Mix the mustard, horseradish sauce, olive oil, and bread crumbs in a bowl and set aside.

Tenderloin:

Cutting the round tenderloin into a flat sheet can be tricky, so if you don't master it the first time, hang in there; it took me a few times to get it right. Using a sharp knife, make a shallow (about 3/8'' deep) cut down the length of the tenderloin. This will start our "peeling process," which should result in a flat tenderloin roughly 10 to 12 inches long, depending on the size you buy.

Begin to cut sideways to the left, using the 3/8'' cut as a guide until you have gone 2 to 3 times around the tenderloin, as it unrolls and flattens out. Then spoon a thin layer of pesto sauce onto the tenderloin, add a pinch of garlic powder, and roll up the tenderloin. Place in an oiled baking pan and coat the outside of the tenderloin with the mustard sauce you have prepared in advance. Cook at 350° F for roughly 2 hours or until tender.

Let cool, slice, and serve. We like to accompany this dish with a potato–carrot sidedish. The potatoes are peeled and cut into thin slices; the carrots are left unpeeled and sliced. Place vegetables into a deep sauce pan and add 1 can of vegetable broth, a splash of Sherry, and one chopped clove of garlic, and cook on low heat until the vegetables are tender.

PASTA DISHES

PASTA TUSCANY

Preparation time: 2 hours

Serves: 6

This hearty pasta dish could serve as a meal on its own, but it goes well with meat or chicken entrées. While the ingredients simmer, the house is filled with a wonderfully unique aroma that'll make everyone's stomach growl.

1	MEDIUM ONION, DICED
2	GARLIC CLOVES, MINCED
2	SPRIGS FRESH ROSEMARY, FINELY CHOPPED
¼	CUP PARSLEY
1	CELERY STALK, DICED
	CARROTS, DICED
3	TABLESPOONS BUTTER
4	OUNCES GROUND BEEF
4	OUNCES GROUND PORK
2	LINKS SWEET ITALIAN SAUSAGE OR 4 OUNCES GROUND SAUSAGE, IF AVAILABLE
1	CUP BECKER CHARDONNAY
¼	CUP FLOUR
1	28-OUNCE CAN WHOLE TOMATOES (PUREE IN ADVANCE)
2	CUPS WATER
1	CHICKEN BULLION CUBE
1	SMALL CAN GREEN PEAS
1	POUND GREEN AND WHITE FETTUCINI
2	TABLESPOONS OLIVE OIL
¼	CUP PARMESAN CHEESE

Combine the onion, garlic, rosemary, parsley, celery, and carrots in a large saucepan with butter and simmer to soften. Mince the beef, pork, and Italian sausage and add to the vegetables and brown slightly. Pour in Chardonnay and allow to simmer for 10 minutes. Sprinkle in flour, stirring to prevent clumping.

Add the tomatoes, water, and crumbled bullion cube. Bring to boil, reduce to a simmer, cover, and cook for 1½ hours. Stir occasionally and add water if necessary. Add the peas 15 minutes before the ingredients have been completely cooked.

Cook and drain the pasta, add in two tablespoons of olive oil, then mix in the other ingredients. Sprinkle the Parmesan cheese on top of the completed dish. This dish goes well with either the Becker Chardonnay or Pheasant Ridge Pinot Noir.

MAKE-BELIEVE GOULASH

Preparation time: 30–40 minutes

Serves: 4

There were few, if any, Hungarian families living in my childhood neighborhood. In an effort to keep four children with voracious appetites fed on a small budget, my mother created what she called "goulash." To us, it sounded exotic and tasted great; to her, it was inexpensive and filling. Now I'm making it for my son.

This is a great dish for the kids or for those evenings when you don't have the energy to prepare a big meal or go out for one. It is easy, fast, and delicious and also tastes just as good after a night in the refrigerator.

1–1½	POUNDS GROUND BEEF
1	SMALL ONION, FINELY CHOPPED
1	CLOVE GARLIC, SLICED
2	CANS TOMATO SOUP
2	SOUP CANS WATER
¼	TEASPOON OREGANO
1	CUP LA BUENA VIDA MERLOT L'ELEGANCE
1	POUND MEDIUM SHELLS OR ELBOW MACARONI
	OLIVE OIL
	SALT AND PEPPER, TO TASTE

Brown the beef with the onion and sliced garlic. Thoroughly mix the tomato soup with water in a bowl, then add to the meat. Sprinkle in the oregano, pour in the Merlot L'Elegance, and allow to simmer for 20 minutes. The wonderful aroma coming from this dish is best enjoyed with a glass of Merlot L'Elegance.

Meanwhile, in a pan of water to which you've added salt and olive oil, boil the pasta *al dente,* drain, and set aside. When the 20 minutes are up, stir in handfuls of the pasta, until there is a good balance between the mixture and the pasta. Add a pinch of salt and pepper, stir, and let simmer for 5 minutes. Serve with the Merlot L'Elegance.

LA PASTA

Preparation time: 15-20 minutes

Serves: 6

This light dish can be served as a hot side dish or a cold pasta salad.

2	TABLESPOONS MARGARINE
¼	CUP OLIVE OIL
1	POUND ANGEL HAIR PASTA
6	CLOVES GARLIC, MINCED
½	CUP CAP*ROCK DIAMOND ROYALE (SAUVIGNON BLANC)
¼	CUP LEMON JUICE
¼	CUP LIME JUICE
	SALT AND PEPPER, TO TASTE
¼	CUP PARMESAN CHEESE
¼	CUP CHOPPED PARSLEY

Combine the margarine, olive oil, and garlic in a saucepan and cook for 1 minute. Add the Diamond Royale, lemon juice, lime juice, and salt and pepper. Bring to a boil, then pour over the angel hair pasta, toss, sprinkle with Parmesan cheese, and serve immediately.

STUFFED SHELLS

Preparation time: 2 hours

Serves: 6–8

Cheese-stuffed pasta is a weakness of mine. Never mind the pasta shape: shells, manicotti, or lasagna. If it has cheese inside, it's mine. Today this dish can be prepared the traditional way or a heart-healthy way. The two main cheeses used here are now available in a low-fat version.

1	PACKAGE LARGE SHELLS
	OLIVE OIL

SALT

1   POUND RICOTTA CHEESE

12   OUNCES MOZZARELLA CHEESE

½   CUP PARMESAN CHEESE

1   EGG

1   TABLESPOON OREGANO

1   TEASPOON BASIL

1   TEASPOON GARLIC POWDER

¼   CUP HOMESTEAD MUSCAT CANELLI

SPAGHETTI SAUCE (SEE FOLLOWING RECIPE)

Boil pasta in water containing olive oil and salt. When shells are done, rinse and set aside. Combine the ricotta, mozzarella, and Parmesan cheese with egg and stir in the oregano, basil, and garlic powder. Slowly pour in the Muscat Canelli, stirring constantly. Chill in the refrigerator for about 20 minutes.

Select only the unbroken pasta for stuffing, setting aside the broken ones for later. Using a spoon (or your fingers like I do), fill each shell to the top with the cheese mixture and place in a casserole containing a thin layer of spaghetti sauce. Top the shells with a small amount of sauce and sprinkle on some Parmesan cheese for presentation. Cover and bake for 30 minutes at 350°.

The broken pasta can be used to hold off famished children who just can't wait for dinner to be ready. Break the pasta into smaller pieces in a small casserole dish. Pour a spoonful or two of spaghetti sauce on top, sprinkle with Parmesan cheese, and heat for a few minutes.

Try serving this dish with Cabernet Sauvignon, or for something different, a Pinot Noir from Pheasant Ridge.

MY SECRET SPAGHETTI SAUCE

Preparation time: 6 hours

Serves: lots of folks for days and days

This spaghetti sauce is a combination of ingredients from at least four different recipes I've enjoyed over the years. The resulting sauce is thick and mildly sweet, despite the addition of

Italian sausage. For variety, I sometimes add ¼ pound of ground beef to create a meat sauce. What I like about this sauce is that it never tastes exactly the same each time I make it, but it's always delicious.

3	**28-OUNCE CANS WHOLE TOMATOES, PUREED**
3	**28-OUNCE CANS TOMATO SAUCE**
1	**12-OUNCE CAN TOMATO PASTE**
1	**TEASPOON GARLIC POWDER**
1	**TABLESPOON OREGANO**
1	**TABLESPOON BASIL**
2–3	**TABLESPOONS SUGAR**
5–6	**LINKS SWEET (MILD) ITALIAN SAUSAGE**
4–5	**LARGE CLOVES GARLIC, CHOPPED**
	OLIVE OIL
1	**LARGE ONION, CHOPPED**
1	**YELLOW BELL PEPPER, CHOPPED**
1	**RED BELL PEPPER, CHOPPED**
2	**CUPS MESSINA HOF MERLOT**
1	**CUP MESSINA HOF OR VAL VERDE PORT**
	SALT, TO TASTE

Puree the whole tomatoes and combine them in a large pot with the tomato sauce and tomato paste, mixing thoroughly. Stir in garlic powder, oregano, basil, and 2 tablespoons of sugar. Heat until almost boiling, cover, and simmer on low heat for 2 hours. If you are cooking on an electric range, place a spacer between the pot and the stove element to prevent the sauce from burning.

In the meantime, sear the Italian sausage links and 1 clove garlic in olive oil. Simmer on low heat for 15 minutes and set aside, leaving the juices in the pan. Using these juices, add in the remaining garlic cloves, chopped onion, red and yellow bell peppers, and a cup of Merlot. Simmer to slightly soften the vegetables. We're only going to use two cups of Merlot in the sauce. The rest of the bottle is for the cook, so pour yourself a glass and relax for a while.

Next, add the vegetables, Port and Italian sausage to the sauce. Cover and simmer for 2 hours, stirring occasionally. During this period sample the sauce for taste. If desired, add a few pinches of salt. When 2 hours are up, pour in the last cup of Merlot, stir, and sample the sauce. Depending on the taste, you may want to add a bit more oregano and a pinch more sugar. Leave uncovered and simmer for two final hours, stirring often. The sauce can be served immediately, though it tastes even better the next day.

My "Can-I-Have-Some-More-Please" Sausage, Onions, and Peppers

Since it's not necessary to keep all five links of Italian sausage in the previous Spaghetti Sauce recipe, after cooking is complete, you can use a few of them to make a tasty side dish that always disappears when I serve it.

When I visit my Italian friends on New Year's Eve, the family always sits down at midnight to share a plate of sausage, peppers, and onions. The original recipe combined all three in a saucepan with olive oil, garlic, and a pinch of salt—a simple, delicious dish. My version includes some spaghetti sauce for a little extra flavor.

3–4	ITALIAN SAUSAGE LINKS, COOKED IN THE SPAGHETTI SAUCE AND SLICED LENGTHWISE
2	CLOVES GARLIC, CHOPPED
	OLIVE OIL
1	LARGE ONION, SLICED
1	RED BELL PEPPER, SEEDED AND SLICED LENGTHWISE INTO THIN STRIPS
1	YELLOW BELL PEPPER, SEEDED AND SLICED LENGTHWISE INTO THIN STRIPS
½	CUP STE. GENEVIEVE WHITE ZINFANDEL
1–2	CUPS SPAGHETTI SAUCE

In a saucepan, brown the sliced sausage links and garlic cloves in olive oil. Reduce heat, stir in the onion, bell peppers, and White Zinfandel, cover, and simmer for 15 minutes. Pour in the spaghetti sauce, cover again, and simmer for 20 minutes on low heat. Serve immediately as a side dish.

Chapter 8

TEXAS WINES IN THE NEW MILLENNIUM

*W*hat's the future for the wine industry in the Lone Star State? Is it all just a fluke? Will Texas wines continue to garner national and international awards, or fizzle in the new millennium? Will favorable legislation be drafted to allow Texas to compete on an equal footing with other wine producing states? What have we learned about making wine in Texas?

Many in the industry are asking themselves these same questions. At the dawn of the tweny-first century, vineyard owners and winemakers hold a vision based on twenty years of learning, hardships, and breakthroughs. Folks in the industry have learned that what works in California will not necessarily work in Texas. Texas vintners do not, of course, have to start from scratch; many of the techniques and ideas about vineyard production and winemaking are sound. Rather they must learn the proper implementation of these techniques and ideas for Texas conditions, and that has proved to be tricky.

We've also learned that Texas can indeed produce world-class wines on a consistent basis. The vinifera grape (a grape derived from the common European grape) will, in fact, thrive here. Vineyard managers are slowly learning what grapes will survive where in Texas' numerous microclimates. What works in one area of West Texas may not work fifty or one hundred miles away, even though conditions appear to be basically the same.

When we asked Tim Dodd, director of the Texas Wine Marketing Research Institute, what he thought about the future of the industry, he said Texas wines have an enormous potential. He feels that the industry as a whole has to move a notch up, to be competitive within Texas and without. One thing is for certain, Tim stressed, "we need more vineyards." We also need to make the vineyards we have more productive and profitable for the growers in order to encourage increased acreage.

When we visited with Tim for this second edition, he had this to add: "During the last two years of the 1990s, the situation with the industry has stabilized, and there is continued optimism about the industry's steady development. We have several well-established wineries with statewide distribution, well-recognized brands, and a solid financial base to further expand. A number of smaller wineries have specialized in producing premium products and often have a strong following in their local area. Many of these wineries focus on tourists and do an excellent job of exposing people to our industry.

"Those involved in making Texas wines and in the promotion of those wines have a number of challenges that must be overcome in the next few years. While there is a solid core of consumers who have developed a loyal following for Texas wines, too many other Texans have been unwilling to try local wines. These attitudes need to change if we can gain the growth that those in the industry desire. The future of the industry is bright, but we will need to continue to learn more about what viticulture and oenology practices we need to use in this state. As consumers continue to search for new varietals and styles of wine from different regions, the Texas industry is well positioned to succeed in the market."

Programs underway such as the campaign to research and conquer Pierce's disease and the Department of Agriculture's Vintage Texas program to market Texas wines lay a solid framework for solving problems and increasing awareness of Texas wine beyond the state.

WEB RESOURCES

TEXAS WINERIES AND ORGANIZATIONS

Alamosa Wine Cellars	www.alamosawinecellars.com
Becker Vineyards	www.beckervineyards.com
Bell Mountain Vineyards	www.bellmountainwine.com
Blue Mountain Vineyards	www.texaswinetrails.com/blue.htm
Bruno & George Wines, Inc	www.texaswinetrails.com/bruno.htm
Brushy Creek Vineyards	www.brushycreekvineyards.com
Cana Cellars	www.texaswinetrails.com/cana.htm
Cap*Rock Winery	www.caprockwinery.com
Chisholm Trail Winery	www.chisholmtrailwinery.com
Comfort Cellars Winery	www.texaswinetrails.com/comfort.htm
Cross Roads Vineyards	www.crossroadsvineyards.com
Cross Timbers Winery	www.crosstimberswinery.com
Delaney Vineyards	www.delaneyvineyards.com
Dry Comal Creek Vineyards	www.drycomalcreek.com
Fall Creek Vineyards	www.fcv.com
Flat Creek Estate	www.flatcreekestate.com
Fredericksburg Winery	www.fbgwinery.com
Grape Creek Vineyards	www.grapecreek.com
Haak Vineyards	www.haakwine.com
Hidden Springs Winery	www.hiddenspringswinery.com
Homestead Winery	www.homesteadwineries.com
Kiepersol Estate Vineyards	www.kiepersol.com
La Bodega Winery	www.texaswinetrails.com/bodega.htm
La Buena Vida Vineyards	www.labuenavida.com
Llano Estacado Winery	www.llanowine.com
Lone Oak Vineyards	www.texaswinetrails.com/lone.htm

McReynolds Wines	www.mcreynoldswines.com
Messina Hof Wine Cellars	www.messinahof.com
Pheasant Ridge Winery	www.pheasantridgewinery.com
Pillar Bluff Vineyards	www.pillarbluff.com
Piney Woods Country Wines	www.texaswinetrails.com/piney.htm
Pleasant Hill Winery	www.pleasanthillwinery.com
Poteet Country Winery	www.poteetwine.com
Red River Winery	www.redriverwinery.com
Sister Creek Vineyards	www.sistercreekvineyards.com
Spicewood Vineyards	www.spicewoodvineyards.com
Ste. Genevieve Wines	www.texaswinetrails.com/gen.htm
Texas Hills Vineyard	www.texashillsvineyard.com
Val Verde Winery	www.texaswinetrails.com/val.htm
Wimberley Valley Winery	www.wimberleyvalleywinery.com
Woodrose Winery & Retreat	www.woodrosewinery.com

Texas Wine and Grape Growers Association	www.twgga.org
Texas Wine Marketing Research Institute	www.hs.ttu.edu/TEXASWINE/default.asp

TEXAS TRAVEL INFORMATION SITES

Texas Mileage Guide	www.window.state.tx.us/comptrol/texastra.html
Texas Parks & Wildlife	www.tpwd.state.tx.us/
Texas Road Conditions	www.dot.state.tx.us/hcr/main.htm
Texas Weather	www.weather.com/weather/us/states/Texas.html
	www.wxusa.com/TX/
Travel Texas	www.traveltx.com
Info Texas	www.infotexas.com
Touring Texas	www.touringtexas.com/index.htm
Texas Wine & Food Festival	www.texaswineandfood.org
Grapefest	www.tourtexas.com/grapevine/gpvevents.htm
Gruene, Texas	www.gruene.net
Fredericksburg, Texas	www.fredericksburg-texas.com
Luckenbach, Texas	www.luckenbachtexas.com

GLOSSARY

APPELLATION. A United States viticultural district defined as a grape-growing region that has geographic features that make it distinct from other nearby areas.

AROMA. The smells coming from the grape itself rather than the aging process.

BALANCED. When all aspects of a wine come together, no individual feature of the wine stands out.

BIG. A term used to describe a high degree of flavor and body of a wine.

BOUQUET. The scent that wine develops from aging in the bottle.

BOUTIQUE WINERY. A term used to describe a small winery producing quality wines.

BRIX. A density unit based on grams of sucrose per 100 grams of solution. Used for classifying Late Harvest wines.

BUTTERY. A taste that is reminiscent of butter; usually associated with white wines.

CABERNET FRANC. A cousin of Cabernet Sauvignon. The juice of this red grape is usually blended with Cabernet Sauvignon and Merlot. Cabernet Franc lacks the tannin and acidity of its cousin, and produces a softer, lighter colored wine.

CABERNET SAUVIGNON. The most famous red grape in the world, it is planted in every country with enough sun to ripen it. Often referred to as simply "Cab," the grape produces a dark tannic juice that is beautifully enhanced by the vanilla and buttery spices it draws from oak barrels during aging. The young Cab is often harsh, but has an excellent capacity to mature in the bottle.

CALIFORNIA STYLE. From one perspective, the California style is no style, in that, as a young wine region, California is still looking for its own signature style. From another perspective, the California style refers to the modern wine technologies developed in the twentieth century and the experimental nature of the industry.

CHARDONNAY. This green-skinned grape is considered the finest grape variety in the world. In France it is usually blended with Pinot Noir to produce Champagne. Champagne made from 100 percent Chardonnay is referred to as *Blanc de Blanc*. Popular as its own varietal in the United States, this wine benefits more than any other white wine from oak aging. It produces an aroma of figs and apples, an it exhibits a buttery flavor from the oak and malolactic fermentation.

CHENIN BLANC. This green-skinned grape is known for predictable quality. It produces long-lived wines that mature to a marvelous sweetness.

COMPLEX. A wine that imparts many levels of flavor on the palate.

DRY COUNTY. An area in Texas that partially restricts or completely prohibits the sale of alcoholic beverages.

DRY WINE. A dry wine seems to have no sweetness. The yeast in the wine has consumed all the sugar, converting it into alcohol.

ELEGANT. A flavor of wine that is not aggressive to the taste; often used to describe lighter wines.

ENOLOGIST (Oenologist). One who practices the science of viticulture and winemaking.

EUROPEAN STYLE. Best summarized by the word "tradition," it embraces the winemaking techniques that have been used for centuries in Europe. Unlike California winemakers, their European counterparts lack the freedom to experiment with blends of new types of wine. Such actions are prohibited by some European wine control laws.

FAVORITE. Believed to be a cross between the Black Spanish and Herbemont grapes. It is less acidic than the Black Spanish and produces a beautiful dark purple juice. Because of its disease resistance, it holds great promise in south and southeast Texas, with potential for producing a great blush wine.

FINED. A wine that has undergone the fining process.

FINING. The addition of albumen-type substances (i.e., egg whites) to the surface of wine which then descend slowly through the wine taking any solid matter with them.

FRUITY. A term referring literally to the fruit element in a wine. It may be the flavor of strawberry, apple, or figs.

GAMAY. This red-skinned grape is often a source of confusion with the Gamay grape of France's Beaujolais region, which it is not. It is a clone of the Pinot Noir grape and produces light-to medium-body wines.

GERMAN STYLE. Traditional German wines are produced by fermenting the wine until the sugar has been consumed by the yeast. Sterilized grape juice is then added back to a certain level of sweetness.

GEWURZTRAMINER. In German the term *Gewurtz* means spicy, a clue to the character of this wine. It is a white wine that produces a spicy, flowing aroma with a fruity flavor.

HERBEMONT. A grape similar to the Black Spanish (Lenoir) that are both part of the *vitis borquiniani* species. The grapes' aromatics, color, and tannin content are quite different from *vitis vinifera* grapes. The white juice is often used in a dry wine and a semi-sweet amber white.

LATE HARVEST. Refers to the sugar level of the grapes at harvest. Measured in BRIX, Late Harvest wines require a minimum of 24° Brix, while Select Late Harvest wines have a 28° Brix and Special Select Late Harvest require that the grapes be picked at a minimum sugar content of 35° Brix.

LEES. The sediment found at the bottom of a fermentation vessel.

LENOIR. Also known as the Black Spanish Grape, it has been cultivated for centuries in Texas. A thick-skinned red grape that is resistant to disease and the humidity of southern Texas, the grape is used to produce a variety of wine, the most notable of which is the fine Ports made from it.

MALOLACTIC FERMENTATION. A secondary fermentation process that occurs naturally after alcoholic fermentation, when the sugar is converted to alcohol. In this second stage, the harsh malic acid is converted into the softer lactic acid.

MERLOT. A red grape that ripens early producing a minty, pleasant wine. Traditionally used only for blending with Cabernet Sauvignon and Cabernet Franc, Merlot has experienced increased popularity on its own. It offers a lighter, less tannic wine that is drinkable at a young age.

METHODE' CHAMPENOISE. The traditional process used in the Champagne region of France in which secondary fermentation takes place in the bottle. The yeast sediments are then removed from each bottle individually.

MUSCADINE. A native grape of southeastern United States, this hardy disease-resistant grape is a rapid grower. These grapes produce a specialty wine with a distinctive flavor and bouquet.

NOSE. A term used to describe both the aroma and the bouquet of a wine.

OAKY. A slightly sweet vanilla flavor developed by maturing wine in oak barrels.

PETIT SIRAH. Long used as a blending wine this grape produces a dark, high-tannin wine with an aroma of spices.

PHYLLOXERA. A louse that attacks vine roots, sucking the life out of the plant.

PINOT NOIR. This red-skinned grape has long been a component of French Champagne. It is often referred to as the "headache grape" because it is difficult to grow and work with. Less tannic than Cabernet Sauvignon, this dark-colored wine often costs more than other varietals because of the extra expense of growing the grape.

RIESLING. A white wine. Normally produced in a sweet style, it is sometimes found as a dry wine.

RUBY CABERNET. A clone of the Cabernet Sauvignon grape developed in California. Ruby Cab has a better color, is less acidic, yet has a strong Cabernet-like character. It is mainly used for blending with Cabernet Sauvignon and Cabernet Franc.

SAUVIGNON BLANC. Traditionally used as a blending wine, it has seen recent popularity when made dry and unblended. Sauvignon Blanc is sometimes referred to as Fumé Blanc, referring to the use of a short oak aging to remove the grapes' sometimes grassy flavor.

SEMILLION. Resistant to vineyard diseases and producing a good yield, this white grape has struggled to be popular with winemakers in America. Thin-skinned and susceptible to rot, this grape can produce a honeyed, apple-and-cream flavored dry wine.

SPICY. This term describes a range of flavors from exotic fruit to peppery or clovy.

SURLIE. French for "on-the-lees." The term describes a wine that is left with the lees in the same container during part of the fermentation.

SYRAH. Producing a smoky, rich flavor, this wine historians believe originated in what is now Iran, near the town of Shiraz. Australians today call this wine Shiraz. Normally used as a blending wine. When used unblended, it requires careful control and aging on oak.

TABLE WINE. Usually the lowest tier of a winery's products, these low-priced wines are made for immediate consumption. These wines are often labeled with generic names such as Chablis, or Rose.

TANNIN. This bitter, mouth-puckering part of red wine is derived from extended contact with the skins and stems of the grapes. It is crucial to a wine's ability to age in the bottle.

TRELLIS. The system of wood or metal stakes and wires used to support the grapevines.

VARIETAL. A type of wine named after the primary grape in a bottle. For example, a bottle of Cabernet Sauvignon must contain 75 percent by volume of wine made from the Cabernet Sauvignon grape.

VINIFERA. A species of grape also known as Old World or European. Varieties belonging to this species produce more than 90 percent of the world's grapes.

VINTNER. A person who makes or sells wine.

WINE STYLE. Refers to the characteristics of the grapes and the winemaking techniques. There are so many variables in making wine that winemakers can create many styles from the same grape variety.

WOODY. A flavor brought about from the aging of wine in wood barrels.

ZINFANDEL. This grape produces fine, robust red wines. Most Zinfandel finds its way into "White" Zinfandel, which is actually a pink wine. True Zinfandel wines range from rich, intense flavors to light, fruity wines. Made almost exclusively in the United States, this chewy, mouth-filling wine is finding increased popularity.

INDEX

About the Authors

C'è vita soltanto dove c'è amore.

Life exists only where there is love, a motto that Thomas and Regina use to guide them through their busy lives.

As active travelers and avid wine buffs, this husband and wife team has enjoyed the romance and culture of wine regions across the United States and Europe. Their experiences have shown them that wine is the result of not just the fruit or the location, but the passion of the people who create the wine. As long-time residents of Houston, Thomas and Regina have been in a perfect position to watch the Texas wine industry develop from a handful of passionate, pioneering winemakers to one of the fastest-growing wine-producing regions in the country.

To help promote Texas wines, Thomas and Regina have combined their creativity and varied expertise to create a variety of print and online marketing tools. In the first edition of *Touring Texas Wineries* (published in 1998), they introduced the concept of *wine trails* to the Lone Star state by creating several trails, each combining a handful of wineries for easy travel. Since 1995, the couple has hosted a website, called Texas Wine Trails® (www.texaswinetrails.com), covering the entire Texas wine industry and winning numerous awards for content and design. In addition, Thomas and Regina have created a Texas Wine Trails® jigsaw puzzle, poster, and trail booklet.

They have published numerous wine-related articles and over the years have appeared on various television programs across the state to discuss Texas wine and prepare recipes featuring Texas wines. Thomas and Regina have also worked with the Department of Agriculture on promotional materials for national and international events.

In addition to being an author, Thomas is an architect, artist, philosopher, and amateur chef. Regina is an author, business consultant, computer expert, and accomplished gardener. Their love of wine and travel has allowed them to meet a fascinating collection of people in the wine industry and enjoy some of the finest wines in the world. Yet Thomas and Regina stress that they are not wine critics—their goal is simply to inform and educate folks about Texas wine.